modern
social theory

Percy S. Cohen

Reader in Sociology, University of London

*Dean of Undergraduate Studies, London
School of Economics and Political Science*

Heinemann
London

Heinemann Educational Books Ltd

LONDON EDINBURGH MELBOURNE AUCKLAND TORONTO
SINGAPORE HONG KONG KUALA LUMPUR
IBADAN NAIROBI JOHANNESBURG
NEW DELHI LUSAKA KINGSTON

ISBN 0 435 82181 4 (paperback)

First published 1968
Reprinted 1968, 1969, 1972, 1973, 1975, 1978

Published by Heinemann Educational Books Ltd
48 Charles Street, London WIX 8AH
Printed in Great Britain by Morrison & Gibb Ltd
London and Edinburgh

HEINEMANN BOOKS ON SOCIOLOGY

General Editor: Donald Gunn MacRae

99p

---

modern social theory

Contents

Introduction

THIS BOOK is, first and most important, a contribution to its own subject matter. I have no doubt that it will be long and widely used by students of the social sciences, not only but especially in sociology and anthropology. For them it will prove useful as a text, clear, swift-moving, austere and critical, but also sympathetic and—a point to which I return—remarkably unified. But Dr Cohen has not only provided an admirable text—and that is a rare achievement—he has made in his selection and ordering of topics, in his learning and rigour, and through his own work and thought a real addition to the contemporary theory of society. He has also in part hidden what he has done.

By this I mean something more than that his exposition is logical, balanced and operates through an essentially philosophical sensibility. Quite specifically in his fourth, fifth and sixth chapters there is a great deal that is the author's. It is congruent with what I may call the best sociological consensus of our time, but it goes beyond this consensus in two ways. Dr Cohen clears up some important but far from obvious muddles and inconsistencies. Further he makes a contribution of his own which in chapter six puts the answer to the central question of all social theory, 'How is society possible?' on a firmer footing than, I believe, will easily be found elsewhere. The reader who is not a student but a professional social theorist will recognize and applaud: students and the general reader—to whom Dr Cohen, jargon-free and direct, is easily accessible—may fail to perceive an originality which the author's modesty disguises, but which is the most valuable feature of his work.

It is a striking fact that such a book is now possible. The complementarities and convergencies in the work of the sociological 'classics' of the late nineteenth and twentieth centuries were remarked by such different writers as Morris Ginsberg and Talcott Parsons in the thirties. That out of them a rational, if imperfect, unity, could be developed and could incorporate new advances was far from obvious. By the late fifties the oral tradition of sociologists adumbrated a unity out of these *discordia semina rerum*, but 'conflict' theory, various forms of marxism—the 'young' Marx, neo-marxist revisionism, etc.—and some new arrivals like exchange theory, posed new problems apparently irreconcilable to synthesis. And old problems in new forms (such as development and modernization of the social order) raised novel difficulties for sociologists in mature industrial societies. Dr Cohen can show us that a unity which is not merely manufactured but genuine is possible and, indeed, is largely achieved, even though, of course, problems and weaknesses must and do remain. (After all, any discipline which is not spurious and is alive, manifests a like untidiness.)

Am I then suggesting that social theory is today in a position like that of economic theory about 1890—the time of Marshall's *Principles* —and that we may expect a comparatively long period of quiet, logical refinement, and cleaning-up operations? Very possibly, but I hope not. The theory of social structure is still far from being in satisfactory order. The theoretical issues of societal classification are not far advanced from what is to be found in Hobhouse. The interconnections of social composition and population distribution with social structure are only partly understood. The sociological theory of culture—at least as important as the theory of structure—hardly exists. And so on and on. . . . Nevertheless this book is fortunate in its timing, both because of that unification of theory to which it contributes, and because of the lull that must for some time be expected and in which the newest generation of sociologists can and will be educated.

I differ from Dr Cohen in that I believe that certain very imperfect macro-sociological theories of change are worth discussion and that socio-linguistics already makes an offering to social theory in no way discordant with his analysis, but greatly extending it. At many points, too, I would offer a very different emphasis. But all this is merely to say that this is a book which is stimulating as well as instructive, a basis for argument and for new thinking. I return to my initial point: without parochialism, but clearly and individually, we are given here an excellent textbook which is at the same time a true development of its theme of social theory. Beyond its purpose there are problems both for sociology and for social philosophy. I hope and expect that Dr Cohen will find the opportunity to turn to these and to speak to us directly not only through the hard task of exposition, but with his own voice.

Palo Alto, 12 February 1968   DONALD G. MACRAE

Preface

THERE ARE several ways of writing a book on modern social theory. One is to treat each of a number of individual authors separately. The advantage of this is that one can assess each idea as part of a total system. The disadvantage is that one must expound and assess detailed arguments, some of which may be neither original nor particularly interesting.

The second possibility is to divide authors into schools, and to assess the relative merits of each school. This has obvious advantages; but there is one major difficulty: authors do not fit neatly into schools. For example, Professor Parsons has been criticized for 'holism' as well as for 'atomism'; Marx has been acclaimed as 'paleo-functionalist' and as a 'paleo-action-theorist'. This is not surprising; most of the important contributors to social theory have occupied a number of different positions simultaneously or successively: after all, psychological space is not the same as physical space and, in any case, the different views are not necessarily inconsistent with one another.

A third possibility is to write an original treatise, from beginning to end. In my judgement there are already far too many of these. Some are less original than they claim to be; and others are none the better for their originality. Apart from the fact that I do not pretend to have enough to say which could be in any way described as the substance of an original treatise—even one occupying a very slim volume—I feel strongly that what is needed is something quite different; I have therefore opted for a fourth way of writing this book. The purpose of this book is to deal with a number of closely related themes in theoretical sociology. In discussing these I have tried to present a critical evaluation of certain ideas which have been formulated and developed by a number of writers, some of whom are not always considered modern social theorists. It is perhaps true, as some contemporary sociologists think, that the ideas of Marx and

Durkheim, for example, are too faulty to be considered as part of the corpus of modern social theory; but it is no less true that a number of comtemporary ideas are equally at fault, without being anything like as interesting as those which they are thought to have replaced.

As I see it, a number of ideas of Marx, Durkheim, Weber, Pareto and Simmel, as well as those of more recent writers, have a claim for contemporary consideration—provided such consideration is vigorously critical—simply because they have not yet been improved upon, nor adequately refuted. If one writes a book on this assumption, then one must treat a number of authors as though their ideas, at least, were fully alive.

One of the difficulties which I have experienced in doing this is that I have so internalized certain modes of thought that I am often led to present them—in modified and, I hope, improved form —as though they were my own. In fact, it is my firm belief that any valuable ideas which I hold on social theory are derived from criticism of Durkheim's theories in the light of others.

Some readers may note, with surprise, that I have neglected large areas of social theory and ignored many writers. If I have omitted all reference to some authors it is either because I do not consider their theories entirely germane to the principal themes of this book, or because I am ignorant of their relevance; I confess that I have ignored others because I cannot see what purpose their so-called theories serve. (If any of them finds that this cap fits he has the opportunity to retaliate.) In my view a sociological theory must itself explain, or suggest ways of ex- plaining, why social phenomena have the characteristics which they do have; if it does not do this, but simply provides yet another set of categories or boxes or paradigms, then it does not deserve serious consideration. Of course, most social theorists would insist that their ideas do have explanatory value; but I do not understand how some of them can know this when they do not appear to have any problems in mind in which their theories are designed to explain.

However, the fact that an author receives no mention here does not signify that he has nothing to contribute to modern social theory. In a book of this length one can only deal with those authors whose writings have had the greatest influence on one's own ideas, and one can only illustrate a mode of thought with one or two principal examples. The bibliography is not meant to be exhaustive on any subject; it is intended principally as a guide to further reading. It is for this reason that English translations are cited wherever they are available; it is no use pretending that the average reader of a book of this sort can master texts in French *and* German *and* Italian: as an author I try to make no demands on my readers that I do not make on myself.

The most difficult task for a writer is to acknowledge his indebtedness to others. I have already mentioned the difficulty concerning other authors, living and dead. But if one neglects an author whom one did not or does not know, one can offend his memory, or him, without being too concerned. If one neglects an acquaintance or worse, a friend, it is very serious. To avoid this problem I propose to mention only a few names and to ask all my colleagues who recognize the influence of discussions which I have had with them, to accept an implicit acknowledgement of their help. I want to thank Mr E. I. Hopper for reading some of the original manuscript and, particularly, for criticisms which prompted me to re-write Chapter IV in very different form. To Professor Donald MacRae I owe more than I can easily express, especially for his suggestion that I write this book and for his constant encouragement. Finally, I owe an immense debt to Ruthie, Omer-li, Thalia and Dina for their readiness to forgive what can only be described as insufferable behaviour. Only they can judge whether the result justifies this.

London, December 1967 PERCY S. COHEN

For AARON and JULIA COHEN

1.

The Nature of Sociological Theory

Introduction

THE WORD 'theory' is like a blank cheque: its potential value depends on the user and his use of it. To call a statement a theory is sometimes intended to increase its value by suggesting that it transcends 'mere facts'. When a man says 'I have a theory about her', he means that he is not deceived by her. But sometimes the word is clearly used to reduce the value of a speculative idea by denying it a close connection with reality. In this sense things are 'all right in theory, but not in practice'.

Theories would certainly have no value if they did not go beyond facts. Facts are nothing more than statements which we believe to be true about particular events which have occurred. Theories are not meant to be about particular events but about whole categories of events. It is sometimes said that theories, or some theories, are nothing but general facts. A statement of a so-called general fact would be either a shorthand statement of a number of statements of events of the same type, or a general statement of the characteristics of a type of event. If it is the first, then it is not a theory. If it is the second, it is not factual. If one states that one has observed a falling leaf, one has stated a fact. If one states that one has *often* observed falling leaves, one is simply adding together a large, but unspecified, number of statements of particular events, which constitute a complex fact. If, however, one states that *all* leaves must fall, one is stating not a fact, but a theory: for what one says about all leaves is not what one has observed; no one can observe all leaves, for there are an infinite number of them which may fall.

All theories, it is true, go beyond facts. But not all statements which go beyond facts are theories. If I say that the Norman conquerors of England established feudal institutions which would otherwise not have developed, I am going beyond facts:

for no one can know what institutions would have developed in England if there had been no Norman conquest; but one can guess; and one's guess is an hypothesis. This hypothesis is not a theory, for it states something about particular events, or particular complexes of events; but says nothing in general about the characteristics of military and political conquests.

If theories go beyond facts, do they have a connection with reality? In fact, we would have no experience of reality worth recording, or which we could record, were it not for theories. The most elementary theories, which we use unconsciously, are those embedded in our language; for, all language must use certain universal categories; and to use a universal category is, in effect, to use a theory. If I say 'this typewriter is heavy' I presume certain universal characteristics associated with heaviness, as opposed to lightness. Without universal categories there can be no communication. And without communication there can be no culture, no society, no science, no technology, no shared experience of the world of reality.

Types of Theory

Systematic theories, which are general ideas consciously formulated for some purpose or purposes, are of four broad types. First, there are analytic theories, like those of logic and mathematics, which may state nothing about the real world, but consist of sets of axiomatic statements which are true by definition, and from which other statements are derived. Second, there are normative theories, which elaborate a set of ideal states to which one may aspire; such theories, like those of ethics and aesthetics, are often combined with theories of a non-normative nature to constitute ideologies, artistic principles, and so on. The third type of theory is scientific and the fourth is metaphysical or programmatic. For the rest of this chapter and, indeed, for the remainder of this book, I shall be concerned almost entirely with the third and fourth types. But I mention the other two because some sociological theories have much in common with them.

A scientific theory is, *ideally*, a universal, empirical statement.

which asserts a causal connection between two or more types of event. At its simplest, it has the form, 'whenever X occurs, then Y occurs'. A scientific theory is universal because it states something about the conditions under which some event or type of event always occurs. It is often said, nowadays, that many scientific theories are not universal at all, but are statistical. This means that they only state the conditions under which some type of event is likely to occur. A formal example of this would be the statement 'on 70 per cent of the occasions that X occurs, Y also occurs'. If this statement is to qualify as a scientific theory it cannot have the form 'on 70 per cent of the occasions that X occurred, Y also occurred', for this would simply be a statement of a number of facts. A scientific theory with this statistical form must assert that *whenever* one takes a large enough sample in which X occurs, it will be found that Y occurs 70 per cent of the time. *Thus a scientific theory with a statistical form is also a universal proposition:* it does not simply state the number of times out of one hundred on which it was found that X was the condition for the occurrence of Y; it states that *invariably* there will be a certain probability of X being the condition for the occurrence of Y. The invariance refers to the *infinite* possibility of selecting samples in which this type of relationship will occur.

Scientific theories must also be empirical. This does not mean that they are merely the product of empirical observations. Empirical observations are of particular events. Theories have universal applicability, so they cannot be statements about particular events. But scientific theories are empirical in the sense that statements can be deduced from them which are about particular events, and which can be checked by observation. To deduce statements of particular events from scientific theories, and to check these by observation, is to test a theory; a theory is empirical if it can be tested. But the essence of testability is that statements derived from a theory should state unambiguously what observations will confirm them. This means that a theory must enable one to deduce statements which, if they do not agree with observations, would lead one to modify or reject the theory. It is for this reason that K. R. Popper has said that a theory is empirical if it can, in principle, be *refuted* by empirical observation.[1] If it is irrefutable by observation, then it is not strictly empirical.

This does *not* mean that a theory is not empirical if it is not refuted. A theory may be refutable, in principle, but remain unrefuted. The statement 'no man can live longer than two hundred years' has never been refuted; but it would be refuted if someone succeeded in living for more than that time, and is therefore refutable. Nor does one imply, if one states that a theory is refutable, that it can in fact be put to the test at any particular time. One may at present have no means to refute the theory which asserts that all psychosis is genetically inherited. This does not make the theory irrefutable; for one may know what kind of evidence one would want before being compelled to give up or modify this theory.

A scientific theory should be causal. This means that it should assert either that some conditions are *sufficient* for the occurrence of certain types of event, or that some conditions are *necessary* for the occurrence of certain types of event. The first type of causal statement has, at its simplest, the form 'whenever X occurs, Y occurs'. The second type has, at its simplest, the form 'whenever Y occurs, X must have occurred'.

Some writers on methodology would say that not all scientific theories have a causal form[2]; others would say that no scientific theories have a causal form[3]; and yet others would assert that all scientific theories have a causal form.[4]

The first group of writers distinguish between causal theories and those which merely assert a statistical probability that certain events will occur together. They argue that if a statement asserts that X is the cause of Y, then X must *always* be accompanied by Y, for this is the meaning of causation; if X is only *sometimes* associated with Y, then it cannot be the cause in the true sense. This argument is untenable. If one observes that X is only sometimes associated with Y, and yet one nevertheless asserts that X and Y are casually connected, one may simply mean that there are other conditions which have to be present in order for X to produce Y. If one does not, or cannot, in some cases, know these other conditions, then one is left with an incomplete theory of the causal connection between X and Y; that is all. It does not follow that the connection between X and Y is not causal; nor does it follow that events of type Y can occur without being caused.

The second group of writers completely reject the idea of

causation on the grounds that all scientific theories are really probability theories. But even if they *are* right in characterizing *all* scientific theories as probability theories, they are not necessarily right in rejecting the idea of causation; for probability theories can be interpreted as incomplete causal theories.

This leaves the third group. They argue that the primary task of science is to explain why or how events occur and that it cannot do this by showing that these events are simply associated with others, for that is not an explanation of how and why either set of events occurred, but must show that some events occur *because* others have occurred, or that some events fail to occur *because* others have failed to occur.

All of this constitutes an *ideal* description of scientific theories. Real science is far from being so neat. Few scientific theories of interest ever have the form 'whenever X occurs Y will occur'; for there is always a number of conditions which must obtain for a theory to be true. Then again, there is often a good deal of doubt about the meaning of scientific tests: if a scientific observation does not support a theory, it may well be that the *observation* is wrong, not the theory; and even when it is accepted that the observation is right, scientists can never be certain whether such an observation really refutes the theory which is being tested, rather than one or more of the other assumptions which are not being tested.

The fourth type of theory is the metaphysical. The chief distinction between metaphysical and scientific theories is that the former are not strictly testable, though they may be subject to rational appraisal. Some metaphysical theories have little or nothing to do with science. But others are clearly part of science.[5] They constitute useful assumptions which have a programmatic or suggestive role: they may delineate a broad field in which more precise formulations can be made; they may provide ways of interpreting evidence which is used to test more precise theories; or they may sensitize an observer to the kind of factors which are relevant to explaining a particular phenomenon.

An interesting example of a metaphysical theory which plays a role in science is the theory of natural selection. This theory states that if a species survives for long, then it must possess characteristics which are well adapted or adaptable to a particular environment; and if it fails to survive for as long as other species in a particular environment, then it must possess characteristics which make it less well adapted or adaptable to that particular environment than other species.* To be testable, this theory would have to state the kind of evidence that could be treated as refuting it: instances of species which had survived without being well adapted to a particular environment; or instances of species which were well adapted to a particular environment, but which had not survived. In fact, one could scarcely conceive of such evidence. For, in the final instance, the criterion of adaptability is the capacity for survival. One does not really know how adaptable a species is until one has already *observed* its capacity for survival.

The fact that such a theory is not strictly testable does not mean that it has little value. Its value lies in directing the inquiries of the student of evolution. In conjunction with other theories, some of which are highly testable, it has enabled evolutionary biologists to explain a great deal. Its own role is programmatic. It says 'if you are making inquiries of this kind, look out for those characteristics which make a species more or less adaptable in a particular environment'. This has proved invaluable.

This last example is deliberately chosen. For it is commonly assumed that only the social sciences attempt to make do with theories which are not strictly testable.

Some Characteristics of Sociological Theory

There are a number of reasons why many sociological theories do not meet the ideal criteria of science. First, some are almost like analytic theories; they are near tautologies which cannot be tested empirically. One such theory asserts that the various parts of a social system are necessarily interdependent. This theory *must* be true. For what else can one mean by saying that something is part of a system than that it must, to some extent, affect, and be affected by, other things within the same system? If one part of a social system in no way affects, or is in no way affected by,

* To say that such a theory is in one sense metaphysical, does not mean that it is metaphysical in the Comtian sense of attributing some hidden essence to some thing or process.

any of the others, then it cannot be considered part of that system. If, however, one were to state that social systems differed in the *degree* of interdependence exhibited by their parts, one would be moving away from the tautological. And if one were to state the *conditions* under which different degrees of interdependence were found, one would be moving clearly in the direction of scientific testability.

The second reason why many sociological theories are not testable is that they are really neither genuine universal statements nor statements of fact. Consider, as an example, the theory that social order rests on the acceptance of common values. This appears to have the truly universal form: 'there can be no social order without the acceptance of common values.' But it does not really have this form; for it does not deny that order can sometimes rest on force, rather than on value-consensus. The theory only states that order *usually* rests on value-consensus, since force is a poor long-term basis for it. The discovery of cases in which order does not rest on value-consensus does not lead to a rejection of the theory. This quasi-theory could be made genuinely universal if it stated the conditions under which value-consensus did produce order, or the conditions under which its absence failed to do so.

The final reason why many sociological theories are difficult to test is that they predicate something too vague to allow for any rigour in testing. For a theory to be highly general in one respect is a merit. A theory which asserts that something is characteristic of a broad category of societies has greater value than one which asserts that the same thing is characteristic of a narrower category of societies. For example, the statement 'all *industrial* societies have sectional conflicts over the distribution of income' is more valuable than the statement 'all *capitalist* industrial societies have sectional conflicts over the distribution of income'. The reason for this is that the term 'capitalist industrial societies' is subsumed by the term 'industrial societies'. Clearly, what one can say of *all* industrial societies applies also to particular types of industrial society. Thus, one theory is more valuable than another if it has a greater level of generality. But for a theory to be too open or vague *in what it predicates* is not a merit. For example, the statement 'all industrial societies have sectional conflicts' is of less value than the statement 'all industrial societies have *sectional conflicts over the distribution of income*'. The term 'sectional conflicts' subsumes the more specific one 'sectional conflicts over the distribution of income'. But to use the more specific one is more valuable than to use the more general one. For, if one states that societies have a specific type of sectional conflict, it follows that they have sectional conflict; but to state that societies have sectional conflict does not imply that they have a specific form of it. Thus one theory may be logically superior to another in that it is a statement whose subject is more general than that of the other; but a theory may be logically inferior to another if it is a statement whose predicate is more general than that of the other.*

It is one of the chief weaknesses of many theoretical statements in sociology that where they gain in generality of subject, they seem to lose in lack of specificity of predicate. A characteristic example is one of the propositions in Marx's theory of social change. This states that the class and institutional structures of society must change radically when they can no longer contain further developments in the technology and organization of production. The theory seems to be valuable because it is saying something about the processes of change in all societies, or at least in all societies of a particular type. But *what* it is saying about them is far too vague for testability. Thus, if vast technological changes are not accompanied by 'radical' changes in the structure of societies, then it can be said that these structures can still contain these techological changes. If, on the other hand, there are changes in the class and other structures, then it can be said that these could not contain further technological changes. And even if these *are* changes in the structure of society, but they are not of the kind expected by Marxists, it can still be said that these are not really radical changes, and that the structure can still contain more technological change. A theory of this sort is right, whatever the circumstances; and is, therefore, not strictly testable. This is not to deny it any value. It may be, like

* The formal exposition of this is as follows. The statement 'if X then Y' has greater explanatory power than the statement 'if x then Y', where x is a sub-class of the class Y; but the statement 'if X then y' has greater explanatory power than the statement 'if X then Y', where y is a sub-class of the class Y. If the choice is between 'if X then Y' and 'if x then y', the greater generality of the first is off set by the greater precision of the second.

many other programme theories, highly suggestive. But it is a mistake to treat it as anything more than this.*

Not all sociological theories are of this kind. Some are genuine, testable theories. An example of this is: 'The degree of social mobility in industrial societies varies directly with the degree of industrialization achieved.'[6] This statement *is* theoretical—that is, it does not state a fact, but an invariant relationship—it is empirical, and it is causal. It may not be true; but that is a separate matter.

Few of the propositions which are called sociological theories are quite as precise as this. But many of those which are very vague can be, and have been made, more precise. For example, it is often assumed by sociologists that there is some connection between social cohesion and institutional integration. The term 'social cohesion' refers to a condition of inter-relationship between individuals and groups, such that they will remain part of a wider unit. The term 'institutional integration' refers to a condition of social systems, such that the different institutions are somehow interrelated with one another so that changes in one will produce changes in another. To say that there is a connection between these two variables is very vague; it is simply tantamount to saying that all societies have some degree of both characteristics, and that these two characteristics coexist. However, one can go further and say: a high degree of institutional integration, X, is necessarily associated with a high degree of social cohesion, Y; though a high degree of Y is not necessarily associated with a high degree of X. This statement, whether it is true or not, is a vast improvement on the vague formulation. For it appears, in principle, to be eminently testable. But a major difficulty arises just at this point. For, to test a theory there must be a minimum of ambiguity concerning the kinds of observations that will be treated as confirming or failing to confirm it. This particular case requires some criteria for measuring various degrees of cohesiveness and of integration; for, in the absence of these there will be ambiguity concerning the nature of the evidence. This is a general difficulty in sociology.†

* Marxist theory is far from being the only type that has this untestable form. It happens to provide examples which are interesting.

† Even the theory of social mobility is not *easily* testable; for different observers may opt for different criteria of industrialization to say nothing of social mobility itself.

Sociological 'Meta-Theories'

There is one important advantage which social theorists may have over theorists in the natural sciences: they can be more confident that their 'meta-theories' are correct.

In both the natural and the social sciences there are certain theories, at the highest level of abstraction, which provide a set of ideas in which the more concrete speculations are carried out. Sometimes these 'meta-theories' are scarcely formulated. But it often happens that these ideas exist in formulated systems, as part of metaphysics proper, and that they influence the development of science by *suggesting* problems and solutions. The line of demarcation between science and metaphysics is by no means as clear as some philosophers have claimed. Of course, 'meta-theories' are not themselves tested in the way that genuine scientific theories are. They are modified in the light of experience; but, on the whole, they do more to structure experience than experience does to test them.

All of this is true of both the natural and the social sciences. But there is one important difference between them in this respect. Whereas in the natural sciences, there is always a possibility that some, or all of the meta-theoretical assumptions, are seriously at fault, in the social sciences this is unlikely to be the case. This does not mean that metaphysical theories of nature *are* commonly mistaken or false, only that they *may* be sufficiently wrong or defective to mislead. Nor does it suggest that there is never any room for improvement in meta-social theories.

There are, I think, three reasons for this important difference between the meta-theories of the natural and of the social sciences. First, by participating in social life men have a far greater chance of comprehending certain features of its fundamental reality, than they do by participating in the natural world. The fact that men are physical objects does not give them access to the nature of matter or life. The fact that men are social subjects, as well as objects, does give them an opportunity to gain some idea of the nature of social relationships and of the wider contexts of these. For social reality does not have mechanisms which are *necessarily* hidden from the observation of all those who participate in it.

The second reason, which is related to the first, is that in participating in social life men are *encouraged* to form certain ideas about its reality. Of course the same is true of their participation in the natural world: to control and forecast natural events, men must have some idea of their nature. But there is a difference. Men do not, for the most part, create either the natural world or its mechanisms. They *do* create their social world, even if, for the most part, they do so unwittingly. But, insofar as their actions and interactions are responsible for the creation of the social world in which they participate, men may be encouraged by their situations to comprehend these fundamental realities, to the best of their ability.

The third reason, which is related to the other two, concerns the nature of social reality itself. Whereas men may be right to assume that the nature of physical reality is independent of their ideas of it, they would be wrong to assume this of much of social reality. This does not mean that social reality would cease to exist if some men ceased to believe in its existence; for men are incapable, unless they are psychotic, of ceasing to believe in the existence of social reality for as long as it does exist. But part of social reality is the set of ideas which men have within it.

These arguments can be easily misconstrued. They do not assert that all men, under all circumstances, come to grips with the fundamental nature of social reality. They assert only that some men can, under certain circumstances, come to grips with it. Nor do these arguments assert that when men begin to comprehend the nature of social reality that they comprehend all of it. On the contrary, they do this little by little; and there is no end to the process. For one thing, they may discover that what they thought was true of all social reality is true only of a part of it.

The Nature of Social Reality

The most fundamental idea concerning the nature of social reality is that the properties of the elements of social phenomena obtain many of their characteristics from the larger phenomena of which they are a part, while the larger entities obtain their characteristics mostly from the relations between the parts of which they are composed. This difficult paradox has been the cause of much irritation to social theorists. For a long time, they failed to grasp its full implications, though they always managed to grasp some aspects of these. The idea *is* difficult to grasp; but grasp it one must, for it expresses the quintessential difference between the nature of social and of physical reality. This requires some amplification.

In the physical world there are entities which are composed of the relationship between parts; and it is often said that these entities are more than the mere sum of their parts. This means that the entities have properties which are not found in the parts taken separately, but which *are* found when the parts are related. *But these parts do have characteristics which exist independently of the entities in which they participate.* The parts of an organism are cells; and these cells have characteristics which are quite independent of their existence in organisms. The parts of cells are molecules; and these molecules have characteristics which are quite independent of their presence in cells. The parts of molecules are atoms; and these too have characteristics which are quite independent of their presence in molecules.

But with social entities—societies, organizations, families, markets, states, economies—this is hardly so. These entities are structures of relations between elements; *but many of the characteristics of these elements are inconceivable apart from their participation in the whole.* Families consist of spouses, parents, children and siblings; but the characteristics of spouses, parents, children and siblings cannot exist outside of families. Economies consist of producers, consumers, arbitrage brokers, advertisers, and so on; but the characteristics of producers, consumers, etc., cannot exist outside of an economy. Political systems consist of leaders, followers, factions, parties, legislatures, and so on; but none of the characteristics of these things can exist outside of political systems.

At the same time, all social wholes are, ultimately, sets of social statuses and roles; and these are filled and performed by, individual men, or collectivities of individual men. Social wholes may be inconceivable without individual men in social positions; but the social positions of individual men are inconceivable without social wholes.

Social wholes are, clearly, different in this important respect, from the wholes studied by any natural science. But why are they? The reason is that they are, in important respects, mental rather than physical entities.* If they were merely physical entities, then their characteristics would be reducible to the complex structures of interaction between parts, whose characteristics were independent of their presence in the whole. But it is because social phenomena are, to a considerable extent, mental products, that they have this peculiarity which they do not share with physical phenomena. Social relations are, fundamentally, sets of mutually adjusted expectations of reciprocal social actions. These expectations define rights and obligations. Sets of interrelated rights and obligations define social statuses and roles. But these definitions must imply mutuality at the outset. One man's rights are, *simultaneously*, another man's obligations.

To say that social phenomena are, for the most part, mental products, is not to say that they are necessarily the direct products of men's deliberate intentions. If this were so, then the characteristics of social phenomena would be present, as ideas, in the minds of individual men, before they were actually formed. In that case, it would be possible to explain the characteristics of society simply as emanations of individual ideas. But it is not usually possible to do this. Social phenomena are produced by the interaction of minds. But the process of interaction immediately produces *a change in the mental characteristics* of those who are parties to the social interaction. *Thus, the creation of the characteristics of the parts of social wholes occurs simultaneously with the creation of the characteristics of the wholes.*[7]

Two Approaches to Social Reality

In view of what has been said above, it is not surprising that there are two different approaches to the study of social phenomena. The first may be called 'holistic', the second 'atomistic'.

* I do *not* mean by this that social wholes exist solely in the imagination of individuals. The term 'mental' is used to imply that social wholes can be observed by the sociologist *only* insofar as he imputes certain mental characteristics to individual men.

The 'holistic' approach has tended to treat societies or social wholes as having characteristics similar to those of organic matter or of organisms; it also stresses, what might be called the 'systemic' properties of social wholes. The atomistic approach has tended to treat social wholes as having characteristics similar to mechanical objects—being made up of identical or replaceable parts which can be assembled in different ways; it stresses the importance of understanding the nature of the individual units which make up the social wholes. The first approach has come to be known as functionalism, or structural-functionalism; the second has come to be known as the action theory of society.

If one accepted that these two approaches simply emphasize different aspects of social reality, then one might expect them to be complementary. But, in fact, there has been and is a source of tension between the two approaches. The reason is as follows. If the characteristics of individual men were purely determined by their social statuses and roles, then to start from the characteristics of the part would bring one ultimately to the working of the whole—to start from social actions would bring one to social functions—and, similarly, to start from the functioning of the whole would bring one ultimately to the actions of the individual parts. For the characteristics of the smallest parts would be moulded by their relations within the largest whole. But one cannot make this assumption. Individuals are not just social in the sense that whatever they do is fitted to the demands of social wholes. Firstly, individuals have biological characteristics as well as others which are the product of those features of their environment which they do not share with all other individuals in a society; thus, the actions of individuals may be governed by factors other than those of the wholes of which they are a part. Secondly, even if individuals had no biological and other characteristics which influence their actions, these last would still not be completely determined by their participation in the whole; for different parts of the whole may make different demands on the actions of the individual. This being so, the individual must, in many cases, make choices between these different demands. These choices may be influenced by participation in the wholes, but they are not determined by it; if they were, they would not be choices. It is for these reasons that the claims of the proponents of the two approaches are not always reconciled. However, there *are* instances of such reconciliation; and these have achieved a great deal in furthering the aim of sociological explanation.

Explanations and Problems

The achievements of any science are prompted largely by the desire to explain. But this desire only occurs when there is a recognition of something which has occurred which calls for an explanation. Explanations are devised to deal with problems.

To explain something is to show that a statement which describes it can be deduced, by valid logical procedures, from other statements. A fundamental rule of logic is that every scientific explanation must have at least one premise which is a universal proposition. When a universal proposition is empirical and casual, it is called a scientific theory.

Explanations also, usually, make use of models.[8] The term model is commonly used in two senses. In the first sense it refers to the use of analogies which facilitate explanation by suggesting certain similarities between unknown or unobservable processes and others which are better known. In the second sense, the term refers to a set of assumptions which are used to circumscribe and insulate a number of interrelated processes which can then be treated as though, for certain purposes, they constituted an autonomous area of reality. In sociology the two senses are closely related: to theorize about the nature of social systems or types of social system requires the use of a number of assumptions which link certain processes as though they constituted real entities; but to do this is also to use the physical or biological analogy in thinking about social reality. Much of what is called sociological theorizing consists in building theoretical models of social reality. These do not have the precision and elegance of those of the physical sciences or of economics; but they are, for all that, models.

Theories and models are invented by men because they are logically necessary for explanation. And the need for explanation results from the discovery of problems, or of things to be explained. But problems do not usually arise unless those who discover them already have certain theories which lead them to problems. Thus, the nature of theories and models is intimately linked with the nature of the problems to which they give rise and which give rise to them.

Every discipline or science has many problems. But if these problems were not interrelated in some way they would not belong to the same science. A science has a separate identity because it deals with a set of interrelated problems. When the attempt to solve problems in one science becomes, in any way, dependent upon the attempt to solve problems in another, then the separate identities of sciences break down, and new identities emerge.*

Because the different problems of a science are, necessarily, interrelated, if only by the most tenuous links, it is sometimes possible to select one or more central problems to which all or most others are related. This can, I think, be done for sociology, whose *central* problem is, I believe, that of social order. The holistic and the atomistic approaches are attempts, at the highest level of generality, to come to grips with this problem: this means that they suggest ways of explaining the general characteristics of social order, and accounting for variations in the forms of it, and in the degree to which it is found.

The interest in social order was not founded simply on scientific curiosity. It almost certainly stems from a practical and moral concern. And this concern is itself a product of circumstances in which order is difficult to obtain, and in which some men become increasingly conscious of the fact.

NOTES

1. K. R. Popper: *The Logic of Scientific Discovery*, Hutchison, London, 1959, pp. 40–2.
2. See N. S. Timasheff, 'Order, Causality, Conjuncture' in Llewellyn

* Those who constantly call for the unity of science—particularly for the unity of the social sciences—fail to recognize that when particular barriers between sciences break down this always results in the creation of new scientific identities. The creation of biochemistry for example has led to new specializations within chemistry and biology not to the total merging of the two disciplines.

Gross (ed) *Symposium on Sociological Theory*, Row, Peterson, 1959, p. 147.

3. Cf. Stephen Toulmin, *The Philosophy of Science: An Introduction*, Hutchison, London, 1953, pp. 119–25.

4. See for example, K. R. Popper, *The Open Society and Its Enemies*, Routledge, London, Vol. II, pp. 342–3.

5. See Joseph Agassi, 'The Confusion Between Physics and Metaphysics in Standard Histories of Science', *Ithaca*, 26 VIII—2 IX, 1962, pp. 231–8.

6. S. M. Lipset & R. Bendix, *Social Mobility in Industrial Society*, Univ. of California Press, 1959, p. 11.

7. Cf. M. Ginsberg, 'The Individual and Society', *On the Diversity of Morals*, Heinemann, London, 1956.

8. Cf. R. B. Braithwaite, *Scientific Explanation*, Harper, New York, 1960, pp. 89–96.

2.

The Central Problems of Sociological Theory

The Problem of Order

To ASSERT that sociological theory centres around the problem of social order is to invite the charge of a conservative ideological bias; for to emphasize order is, on some views, to affirm its desirability. Although people in most societies do, I think, desire order—they may not accept any kind of order at all costs—this is not a sufficient reason for placing the problem at the centre of theoretical inquiry. This is done, rather, for the following reasons: first, order is itself something positive and its opposites are only conceivable in terms of it; second, the very idea of human society presupposes order; third, the existence of social order is problematic and cannot be taken for granted; and fourth, the investigation of the problem of order illuminates the nature of disorder in its various aspects.[1]

Aspects of Social Order

The term 'social order' can mean a number of things. The first meaning refers to the existence of *restraint*, the inhibition of impulse or, more specifically, to the control of violence in social life. The second meaning refers to the existence of *reciprocity* or *mutuality* in social life: the conduct of each individual is not random or haphazard but reciprocates or complements the conduct of others. The third meaning refers to the element of *predictability* in social life: men can act socially only if they know what to expect of one another. If these expectations are to be fulfilled then they must be fairly consistent with one another; the fourth meaning which can be attached to the notion of social order is that of *consistency*. The fifth meaning is that of *persistence*; there can be no predictability and consistency in social life unless its forms endure.

All of these meanings are both logically and empirically related. To say that men do not always act towards one another on impulse, but restrain themselves, is to imply either that they inherit their constraints genetically, or that they learn to internalize them during a process of social education. As far as we know men do not have genetically inherited social instincts; but they do have culture and the ability not only to be influenced by it but to create it.* An important part of any cultural heritage are the sets of reciprocal rights and obligations which men exercise in their dealings with one another. If men are to restrain themselves in these dealings they must also have some means of knowing the demands of others; and if they are to deny themselves certain courses of action they must have some recompense, in the form of mutual assistance or, at least, mutual non-interference. All of this implies the existence of rules or norms. Rules are, of their very nature, general; they cannot be made to fit any and every situation; indeed, their function derives from their generality, and generality implies predictability. If what A does is dependent upon what B does, then A must have some expectation of what B will do; and, if what A chooses to do, or is forced to do, is affected by what B does, then A must have some idea of the relevance of B's actions for his own; and if the expectations of B are similarly dependent upon, or influenced by, those of A, then there will be certain common or corresponding expectations guiding the conduct of both A and B in certain situations, or types of situation. The establishment of norms increases predictability in social life by specifying a fairly limited range of expectations for particular types of occasion. But if predictability is to be maintained, the different sets of expectations in the same or linked circumstances must be kept reasonably consistent with one another; or, putting it another way, the different norms, or sets of norms, must be integrated as a system. This is not to say that the different social norms must 'reflect' one another: the inequalitarian norms which govern or define the relations

---

* Culture is, of course, not only negative, it does not merely constrain 'animal' behaviour, but transforms it and adds to it; it does not merely inhibit motivation but creates new motivations.

between parents and young children are in no way incompatible with the equalitarian norms which define the relationships between certain categories of adults in certain situations, even when these adults are also parents and children to one another. However, norms which accord to parents total control over the conduct of their children may well be incompatible with those which accord to the State certain rights over its subjects. If such conflicting norms exist then, in certain circumstances, men do not know what to expect; predictability and, indeed, reciprocity may break down. Such circumstances are common enough; but if they were typical of all social life there would be chaos.

Persistence is implied by predictability. This only means that on two or more successive occasions the same norms will prescribe conduct for the parties concerned. But persistence goes a good deal further than that; in most societies *some* norms persist unchanged, or relatively unchanged, for several generations; and in some societies *most* of the norms persist for several generations. There are a number of reasons for this. First, some of the norms of family life, specifically those which govern the relations between the old and the young, actually exist to bridge the gap between the generations; although these may change with changes in the nature of this gap, they do not change entirely; for the older generation have learned how to deal with the younger only by internalizing such norms from their own experience. Second, those who assume positions in existing social institutions do not create these institutions in their own image; there are no complete revolutions.

Each meaning of the term 'social order' is, in fact, an aspect of it; and each such aspect has its opposite. If men commonly suppress those drives, whims or impulses which go against the normative constraints, they also frequently allow them expression. While there is a good deal of reciprocity and even cooperation in social life, there is, equally, a good deal of opposition and conflict; indeed, reciprocity, cooperation, opposition and conflict may be compounded in the same relationships, as anthropologists and psychoanalysts have shown in their studies of the human family. While there is much that is predictable and consistent in social life, there are always some areas of uncertainty and inconsistency resulting from conflicts of principle, or conflicts between the expected and the possible. Finally, though all societies are in a process of constant change, this is more marked and more rapid in some circumstances than in others; and it always affects a given order of society unevenly; both persistence and change are characteristic of social life.

That societies simultaneously possess these opposed characteristics may be perfectly obvious. Yet it does not appear to be obvious to those who constantly proclaim that it is in the nature of societies to be riven by conflicts of interest and principle and to be in a constant process of change, while overlooking the fact that it is equally in its nature to be orderly and persistent.

Explanations of Social Order: The Coercion Theory

In general there have been four main types of theory to explain the existence of social order: the first has emphasized the factor of coercion, the second that of interests, the third that of values, and the fourth that of inertia.

The coercion theory itself may emphasize the use, or threatened use, of physical coercion or the use of symbolic and moral coercion. According to this theory, order exists in society only, or largely, as a result of the power which some men have to command compliance from others; men do what is expected of them because they are compelled to do so by those who monopolize some means of coercion.* If they do not comply, they are threatened with some form of physical punishment, deprivation of property, resources or rights, or with some social stigma or supernatural sanction. This type of theory is often associated with a conspiracy theory which asserts that what occurs in society is the direct outcome of the wishes of some men who impress their will on others. But it is not necessarily wedded to such an assumption; for it may assert that those who command compliance do so in the name of all men.[2]

This theory can explain the various aspects of social order.

* It should be noted that the English word 'order' can also mean 'command'; the confusions of etymology may well reflect popular social theories.

Men restrain their impulses and abide by norms because they fear the consequences of doing otherwise, or because they are constantly reminded of their moral need to do so by those who command them. They carry out their obligations and can expect others to do the same because a failure to do so will be punished by authority. Predictability is ensured in the same way. There must be consistency between different norms because if there were not this would come to the notice of those who command. And there must be persistence because it is, on the whole, in the interests of authority to maintain society in unchanging form for as long as possible; this makes their task easier and ensures continued power, prestige and other privileges for themselves.

The theory can also explain disorder, conflict and change. In all societies there are at least two sorts of conflict. First, there is conflict between men contending for positions of power: since order is based on nothing but coercion, any show of weakness on the part of the powerful will produce a struggle for succession among those close to power; this is most likely to occur when authorities are weak or under pressure. Second, there is conflict between the powerful and the powerless: whenever coercion fails or exceeds certain limits it produces a reaction against it to abolish it; these reactions are often successful when accompanied by struggles within the ruling group. During such periods of conflict all types of disorder occur: if there is no one able to uphold the norms they are not adhered to; the result is that 'instinct' and impulse re-emerge and chaos and violence ensue. In such conditions, social change may occur; though change may also occur if the powerful foresee such consequences: planned changes may result in greater repression or in less.

The coercion theory explains order in its various aspects and also explains the breakdown of social order and the occurrence of change. This is a great deal; but, for all that, the theory has serious weaknesses.

If it states that coercion is a *necessary* condition for social order, it can seemingly be refuted by examining those societies in which order exists without a single centralized authority which can coerce all of its members; these are the tribal societies which have been termed 'stateless' or 'acephalous'.[3] In such societies there are positions of authority within the domestic group or family, within the local community, within lineal segments or whole lineages; but there are scarcely any for the society as a whole; and commonly there are none even for the larger political units within the society. In these societies, the maintenance of order in the relationships between members of different segments is dependent upon a number of conditions. First, there is the potential use of force to settle disputes between members of different lineages or clans (or even larger units such as tribes) who can attempt to mobilize support from other members of the same social segment. Second, there are ties of various kinds, particularly those of marriage and extra-segmental kinship—if men marry outside of their lineages and clans this creates affinal ties for themselves and cognatic ties for their descendants— which cut across other kinship ties; these cross-cutting ties of kinship, or of ritual or political association, serve to restrain those who seek to mobilize force in the settlement of disputes; they also create a cohesive network of ties which, if strong enough, prevent the secession of segmental units from the larger whole. Third, there are sometimes intermediaries, who may have ritual status, who mediate between conflicting parties. An important aspect of the pattern of feuding is that internal segmentation within segments and the cross-cutting ties between them, tend to constrain the forces of organized violence; for men are reluctant to use force to seek redress of grievances unless they can mobilize support, since their opponents might meet their attack with strong defensive alliances; furthermore, nominal allies are reluctant to be drawn into states of feud with others whom they may wish to call upon as allies in some other disputes. In addition, various supernatural and moral sanctions set limits to the use of violence; and these are strengthened by rules which specify the social boundaries within which certain forms of redress are to be sought.

These ethnographic facts would appear to refute the argument that coercion is a necessary condition for social order. However, some counter-arguments should be considered. First, it is arguable that order in these societies *is* dependent upon coercive authority *within* each segment; for without this, segments would fragment into smaller units and the control of violence between segments would, in any case, not be possible without leadership. Second, it could be said that the potential use of coercion *between* units indicates that some form of it is necessary for social order, even if it is not exercised from a position of power. Third, it is clear that one of the constraints on social conflict is moral or symbolic coercion: that is, the manipulation of ideas and moral attachments as a means of ensuring conformity or compliance.

The first of these arguments is partly convincing. A society cannot exist without some form of hierarchically organized coercion, even if this is based only on age or kinship seniority; however, this need not extend beyond the range of a segment of the society; and, for this reason, the theory, in its most general form, which postulates a necessary coercive force for the whole society, is rejected. The second argument also has something to commend it: the existence of countervailing coercion as a necessary condition of social order does suggest that some other form of coercion is necessary in the absence of a centralized form. (It could, of course, be said that this pattern of coercion is unstable by comparison with a centralized form: but there is little evidence to support such a view.) The third argument is largely unacceptable. Symbolic or moral coercion can only be exercised if men accept certain common values, and is, in the final instance, an inner coercion or constraint; and the effectiveness of inner constraints does not really support the theory that centralized coercion is a necessary condition for social order. However, it could well be argued, for two reasons, that there must be some form of hierarchically organized coercion resting on the potential use of physical force so that any form of moral or symbolic coercion can be effective: first, there must be some agent to apply sanctions when moral or symbolic influence is neglected, ignored or opposed; second, there must be some coercive agents, such as elders, who supervise the learning of moral standards and the internalization of symbolic meanings.

One can agree that coercion is necessary without agreeing that it is also sufficient for the existence of social order. In the short run, the exercise of naked power may achieve some degree of social order; but in the long run it is bound to provoke opposition or the use of violence to overthrow it. And it is doubtful whether coercion as such is ever sufficient to maintain order even in the short run: the establishment of primitive and even of more complex states through coercion is commonly accompanied by dynastic struggles and sectional hostilities of a particularly violent kind.

If coercion is necessary, though not sufficient, for the maintenance of social order and, particularly, for the restriction of organized violence, then it would seem to be true that the weakening of coercive power is a sufficient condition for the occurrence of social disorder or change. This is difficult to test empirically for there is no society in which coercion disappears entirely. For example, after the removal of the Belgian presence in the Congo there was not a total absence of centralized coercion; there was a replacement of one coercive power by another; this encouraged rival claims to power, which was one of the most important factors leading to a breakdown of social order. But even though a rigorous test of the theory is not possible—at least with present techniques—there are still ways of assessing its explanatory power: for example, one could inquire whether the possible weakening of parental authority resulting from the development of peer-group associations, educational and other agencies, and the legal protection of minors, did or did not contribute to family instability; or, to take a very different sort of example, one could inquire whether the impairment of the coercive power of feudal magnates did or did not facilitate the creation of a state bureaucracy. It seems reasonable to conclude that most evidence supports the view that the weakening of any form of coercive power contributes significantly to social disorder and to social change.

The 'Interest' Theory of Social Order

The interest theory has two main variants. The first explains social order as resulting from a contract between men who find it in their interests to have some social arrangements.[5] This states that men cannot achieve their aims without the cooperation or, at least, the dependability of others. Since this dependability must be relatively predictable it requires the establishment of rules which accord to each party rights and obligations which are mutually beneficial, and which prevent some parties from benefiting excessively at the expense of others.

This theory can also account for disorder and change in the

following way: when circumstances arise which are not covered by the existing rules then disorder and conflict follow, until, in time, the need for new rules is recognized.

There are two important defects to this type of theory. First, it explains social order largely in terms of men's intentions; and it is very clear that many social institutions exist without having been intended by anyone. Second, it fails to explain how these intentions can arise or affect social order prior to the existence of some degree of order which would enable the parties to the contract to devise and establish it. These two objections are related: for it is difficult to see how men can have ideas expressing social intentions before they have the rudiments of social life, particularly language.

The second version of the 'interest' theory is far more subtle and complex than the first, and far more plausible. It states that social order results from the *unintended* consequence of the actions of many men separately pursuing their own interests; it is not that men discover that order is in their collective interests and then establish it, but that they establish it unwittingly and then, subsequently, discover that it is in their interests. The argument, stated more fully, is this: each man pursues his own interests and conducts himself in a way best designed to do this; in so doing, he finds that this inevitably brings him into contact with others, that he must adjust to the conduct of others, and therefore take it into account. This may lead, at first, to clashes. But gradually, each individual will find that his interests are better served, in the long run, by avoiding such clashes with some men, and possibly, by cooperating with them; this leads to the establishment of certain mutual expectations of conduct and to the gradual modification of these until some balance is struck.

This theory, despite its defects, is one of the great contributions to the development of sociological theory; its merit lies just in this, that it does conceive of social phenomena in terms of casual processes which are, to some extent, independent of human will. It can explain the occurrence of social disorder and change with considerable economy: for the adjustment of interests is never *fully* achieved; there is always the possibility that individuals will develop new interests which will lead to conflicts with others and to pressures for new adjustments; and there is always the likelihood that circumstances will arise which could not have been foreseen and provided for in the establishment of any particular set of rules; and, finally, man's 'nature' is such that he will not rest content with the pursuit of particular goals, and his interaction with others may even stimulate or compel him to engage in new activities. Man is, on the whole, capable of rational action in pursuing his goals—though he is also considerably affected by sentiments and passions—but he does not rationally design the form of his social life.[4]

There are two main defects to this theory. The first, which has been exposed by Emile Durkheim[5] and later, following him, Talcott Parsons,[6] is that it does not explain the derivation of interests. Durkheim and Parsons both argue that these are, to some extent, given by society itself; that is, their existence presupposes social order. A defendant of this theory could argue that some interests are given by man's 'nature', by his condition in the natural world and by the bare fact of his coexistence with others; therefore his primary interests depend not upon society but upon nature. This argument could be used to account for some orderliness in the social behaviour of non-human primates, but it cannot account for the type of order which exists in human society, for this at least presupposes linguistic communication; and the rules of language presuppose society.

The second objection to the theory is that it assumes that men adjust to the conduct of one another with almost perfect freedom, their choices being limited only by nature and by the need to take note of one another's conduct. No consideration is given to the power which some men have to determine or influence the manner in which others will take account of their own wishes: in short, the theory so stresses the unintended consequences of actions that it overlooks the degree to which *some* intentions are more significant than others, even when the outcome is not what was intended by any one or more parties.

The process of adjustment of interests is never sufficient for the establishment and maintenance of social order; but it is necessary. Of course, to say this is almost tautological: it is always possible to show that a given order of society expresses some mutual adjustment of interests. Nevertheless, the theory has considerable value in directing attention to an important aspect of social order.

The Value-Consensus Theory of Social Order

The third theory states that order is based on some minimal consensus on certain values, which are predominantly moral but may also be technical and aesthetic.[7] The argument underlying this theory is that if men are committed to the same values they recognize a common identity as against others; they accept common goals and also certain prescriptions and prohibitions concerning the means whereby these goals can be achieved. The choice of conduct made by each individual will be largely governed by these common standards and by the psychological satisfaction which is obtained from such conformity. The commitment to values enables men to devise means for reconciling or adjusting conflicting interests, and for turning coercive force into legitimate authority.

This theory can explain disorder and change in the following way. First, no man is totally committed to common standards and some, because of their upbringing, are never fully committed. When circumstances change radically, many men will abandon their commitments: but when they change even slightly some men will do this more readily. Thus, there are always individuals who are ready to deviate, and they are large in number when circumstances encourage this. The second possible cause of disorder and change occurs when there is a clash of values due to contact between different societies or when new values emerge which are incompatible with the old.

This theory which has, of late, been well favoured is hardly new; it was advanced by Auguste Comte and, to some extent by Emile Durkheim who also recognized its weaknesses as a general theory. Comte argued that disorder in society was due to a lack of consensus on certain fundamental ideas and principles concerning the desired type of society and the proper means of administering it. He considered that concensus was reduced by the growth of the division of labour, which promoted sectional differences and conflict.[8]

Durkheim rejected much of Comte's argument. He considered that a unified system of ideas and morals was possible only in a relatively simple, undifferentiated society. He recognized that the division of labour promoted differences and conflicts, but considered that it also provided a new moral conception of inter-dependence. In highly differentiated societies there could be no consensus based on detailed moral rules and the acceptance of total systems of ideas; there could, however, be a consensus on certain diffuse moral values which prescribed limits within which different sets of rules could exist.[9]

If this theory states that consensus is a *sufficient* condition for the creation and maintenance of social order then it is rather weak. In the first place, it fails to explain how some consensus can be reached without social order. Secondly, it is also false as an explanation of the continuity of order: for there may be widespread consensus in modern society on the desirability of higher living standards; but this is as likely to provoke conflict as to solve it. If there were not this concensus—if different social sectors had different values and only *some* desired higher living standards—then there might be far greater social stability.

But if the theory states that some degree of consensus or commitment to common values is a *necessary* condition for social order, it is far more acceptable. In a trivial sense the theory is almost indisputable; for human social life is simply inconceivable unless men have some common standards and are committed to maintaining them. In a more significant sense, the theory states that, underlying the acceptance of some common rules is the commitment to certain broad principles concerning the desirability of these rules. This implies—indeed, the very term 'value' suggests this—that there is a possibility of choosing between one set of principles and another. This is questionable: for while it may be true in some complex civilizations that men debate different and even opposed views concerning the desirable society and can to some extent choose between different courses of action in terms of these, it is not true at all of most simple societies; in these latter, insofar as there are choices, they are made within a common conception of social order which is relatively unquestioned. Where then does the commitment to common values lie? In those societies where there is a possibility of choice, where consensus is reached with difficulty and can therefore be said to reflect a commitment to one thing rather than to another? Or does it lie where no fundamental disagreement is possible? This is not mere sophistry. The question is aimed to elucidate the following point: if there is fundamental agreement on the nature of society and no alternative is conceivable, is it not trivial or truistic to say that this is based on commitment to common values? Is social order not simply equated with the commitment to common values?

There is a counter-argument to this. It states that the condition of value-commitment, which cannot be directly observed, and can only be inferred from certain objective indices, is phenomenally independent of social order itself. For example, it could be said that Hindu beliefs and values provide a set of common principles which define or justify the different rights and obligations of caste groups, and that this is a necessary, if not a sufficient, condition for maintaining both an orderly relationship between occupational groups and a stable structure of power and prestige. What this argument implies is that without such an underlying commitment, which may be diffuse and even subliminal, men would not necessarily conform to the specific rules of social life but might well choose courses of action which would result in chaos. The difference between simple and complex societies would lie in this: that in the former the alternative would be simply between order and chaos, while in the latter it would also be between different *kinds* of order.

Despite its weaknesses, this theory is not easily dismissed: even if it does approach the tautological, it is of value in directing attention to an important factor in social life. And, as I hope to show later, it can be usefully combined with some elements in the other theories. Its unpopularity in some circles is due largely, and sometimes justifiably, to the inflated claims which have been made for it in one form or another. Comte and Parsons have supported it strongly as an explanatory theory; while men as different as Comte, Mannheim and Marx have held rather Utopian notions concerning the possibility of establishing a complex society on the basis of a vast consensus. Critics have been quick to point out that a commitment to common values and ideas in complex societies is unlikely to be extensive even where it is powerful.

The 'Inertia' Theory of Social Order

The fourth and last type of theory of social order is rather different from all the others in that it seeks only to explain one aspect of social order, namely the element of continuity or persistence in social life. It is also different in that it does not refer to a single factor or process but to any number of them, and does not necessarily compete with any of the other theories. The theory asserts, in brief, that if social order exists it provides the conditions for its own perpetuation. This sounds absurd: either it is tautological, in that the notion of social order implies that of continuity; or it is clearly false, for social order can break down or change, and to say that it sometimes persists is to revert to platitude.

Despite its seeming absurdity the theory has, when formulated more clearly and precisely, much to commend it; for it emphasizes the point that some of the causal processes of social phenomena are often circular. What this theory *should* state is that when social order is maintained by a number of mutually reinforcing processes, it tends to resist pressures for disruption and change, at least from within.

This theory can be combined with any one of the others: coercion, interests and value consensus can each be introduced as factors within the theory or model which uses the assumption of inertia or equilibrium. In fact, all three elements can be combined within a theory or model of an ongoing social order.

Conclusion

A survey of these four types of theory brings one inescapably to two important conclusions. The first is that none of these theories can really explain the *origins* of social order; indeed, this may be an impossible task to carry out in purely sociological terms. (Whether an explanation in partly biological terms is possible, I do not venture to say.) The coercion theory is implausible because it presupposes that those who wield power invent a number of social norms. The contractual theory presupposes the existence of some form of social order within which a contract can be designed and agreed to; it therefore assumes, as part of the explanation, what is to be explained. The second interest theory comes nearest to success, for it assumes a long process of undesigned development from a state of disorder to one of order; but it cannot fully account for the existence of interests without showing that these depend on the existence of society. The consensus theory likewise presupposes the existence of a social order which can promote commitment to certain underlying common values. Finally, the inertia theory makes no claim to explain the *origin* of social order.

The second inescapable conclusion is that *each* of these theories contributes to the explanation of how social order *persists*—rather than how it originates—and how it breaks down and changes. For each theory states a *necessary*, though not a sufficient condition, for the continuity of any social order, once it exists. All social order rests on a combination of coercion, interest and values. This does not mean that every type of social order is dependent, to the same extent, on each of the three factors. In fact, they differ very much in the extent to which they emphasize these different elements.

Similarly, though all societies are characterized by some degree of inertia, they differ in the degree to which this is the case. To understand why they differ in this respect—that is, to understand why some societies are more resistant to change than others—one has to investigate more closely the processes which are said to be interrelated in social systems. One approach to this problem is the 'holistic' one.

NOTES

1. Cf. Talcott Parsons, *The Structure of Social Action*, Free Press, Illinois, 1949.
2. See for example, Thomas Hobbes, *Leviathan* (ed. Michael Oakeshott), Blackwell, Oxford, esp. pp. 107–8.
3. See John Middleton and David Tait (eds), *Tribes Without Rulers*, Routledge, London, 1958.
4. Cf. Friedrich A. Hayek, *Individualism and Economic Order*, Routledge, 1949, pp. 6–13.

5. Emile Durkheim, *The Rules of Sociological Method* (trans. Solovney & Mueller), ed. George E. G. Catlin, Free Press, 1950, pp. 2–3.

6. Talcott Parsons, ibid, p. 460.

7. Cf. K. Davis, *Human Society*, Macmillan, New York, 1959, pp. 143–4.

8. Auguste Comte, *Cours de Philosophie Positive*, IV, pp. 429–31.

9. Emile Durkheim, *The Division of Labour in Society* (trans. George Simpson), Free Press, 1947, esp. pp. 364–71.

3.

Functionalism or the 'Holistic' Approach

Introduction

THE 'HOLISTIC' approach to society is as old as social theory and stems from the Greeks. Some historians of ideas would trace the modern doctrine of functionalism, by which name the holistic approach in sociology has been known in the last three decades, to Montesquieu; but it is probably from Comte that its recent influence derives. Comte recommended, as one part of sociological inquiry, which he called Social Statics, the study of the coexistence of social phenomena.[1] Underlying this was the notion that all of the institutions, beliefs and morals of a society are interrelated as a whole, so that the method of explaining the existence of any one item in the whole is to discover the law which prescribes how this item coexists with all of the others. This, for Comte, was part of a grand scheme of planning the total reconstruction of society; for this could be based only on a theory stating which combinations of social items would be viable. Comte has been much criticized for his grandiose proposals[2] and for his responsibility for encouraging the view of society as a 'seamless web'.[3] But he should also, in fairness, be credited with a number of important insights.

Herbert Spencer contributed something new to the functionalist conception of society. Much has been made of Spencer's specific proposal to draw functional analogies between the processes of organisms and societies, but this was not his fundamental concern, which was to show that sociology should aim to analyse the structure of societies in order to show how each part contributed to the functioning of the whole. Spencer constructed an evolutionary typology of societies which, like organisms, exhibit varying degrees of structural complexity which can be measured in terms of the number of different types of elements of which the structure is composed. Where the structure consisted of a number of like or identical elements, each

34

would tend to be more or less self-sufficient; where it consisted of unlike elements—that is, where the structure is internally differentiated—there is a greater degree of interdependence between the parts. Spencer argued that greater differentiation of structure made for greater integration of the whole, which made it more able to survive by reducing internal disharmony.[4]

Most recent functionalist arguments owe far more to Emile Durkheim than to Spencer. Durkheim, like Spencer, was, at least in his earlier writings, strongly influenced by biological thinking; indeed, his early views were directly influenced by those of Spencer, whom he also strongly criticized.[5] In both his methodological[6] and in his substantive writings Durkheim warned against some of the dangers of functionalist explanation. (He did not use the term 'functionalist'.) In fact, he anticipated many of the recent attacks on it; yet, paradoxically, he helped to make the doctrine attractive and very fruitful to social anthropologists and, subsequently, to sociologists in general.

In his book on the division of labour[7] Durkheim made a clear distinction between the function (as we would call it) of the division of labour and its efficient cause. Its function was the integration or reintegration of society; its cause was the increase in 'moral density' resulting from population pressure. But when one scrutinizes Durkheim's casual explanation some difficulties arise. Durkheim's argument is as follows: when there is increased pressure of population and increased social interaction there is a breakdown of the constraints built into the simple 'segmentary' society and an increase in competition which threatens the social order; this increased rivalry and competition is reduced or even controlled by the adoption of specialized tasks which make men more dependent upon one another and, therefore, more likely to accept a morality of mutual obligation. What Durkheim does not explain is how men come to adopt this solution to the problem of intensified competition. He did not suggest the highly implausible theory that they do this consciously, nor the equally implausible theory that they are guided by unconscious wisdom. Yet he does seem wedded to the view that the division of labour emerges because it is needed to restore order where unbridled competition might otherwise destroy social life. There seems little doubt that Durkheim, in avoiding one trap of functional explanation, has fallen into another.

The same difficulty recurs in a later book on the origins and nature of religion.[8] Durkheim sets out to refute theories which explain religion in terms of the intellectual or emotional characteristics of individuals and seeks an explanation which will show why religion is a social phenomenon. His theory is as follows. Society is a constraining and also a creative force which acts on individual men from without: it constrains them by providing moral rules and other norms to which they must conform; but it is also creative, in that it provides each individual with the cultural resources with which to lead his life. Aboriginal men sense their dependence upon, and submission to this external force, but are unable to express this abstract notion. Yet they have a 'need' to express this; they therefore choose some material object to represent society and their collective attitude towards it. This symbol becomes sacred by virtue of what it represents—the moral order—and must be kept separate in the minds of men from other, profane, objects so that it can evoke a special feeling of reverence. Such objects are central to ritual activities which are, in turn, collective actions whereby certain sentiments of group solidarity are aroused and sustained. The objects of religious worship are thought of as outside of men, because society is sensed as external to the individuals who form the collectivity.

This theory explains religion in terms of a collective need to express a sense of solidarity and an awareness of the social derivation of the moral order; it therefore seems to account for the phenomenon in terms of its desirable consequences. It could, possibly, be rescued from this indictment; but to do so would change it beyond recognition. It seems to be essential to the argument that men have a collective need to express their moral dependence upon society, and that a symbolic expression is necessary for the maintenance of social solidarity. Durkheim cannot escape the charge that the efficient causes he adduces—the sense of dependency and the cognitive inability to grasp this abstract idea—are insufficient to account for religion; he must have recourse also to the social 'need' for this expression.

If one were to defend Durkheim by postulating the assumption that men *unconsciously* feel the need for symbolic expression of their moral dependence upon society and act on this dim awareness, then some very odd and remarkable things follow: for it would seem that men who are incapable of consciously expressing an abstract principle are nevertheless capable of a complex, unconscious, coordinated effort to select an object, treat it as sacred, organize a set of rituals around its sacredness which, together with the attitudes towards it, give it a social value quite different from any practical value which other objects may have, so that it may in turn evoke sentiments which are appropriate to a sense of moral commitment and obligation. All of this would make of aboriginal man a truly remarkable being. Durkheim would doubtless have rejected this postulate. This leaves him with the assumption that the beneficial social consequences of religion partly account for its existence.

If Durkheim did not always heed his own methodological advice, it is hardly surprising that his influence served to establish a functionalist-holistic school of sociology.

Functionalism Established

None of the precursors of modern functionalism referred to themselves by that name. An explicit doctrine called functionalism was, in fact, the creation of Bronislaw Malinowski. But Malinowski's influence has been less significant, in some respects, than that of A. R. Radcliffe-Brown, who repudiated the term 'functionalist' as applied to himself, yet formulated a set of ideas which encouraged a version of functionalist holism.

It is commonly argued that the polemical position adopted by both Malinowski and Radcliffe-Brown was directed against two influential doctrines which had dominated anthropological speculation in the nineteenth and early twentieth centuries: they were evolutionism and diffusionism. There is also ample evidence in the writings of both authors that they considered it a paramountly important task to expose the weaknesses of both these doctrines on specific matters. However, this does not necessarily account for the emergence of functionalism: for it is arguable that they attacked the old doctrines because they had found a new one,[9] not that they created a new one because they found the old one wanting. If this last is true—and I think that it is at least part of the truth—then it still remains to explain why functionalism, as a formulated doctrine which became a highly valuable dogma, was created. This is important not merely in the context of the history of social doctrines—something with which I am scarcely concerned in this book—but as a guide to the constructive evaluation of the doctrine.

Actually, neither Malinowski nor Radcliffe-Brown rejected the view that human societies had developed from fairly simple to more complex forms, nor even that they had passed through certain stages in the process. What they did both criticize were a number of other evolutionist assumptions which had a direct bearing on the study of contemporary primitive and peasant societies: first, that existing primitive societies represented the early stages of human social development; second, that these societies could themselves be placed on an evolutionary scale in terms of certain fixed criteria of development; third, that the evolutionary history of a society, or group of neighbouring societies, could be reconstructed in terms of the presence of certain characteristics which were clues to the past; fourth, that the presence of certain characteristics which did not fit a particular stage of development, could be interpreted as 'survivals' of the past. The objection to the first two assumptions was not so much that they were false but that they directed attention to insoluble problems and away from important ones. The objection to the third and fourth assumptions was that they gave rise to 'conjectural' hypotheses* while ignoring the possibility that existing phenomena could be explained in terms other than these. For example, evolutionists had observed that in some societies inheritance, succession and descent were traced through the female line; they concluded that this must be a sign of matriarchy; and if the societies possessing these institutions were not now matriarchal, then they must have been so in the past. This sort of interpretation was not only guided by an evolutionary scheme but was used to lend support to one. Malinowski and Radcliffe-Brown considered that matrilineality had to be understood for what it was rather than for what it might indicate from a past whose characteristics were not known.

The attitude of these two 'founders' of functionalism towards

---

* The pejorative use of the term 'conjectural' is most unfortunate, for no science, including functionalist sociology, is possible or desirable without conjectures of one sort or another. (See K. R. Popper.[10])

diffusion was, again, similar. Neither disputed the argument that if two or more societies possessed common characteristics this similarity might be due to diffusion rather than to parallel development; and that this was most likely to be true where the societies concerned were contiguous. However, both rejected the rather extravagant hypotheses of some diffusionists who attempted to trace certain institutions and cultural items, as found in different societies in different parts of the globe, to certain common origins. Furthermore, both rejected as trivial the theoretical concerns of the diffusionists.

There was, in fact, a third doctrine which gained considerable popularity both before and after the establishment of functionalism, which could be called psychological universalism, and which was commonly associated with evolutionism. Its chief and most renowned practitioner was Sir James Frazer, who sought to show that there were constant factors in the intellectual and emotional make-up of men which gave rise to certain widespread cultural phenomena. Frazer's method consisted in selecting illustrations of such phenomena from a vast array of existing and historical cultures. It was not so much his evolutionism or even his psychologism which bothered the early functionalists, as his method; they strongly condemned the way in which Frazer allegedly 'tore items from their wider context' thereby doing violence to their meaning. It was this, rather than evolutionism or diffusionism as such, against which Malinowski and Radcliffe-Brown reacted. Yet they reacted not so much because they first saw the weakness of the method, but because their possession of another theory and method sensitized them to the weaknesses of others.

Malinowski's first formulations of the functionalist doctrine appeared after he had carried out ethnographic fieldwork amongst the Australian aborigines and, later, the Trobriand Islanders.[11] As such, they did not guide his researches; they are more in the nature of elaborations of assumptions which he worked out, in piecemeal fashion, either while doing fieldwork, or when reporting it. The fundamental idea is this: if one wishes to understand a particular cultural item one does so by referring (a) to some general principles of human conduct, (b) to some other items in the same society which provide the context within which the particular item occurs. For example, if one wishes to explain why a Trobriand man makes payments in kind (known as *urigubu*) to his sister's husband, one refers first to certain general principles of reciprocity, which govern conduct in all societies, and secondly to the fact that this is a matrilineal society; here a man is succeeded by his sister's son, so that it is his sister who provides him with heirs; the payments signify that women and their children have an interest in the property of the matrilineage. This kind of analysis not only explained what the Trobianders were doing, it also dispensed with speculations concerning stages of development, etc.; and it also helped to debunk the notion that such payments were evidence of matriarchy or of matriarchal survivals; for the *urigubu* payment expresses not female control over property, but the role of the sister in providing an heir.

At this stage, Malinowski's major contributions were of three kinds: he suggested a method of ethnographic inquiry; he developed specific ideas to interpret particular phenomena; and, finally, he attacked the common preconceptions of primitive man as irrational and dominated by custom. For he showed that many of the institutions of primitive society—such as those governing the settlement of disputes or the allocation of resources —did, in fact, meet the same sorts of requirements as do the more specialized judicial and economic institutions of our own society; furthermore, he emphasized that these institutions did permit some choice of options and did not simply compel automatic compliance.

All of this led Malinowski to elaborate a more rigorous system of ideas.[12] He started from the assumption that all men have certain primary needs for food, shelter, sexual satisfaction, exploration, protection, and so on. They meet these by devising techniques for growing or finding and distributing food, erecting dwellings, establishing heterosexual relations and banding together. The process of satisfying these needs creates derived or secondary needs: the need for communication produces language; the need to control conflict and promote cooperation gives rise to norms of reciprocity and social sanctions; the development of conscious awareness of the vicissitudes and dangers of life and of the significant points of change in the life-cycle gives rise to magic and other forms of ritual and belief, such as religion, which allay the anxieties produced by uncertainty. The satisfaction of these secondary needs gives rise, in turn, to the need for more elaborate coordinative institutions: the existence of these creates the need for rules of succession, and for some mechanisms of legitimation of authority, such as myth, which provides a charter for certain central institutions.

Some of Malinowski's arguments are convincing enough. No doubt there are basic human drives or needs to be satisfied; though exactly what they are is still a matter of much dispute. But the scheme, as a whole, raises more difficulties than it solves. First, to say that certain specific items of culture are created to fulfil certain needs is almost tautological; for, if other items had been created it would be as easy to establish that they too met certain needs. Second, even if men do have certain needs, it does not follow that these will be satisfied; clearly, if men do not satisfy certain *biological* needs, then they cease to reproduce; but other needs, if they exist, may remain unsatisfied; what has to be explained is how and why men develop certain ways of satisfying some needs and not others.* Third, explanations in terms of broad, general human needs cannot account for the differences between societies or, for that matter, for the particular features of any society or type of society; these differences are not simply variations on common themes, for some societies possess institutions which others do not have in any form. Fourth, if Malinowski is seeking to explain how societies and cultures function at any particular time, then the needs to which he refers—other than truly biological ones—are in fact learned by the members of society, as he himself emphasizes[13]; thus the need for any cultural item is as much a consequence of its existence as a cause; if, however, Malinowski is seeking to explain the origin of cultural items, then he is engaging in the kind of conjecture which he condemns in evolutionist and diffusionist writers. Fifth, Malinowski's insistence that every cultural item must have a function— that is, it exists because it meets some present need, and would otherwise not be there—is an overstatement of the case; one can only know if an item is of use to anyone by inquiry. Of course, Malinowski was concerned to show that many cultural items that had previously been treated as mere survivals were useful to those who possessed them.

Malinowski's influence on the development of anthropological

* For example, it could be argued that men need a way of settling all disputes without violence; but they do not have one.

fieldwork was remarkable. But the theoretical conceptions which later guided social anthropologists were those of Radcliffe-Brown.

Radcliffe-Brown disavowed the term functionalist as applied to himself; all the same, he espoused a doctrine in some ways similar to that of Malinowski. Like Malinowski he exposed the excesses and weaknesses of evolutionism and diffusionism, and sought to analyse societies in terms of the 'here and now'. But he rejected any attempt to relate items to individual needs, whether biological or psychological; nor did he attempt to derive social needs from these others.[14] Following Durkheim, Radcliffe-Brown argued that the nature of social and cultural phenomena could be explained only in social terms. He started out from a number of assumptions. (i) If a society is to survive, there must be some minimal solidarity between its members; the function of social phenomena is either to create or sustain this solidarity of social groups, or, in turn, to support those institutions which do this. (ii) Thus, there must be a minimal consistency in the relationship between the parts of a social system. (iii) Each society, or type of society, exhibits certain basic structural features, and various practices can be shown to relate to these in such a way as to contribute to their maintenance. On the whole, Radcliffe-Brown treated social structure, and the requirements of it, as something irreducible, in the way that Malinowski treated needs as fundamental and irreducible: he tended, therefore, to explain other things—for example, ideas and ritual practices—in terms of social structure.[15] For this reason he and his pupils referred to themselves as 'structuralists' rather than as 'functionalists'.

Using these ideas, Radcliffe-Brown proceeded to analyse and explain a large number of phenomena in a way quite unlike that of his anthropological predecessors. A classic example is his discussion of the relationship between mother's brother and sister's son in Southern Africa patrilineal societies.[16] In these societies a man will give certain favours to his sister's sons which he would not necessarily grant to his own sons or the sons of his brother; and, furthermore, he will permit his sister's sons to treat him with disrespect and to use abusive or even obscene language, or to take items of his property. Earlier anthropologists had found these practices so bizarre that they could only explain them as survivals of matriliny or even matriarchy. Radcliffe-Brown saw these practices as aspects of patriliny. In such a system a boy is under the authority of his father and other males of his father's generation in the same lineage; he does not submit to the authority of men in his mother's lineage, which must be distinguished clearly from his own. His mother's brother is classified with his mother as affectionate and permissive rather than as demanding obedience; this permissiveness is institutionalized. But there is a clash between the principle of seniority and that of lineage: the mother's brother belongs to the same generation as the father. This tension is managed by ritualizing a 'joking' relationship between mother's brother and sister's son.

There are several parts to this explanation. The first starts with existing principles of social structure, such as seniority, patrilineality and the requirement of lineage exogamy; this last results in the establishment of affinal ties between lineages, and for the offspring, these provide a set of cognatic ties which must be clearly distinguished from agnatic ones. The second part of the explanation consists in showing how these structural features create a potential condition of tension which gives rise to forms of conduct which both express them and contain them. The expression of these tensions has a largely educative value, in affirming the fundamental principles of social structure; but it may also serve to relieve tension within the relationships themselves. The functional element in the explanation lies in showing how such practices not only result from certain structural conditions, but how they contribute to their maintenance and, particularly, to the solidarity of the social group as a whole.

Radcliffe-Brown approached many other problems in this way, and inspired his pupils to do the same. For example, E. E. Evans-Pritchard in his now classical study of the political system of the Nuer tribes, argued that the structure of segmental alliances determined the pattern of feuding or threats of it, while these last in turn contributed to the maintenance of the segmental structure of alliances which, in turn, made feuding relations, in that particular form, possible and likely. The surprising element in Evans-Pritchard's analysis was the assertion that feuding was not necessarily something disruptive in society but might, in fact, support a particular type of social system.[17]

If this example, which resembles many of those given by

Radcliffe-Brown himself, is compared with the analysis of joking relationships, a number of differences between them are immediately apparent. The first is, in effect, an explanation of origins. Radcliffe-Brown is not simply asserting that two or more features of social life coexist, but is explaining why one of them does exist: societies have institutionalized joking relationships because there is a tension between two or more principles of social structure.

In the second example there is no attempt to explain the existence of lineal segmentation or the pattern of feuding: neither the pattern of feuding nor that of segmentation is treated as an independent variable. What is being explained, or partly explained, is simply *a pattern of continuity*.

There are here two rather different forms of functional analysis or explanation. The one is explanation of how things come to be as they are: it is a type of developmental hypothesis. The other answers the question of how social forms persist.

Having examined the contributions of Malinowski and Radcliffe-Brown we can now return to the question that was posed earlier: why did these two anthropologists formulate these doctrines in opposition to others? And why were their doctrines so attractive?

The first obvious point is that pre-literate societies lack written records of the past. They do possess oral traditions, but these often idealize or even falsify the past. Thus, in the absence of evidence of the past there is a temptation to treat existing phenomena as a timeless pattern of interrelated parts.

This temptation is strengthened by the fact that men in primitive societies do not have an historical consciousness in the sense that men do in literate, complex societies. They have a sense of the past; but this, on the whole, relates to certain specific events, often in the very distant past of mythical reality, which account for the conditions of the present which tend to be treated as unchanging. This lack of historical consciousness is, in turn, an aspect of the relative stability of simple social systems; these simply do not change much within a few generations.*

Finally, it is characteristic of the simpler societies that the different institutions, beliefs and symbols are all interrelated in such a way as to appear to constitute a total pattern†; and intensive

* The reasons for this will be examined fully in Chapters 6 and 7.
† The reasons for this will be examined in Chapter 6.

fieldwork, as opposed to superficial acquaintance, reveals this. This revelation discourages the practice of tearing items from their context, as Frazer was accused of doing; and it encourages the belief in a total system, operating as a timeless reality, in which each part is dependent upon the other.

It can be concluded that one of the chief reasons for the formulation of functionalist doctrine was the experience of fieldwork. The doctrine was enormously attractive to anthropologists: it gave them a method of systematizing their observations, and it also provided them with a number of problems to guide their inquiries, which were actually built into the theory and method. And Radcliffe-Brown's doctrine enabled them to seek the explanatory factors of social phenomena in certain crucial or central features of the social structure, rather than posit conditions which are anterior to the existing social system.

Functionalism Continued

Some important recent contributions have been made to functionalist theory in America by Talcott Parsons and others.

For Parsons one of the central tasks of sociology is to analyse society as a system of functionally interrelated variables. This means that the analysis of any social process is conducted as part of a study of a 'boundary-maintaining' system.[18] Parsons combines some of the ideas of Malinowski with those of Pareto and Durkheim, that is, treating the needs of the personality as variables in the social system. This emerges clearly in his analysis of the function of professional rules, particularly the rules of etiquette.[19] Parsons argues that professional rules have certain functions for the profession as a body: they define conditions of entry, demarcate the boundaries of the profession and prescribe the rights and obligations of practitioners in relation to the society, and so on. But, in addition, they facilitate inter-personal relations between the professional practitioner and his client: a practitioner must often have access to information about the client which would normally be the preserve of an intimate;

furthermore, he must obtain such information without becoming too familiar with the client; the rules of etiquette serve to structure the relationship in such a way as to protect the practitioner from becoming involved with the client.

Parsons and others have sought not only to construct a theory for the functional analysis of each social system—and for them a system is any ongoing set of recurrent and interrelated social actions—but also to elaborate a set of 'functional prerequisites' for all social systems; these are the conditions necessary for the operation of any such system. They relate not only to the social system as such, but also to the personalities of its members. At the more obvious level every social system must cater for certain physical needs of its members so that they can survive; it must have some means of allocating material resources. Further, every system must have some process of socializing the young so that they develop either specific motivations to conform to particular norms, or so that they develop a general need to conform to norms. This means that every society must have, in addition to specific norms, certain fundamental values which limit the range within which norms can develop; if it does not, then it is unlikely that personalities can successfully internalize the need to conform or the motivations necessary for certain types of activity; for these fundamental values become part of the personality. Every system must have some organization of activities and some institutional means for ensuring that failures in organization are dealt with, either by some form of inducement or by coercion. Finally, the institutional structures must be relatively compatible with one another.[20]

The search for functional prerequisites, not only of social systems in general but of types of social systems, is intended to facilitate comparison and more precise generalization of how social life operates. But Parsons suggests that this approach is in lieu of the more rigorous one of formulating sets of equations which would describe social systems in terms of functional relations in the mathematical sense.[21] It seems that what he has in mind is something of the nature of a mathematical statement of the equilibrium of a social system, such as the one envisaged by Walras and Pareto for economic systems.

Criticisms: Logical

Functionalism has attracted a good deal of criticism during the past ten years. (It frequently looks as though anyone in search of theoretical acclaim has only to discover one more defect in functionalism to achieve this.) In fact, much of the criticism is largely beside the point, since the chief weaknesses of functionalism were often recognized by those who formulated the doctrine; and, in any case, such criticism often fails to recognize the merits of the functional approach. However, several of these criticisms have genuinely contributed, at a number of levels, to social theory.[22]

These criticisms have been of three kinds: logical, substantive and ideological. It is not always easy to keep these separate, but some attempt will be made here to do so.

The main logical arguments against functionalism are that it encourages teleological explanation, that it suggests hypotheses which are untestable, that it demands a level of scientific inquiry which does not exist in sociology and, finally, that it inhibits comparison.

A doctrine or theory is said to be teleological if it explains the existence of some phenomenon by asserting that it is necessary in order to bring about some consequence; more specifically, teleological theories are said to explain one thing by showing that it has beneficial consequences for another. The principal objection to this is that the explanation treats an effect as a cause. A teleological explanation in astrophysics would be one which explained the movements of the planets in relation to one another by referring to the need to keep the solar system in operation, or by the need to avoid collisions between planets. Similarly, a teleological explanation in sociology consists in showing that religion exists in order to sustain the moral foundations of society, or that the State exists in order to coordinate the various activities which occur in complex societies. In both these cases, a consequence is used to explain a cause; the end conditions of moral order and coordination are used to explain the existence of religion and the State. It is as though one were to say: X produces Y, therefore the occurrence of Y, which is desirable, must explain the occurrence of X. Critics rightly argue that this type of explanation defies the laws of logic, for one thing cannot be the cause of another if it succeeds it in time.

One attempt to save functionalism asserts that its apparent logical defects are simply the result of a misinterpretation. On this view, what functionalism does is to explain in the normal way[23] by demonstrating a circular process of causal connections, such that one condition produces another, which in turn produce others which may themselves become conditions for the occurrence of the first condition, thus: $A \rightarrow B \rightarrow C \rightarrow D \rightarrow A$. For example, the existence of religion maintains moral order; this, in turn, preserves political institutions; these, in turn, coordinate activities; and this favours the persistence of a social structure of which religion is a part.

This defence is powerful; but it still raises difficulties. First, such statements of circular causation can scarcely be made for any society other than the most simple. Second, it is one thing to assert a causal link between one process and another, but it is quite another to establish that this does explain how a system continues to operate.[24]

One well-known argument in defence of teleology states that sciences, like biology, psychology and sociology—as opposed to physics and chemistry—all deal with the phenomena of purposive behaviour; therefore, they are entitled to treat end states as causes: for example, one explains the activity of eating in terms of the goal of satisfying hunger by showing that eating does have the consequence of reducing hunger pangs. But all that this does in fact show is that in the study of purposive behaviour the aims of an organism must be treated as one of the *anterior* conditions of behaviour. This does not involve treating the consequence—the actual reduction of hunger—as a cause; for it often happens that the end aimed at is not achieved. It is the *aim* of reducing hunger which is a cause. In any case, although all human behaviour, and certainly all human social conduct, must be treated as purposive, it does not follow that social phenomena can be explained as the *direct* outcome of purposive conduct. If religion does strengthen the moral code of society, this does not mean that men practise their religion with the intention of strengthening the moral code. Many, if not most, social phenomena are the product of the *unintended* consequences of social actions; these social actions are themselves purposive; but many of their consequences have no direct connection with these purposes. Thus, men may participate in their religion in order to achieve a state of salvation; if this widespread participation has consequences for the moral order, this may be quite unconnected with the purposes envisaged by the participants. This is not to deny that men sometimes deliberately set out to create or destroy social phenomena. Once they recognize that certain social institutions are beneficial, or that others are harmful, they may deliberately create them or destroy them. But whatever men do in this respect, they always unintentionally produce certain social and cultural items which, though they appear to have been devised for certain purposes, were not. One cannot explain the historical development of the price-mechanism in terms of the intentions of anyone; though, one may explain the partial suspension of the price-mechanism in some societies in terms of intentions which are guided by ideology; and, furthermore, one may explain its partial restoration in terms of the deliberate attempt to avoid the consequences of its suspension.

It might be argued in reply to this criticism that there are *unconscious* intentions at work in society; for example, religion may change in response to social 'needs' through the unconscious recognition of these 'needs'. That unconscious motives exist in the human mind can scarcely be doubted. But whereas psychologists may have some means of investigating these in the personality, sociologists do not seem to have any means of doing this in the analysis of social phenomena. In any case, such explanations are often unnecessary; for it is simplest to explain social phenomena that are not consciously intended as unintended consequences of social action. However, there is still the difficulty of explaining why these unintended consequences do contribute to the maintenance of other social phenomena, or do satisfy certain needs of individuals.

Some functionalists would deal with this problem by drawing an analogy between physiology and sociology. They would argue that just as physical organs are necessary for an organism to function in its environment, so social institutions, beliefs, etc., are necessary for social systems to function in their environment. This type of argument makes no doubtful assumptions concerning conscious or unconscious purposes. An example of this would be to say that the family is necessary for the socialization of the young and for the protection of the mother, and it is for these reasons a universal institution.

Plausible though this argument may be, it is, nevertheless, unacceptable. Physiologists may well examine the functions of organs and thereby explain how the organism, or part of it, works; but they do not thereby explain the presence of the organ. This they may do in terms of natural selection. Can sociologists argue in this way? Can they assume that social phenomena arise, in more or less random fashion, and survive by a process of natural selection? For some purposes it would appear that they can. For example, they may explain the survival of some industrial organizations and the failure of others in terms of differences in organizational efficiency; or they may explain the survival of some states, as independent political entities, in terms of superior military or economic organization. But these arguments are fragile. For if one organization or state fails to compete favourably with another it may not disappear but may be absorbed by the more successful organization. There is no analogous process in the world of physical organisms. Criteria of survival of societies or cultures are difficult, if not impossible, to specify.

Another possibility is simply to treat functional analysis as social 'physiology' without any aim of explaining why the particular social phenomena exist in the first place. But even this raises some difficulties. For, in physiology proper, there are some criteria of the health of an organism which can be used to assess the functioning or malfunctioning of its processes. In sociology this kind of analysis is fraught with pitfalls; by some standards the health of a society would be improved by preventing expressions of conflict, but by other standards this would be a sign of ill-health. To make matters more complicated, a society can change its structure to a greater or lesser extent, whereas an organism cannot.

This does not mean that there can be no analogies between sociological and biological thinking. There is an important sense in which one can explain social changes in terms of the adaptation of one set of institutions to others, or in terms of the adaptation of institutions to changes in the external environment. But societies can adapt in some respects and not in others; and what is adaptation from one viewpoint is not so from another. For example, if the caste system survives in India, as it does at present, it might be said that this is maladaptive for economic growth. On the other hand, one could argue that the pressure for economic development is maladaptive from the standpoint of the caste system; in this case, the obstacles to economic development have the function of preserving the caste system. Clearly the whole exercise becomes rather futile in these terms. It is simpler to show how caste inhibits economic development and how economic development leads to the modification of the caste system.

The second logical criticism of functionalist hypotheses is that they are untestable. An hypothesis is untestable not because it lacks confirming evidence—confirming evidence is found only too easily for any hypothesis—but because it does not enable one to deduce statements from it which, if false, in the light of evidence, would lead one to reject or modify the hypothesis. Consider the following example. It is said that the function of the State is to coordinate activities. If this is to be treated as a scientific hypothesis, then it should be agreed that if one finds examples of the State not coordinating activities, or of actually separating different activities, then the hypothesis should be modified or abandoned. But this is where the difficulties arise. For one can argue that the separation of activities by the State is carried out as a type of coordination: thus even when the very opposite of what is expected actually occurs it can be treated as confirming evidence! But even if one abjures this sort of argument the difficulties still remain. Let us say that one does discover cases where the State does coordinate activities and other cases where it does not; one could then argue that although the State does not *always* coordinate activities, it would not exist if it did not *sometimes* do this. In this weakened version the hypothesis would read: State institutions arise as a response to the need for co-ordination of activities; if these institutions entirely fail to coordinate some activities, then they tend to disappear. This is an improved form, but it is nevertheless still difficult to test. First, how does one investigate a condition such as the 'need for coordination'? One suspects that this need is inferred, by the sociologist, from the existence or growth of State institutions; for there are surely many cases where the proliferation of social activities does not, by itself, result in greater coordination; and, one suspects, there are many cases where it is the expansion of State activities which creates a so-called 'need' for coordination; that is, the 'need' is discovered by those who represent the State. Second, there is the difficulty of envisaging a case in which the State coordinates nothing at all; since one can always find *some* respect in which the State coordinates some activities there is little chance of discovering a counter-example to the hypothesis. In short, the hypothesis is bound to be right, whatever the circumstances.

This criticism can be applied to any hypothesis of this kind: there is nothing very special about the one actually chosen. An excellent example is the hypothesis that the function of religion is to provide a moral consensus for social life. If one quotes as a counter-example the divisive effects of religion, it can be argued that religion has powerful divisive effects precisely because it commits its members so firmly to its support. The hypothesis, like the customer, is never wrong.

The indictment of untestability could, presumably, be brought against sociological hypotheses in general, on the grounds that they do not often specify very precisely what evidence would be accepted in refutation.* But the reply to this point could be that it is possible to make other types of hypothesis more testable, while those of a functionalist variety resist such treatment. This verdict seems reasonably just as applied to many functionalist hypotheses. An extreme example is the hypothesis that conflict has the function of stabilizing society. The evidence supporting this is always taken from cases where severe conflict was followed, in the long run, not by a break-up of a social unit but by consolidation. But little attempt is made to assess the significance of such cases in the light of those where the opposite has occurred.†

One aspect of the untestability of functionalist hypotheses that has been remarked upon by some writers is that if they are to be interpreted in an acceptable way they demand standards of rigour in empirical testing which simply cannot be applied.[26] The full argument is as follows. Let us say that what sociological functionalism sets out to do is to examine the contribution made by various social processes to the maintenance of a whole system

* See Chapter 1.
† An exception is provided by I. Schapira.[25]

in a given state, and that as part of this task it seeks to assess what changes will occur in a system when there is a change in any one or more variables in it. This formulation is similar to, if not identical with, that known as the cybernetic model; here one is concerned with an interaction of processes known as 'feedback': a 'negative feedback' is one which cancels out or offsets any process which might produce a change in the system; 'positive feedback' is one which responds to any change in such a way as to produce a new state of equilibrium in which the altered system is once again adapted to its environment. The testing of hypotheses derived from such models requires that one has some measures, preferably precise ones, which tell one whether a system is in a given state at any particular time, or whether there has been a change in that state. A physical system, for example, can be interpreted in this way in terms of energy levels; or an economic system can be interpreted in terms of price-levels, of levels of out-put in relation to in-put, and so on. But how is one to assess the state of a political system, or a family system, or the relationship between the religious system and the the State? How, in these cases, is one to decide where there has or has not been a return to a given state, or a persistence in it, or a movement away from it? To say, without such measures, that a given process contributes to the maintenance of the system is little more than tautology: for if this process were to change, then there would, by definition, be a change in the system.

The final logical criticism is that the holistic approach of functionalism inhibits comparison and generalization. The argument is this, that if a social and cultural item is to be examined within the totality of a society, then it must be treated as unique; for the totality of one society is never the same as another. For example, if the English family can be understood only in the context of English society and culture as a whole, then the English family becomes a unique phenomenon, unlike the French family which, in turn, can only be understood in the context of French society and culture as a whole. An adjunct of this argument is that the comparison of whole societies and cultures is so unwieldy as to be impracticable: imagine the difficulty of trying to compare the family structures of English and French society by examining not only every other known

feature of the two societies but the way in which these interrelate with one another to form a whole.

One retort to this could be that the principal task of sociology
is simply to understand each social whole as a unique system.
But this is indefensible for at least two obvious reasons. First,
though one cannot claim to understand anything without
referring to its context, one can also not claim to understand it,
in any meaningful sense of the term, unless one can compare it
with other things which are like it in at least some respects.
Malinowski may have increased our understanding of Trobriand
institutions by placing them in their wider context; but he would
not have achieved this if he had not also had in mind similar or
comparable institutions or processes in our own society. Second,
and this argument is linked with the first, one can scarcely begin
an analysis of any society without some general concepts or
terms which make it, in some respects, familiar to us. One understands the Trobriand family only by calling it a 'family'. Or, to
take a more interesting example, one understands the Trobriand
Kula by describing it as a system of ritual exchanges, since the
terms 'ritual' and 'exchange' are meaningful to us. Every examination of a society or culture, including that of our own, must
comprise both contextual analysis and wider comparison, even
when this last is only implicit.

It is, of course, important to recognize why so much has been
made of the need for contextual understanding; for without this
one might tend to assume that superficial resemblances between
the features of different societies necessarily indicated that other,
more profound or significant, features were also alike. E. R.
Leach has argued very forcibly that we have been unable to
recognize that our ideas about the family are cultural products
rather than biological ones, simply because we ourselves tend to
confuse these two levels of reality. The implication is that the
use of English terms like 'father' and 'mother' carry connotations
which are out of place in other cultures.[27] But the remedy for
this cannot be to abandon terms like 'family', 'paternity',
'maternity', 'central authority', 'magic', 'religion', simply because
they carry connotations which are not applicable to all societies.
For if we abandon these we shall find ourselves adopting other
general terms with connotations which are equally 'culture-
specific'. The only remedy is to remember that while some

things are common to all societies or to all societies of a particular type, others are not. Contextual analysis helps us to understand what the characteristics of a particular institution are. But this is not the only aim of sociological inquiry, which is also to explain why social life does exhibit so many similarities, and why variations on these similar themes can and do occur.

A recent attempt to solve this problem, within the context of functional theory, has suggested that functionalism be taken ever more seriously and literally than it has been. This argument starts out by agreeing that each culture is a unique whole, and it therefore concedes that the parts of each culture are really unique to it, because they obtain their characteristics from their presence in the larger whole. It recommends that the true items for comparison and generalization are not, therefore, items of social structure and culture, but *functional processes as such*.[28] An example of a functional process—that is, a process which is necessary to serve certain needs of individuals and societies—is education or socialization. In simple societies this occurs within the domestic group, for the most part; but in more complex societies this occurs also in other contexts; so the comparison and generalization should focus not on the contexts as such, but on the process. The author of this view, W. Goldschmidt, does not seem to realize that this raises problems similar to those which he wishes to avoid. For the difficulty now lies in identifying a common functional process in different societies. It is no easier to look for socialization as a universal process in all societies than it is to look for the family, the State, magic, etc., for the nature of socialization—the meaning of the process—presumably varies from one context to another. Goldschmidt tries to solve this problem by falling back on the arguments of Malinowski: that there are certain universal biological needs, and from these certain psychological and social ones are derived. This takes the problem of identifying functions out of the realm of the cultural analysis. But this is not very helpful: human society has travelled a long way from its biological origins; most of its 'needs'—if they can be called this—have an autonomous social and cultural character: for example, the 'need' of an industrial society for a complex bureaucratic structure can scarcely be reduced to any primary or even secondary needs.

Goldschmidt's contribution is certainly an important one in

that it shows that what we are interested in comparing and in explaining are social processes rather than items of social structure.

Of course, the notion that any society or culture is ever really studied 'as a whole' is a misconception, if not a myth. It would be logically impossible to do this, for there is no way of knowing when one has included every single item; there may always be another.

Contextual analysis is necessary for *identifying* social phenomena; but these can then be removed from their contexts and compared. Much functional inquiry consists in relating a small number of processes which are manageable for purposes of comparison and generalization.

Criticisms: Substantive

It could justly be argued that some of the logical objections to functionalism are so damaging as to make others superfluous. But the substantive objections should be listed if only for the reason that some sociologists would reject the doctrine even if it were logically reinstated.

The chief substantive criticisms of functionalism are these: it overemphasizes the normative element in social life; it minimizes the importance of social conflict at the expense of social solidarity; it stresses the harmonious nature of social systems; and, finally, it fails to account for social change and even treats this as abnormal.

The first objection is without foundation. Some functionalists may tend to treat the norms and values of society as the only reality to be considered. But this was certainly not true of Malinowski. There is nothing in functionalism as such which requires the adoption of this position.

The second objection is related to the first. For if men accepted the norms and values of their society, it is argued, there would never be any conflict. For example, if all men accepted the rules of succession to chieftainship there would never be any strife over this. This is mistaken. The strife may occur not because there is any questioning of the rules, but because there are different claimants to whom the rules may apply. This suggests that even if the norms and values were totally accepted there would always be conflict, because the norms are seldom totally unambiguous.

In fact, there is nothing in functionalism itself which encourages an emphasis on unity or solidarity as opposed to conflict. It is true that Radcliffe-Brown, following Durkheim, did seek to analyse a number of phenomena in terms of the function of maintaining social solidarity. He did not ignore conflict, but argued that a society could not operate unless there were some restraints on the expression of conflict and some mechanisms for its resolution. But some of Radcliffe-Brown's pupils, such as Gluckman, have drawn attention to the pervasiveness of conflict situations in primitive as well as more complex societies.[29] The charge that functionalism minimizes the importance of conflict is clearly without foundation.

The complaint that functionalism overemphasizes the harmonious interrelatedness of parts of a social system is more just than the previous two complaints. However, Merton pointed out some years ago that items may be functional for some groups, or for some features of social life, and dysfunctional for others.[30] For example, internal ethnic cohesion may function to protect minority rights; but it may also delay the disappearance of minority status.

Gouldner has also argued that to assert that there is functional interdependence within a society is less significant than showing that the degrees of interdependence may vary within a social system.[31] For example, the distribution of wealth may have a greater impact on the pattern of leisure activities than this latter has on the former.

The final substantive complaint, that functionalism cannot explain social change, is perhaps justified, but not for the reasons that are normally given. The implication of this argument is that functionalism, by emphasizing the conditions of persistence and stability, treats change as something abnormal and unlikely to occur except, perhaps, by accident. This argument appears plausible: if functionalism asserts that all items in a social system reinforce one another, then none can contribute to change, since each is kept going by the others. But in fact, if functionalism could really state the conditions under which social systems persist then it could also explain change simply by showing that some of those conditions are sometimes absent. Clearly, no functionalist has ever denied that social change is 'normal' and that it may result from conditions within the social system itself. This being so, if they really do have a theory of social persistence then they must also have a theory of change. In fact, some functionalist hypotheses are covert, but abbreviated, statements of social change. For example, if one asserts that kinship terminology has a function of categorizing kinsmen in terms of the rights and obligations owing to them and expected from them, then the implication is that a change in the jural content of kinship relations will be accompanied by a change in the system of terminology.

The truth of the matter is that if functionalists have not produced adequate theories of social change this is largely because they have not produced adequate theories of social persistence. Insofar as they have gone some way to explaining why social systems persist, they have also, I submit, contributed to the theory of social change. What has been wrong with functionalism is that it has simply asserted that social systems or certain types of system tend to persist without giving more than a hint at why this occurs. I propose to elaborate these hints in later chapters.

Criticisms: Ideological

The alleged connection between functionalism and ideology should really be irrelevant to the assessment of the doctrine as a theory of society or as a method of inquiry. For, strictly, if a theory has implications which are considered undesirable or unpalatable this should lead one to alter one's notions of how to achieve the desirable, not to a rejection of the theory. But this is a pious and unrealistic hope. It would be surprising if sociologists did succeed in divorcing their ideological criticisms from their scientific ones. However, some of the ideological criticisms of functionalism are also interesting as scientific criticisms.

The chief criticism of this kind is that functionalism encourages or reflects a conservative bias. The argument behind this is that functionalism, by emphasizing the harmonious relationships between different parts of a social system, tends to treat each system as though it were the best of all possible worlds. It is true that Burke was something of a functionalist and that he used functionalist arguments in defence of his conservatism. But, as Merton has shown, functionalism could equally be used to justify a policy of total revolution. For, if all features of social life are completely interdependent, then the only hope for social reform is a total transformation of society; to change some parts only would be impossible, for these changes would be ineffective, unless linked with a totally different system.[32] Despite Merton's arguments, the claim is still made that functionalism is wedded to conservatism, and the counter-claims are made that anti-functionalists disguise radical or Utopian ideologies as scientific theories. The *cause célèbre* of this debate has been the problem of social stratification; and a very appropriate *cause* it is.

The functionalist theory of social stratification, which has been put forward by Davis and Moore,[33] and, separately by Parsons,[34] derives in fact from Durkheim. What these writers have sought to show is that social stratification inevitably occurs in any complex society, particularly in an industrial society, and that it serves 'vital functions' in such societies. This means, in other words, that social stratification is indispensable to any complex society and that any attempt to be rid of it would necessarily require the abandonment of other features of such societies. The argument is as follows. In a society in which tasks are specialized, some of these tasks call for talents which are rare, or are found more abundantly in some individuals than in others. It is necessary that the more talented be attracted to those occupations which require their skills. These occupations demand administrative, entrepreneurial, military, or intellectual skills, which are vital to the society. While anyone can perform unskilled tasks only the talented can perform certain skilled ones; consequently, such tasks must earn higher material and prestige rewards than others; and often they also involve the exercise of greater power. The possession of greater wealth, prestige and power marks off a section of society as a class. Given this, and given the existence of the human family, class privileges will be inherited by one generation from another. But there will also be a certain amount of social mobility; those who are unsuccessful at performing the tasks required of them may lose their class position, while others with exceptional abilities may rise.

The critics of this view, who see in it an apology for the status quo, put forward the following counter-arguments.[35] First, they show that stratification may actually hinder the efficient working of a social system by preventing those with superior, innate abilities from performing certain tasks which are the preserve of a privileged class. Second, they dispute the argument that some tasks are more vital or important to a society than others: the manager is no more vital than the manual labourer, for the one cannot operate without the other. Third, they question the need for large income differentials as a means of attracting men of talent to skilled occupations: they argue, in fact, that if occupations require special skills they will usually give more intrinsic satisfaction than those which do not, so that there should be less need to offer higher rewards, not more. Fourth, they cast doubt on the implicit assumption that actual differentials of reward do reflect differences in the skills required for particular occupations: for example, if a surgeon earns twenty times more than a coal-miner, does this mean that the surgeon's skills are twenty times greater or more valuable to society than those of the miner? The final criticism is that a society without social classes is, in principle, possible if it possesses a value-system which encourages a commitment to equality and public service. Such a society may never exist; but this would be more a consequence of existing stratification than of the requirements of a complex society; for the inheritance of privilege, which is the greatest determinant of class position, also ensures its own continuity.

These criticisms appear unanswerable. But this only means that they are true statements, not that they constitute a refutation of the functionalist theory. For it is at least arguable that the two theories are not really incompatible, since they really answer different questions. Davis and Moore, and Parsons, set out to explain why social stratification must exist in all contemporary complex societies, even if they have no history of stratification, and now have an egalitarian ideology. They assume that the division of labour produces inequality of reward, so that even if the present structures of social class were abolished, there would still be inequalities of occupational status to replace the old class structure. The second part of their answer is that without such inequalities of reward there would be no way of ensuring the continuity of a complex division of labour.

The opposing theory is really an answer to the question: why do social classes perpetuate themselves? The answer given is that such perpetuation may have nothing to do with the so-called 'needs of society', but may lie within the structure of privilege and of the family. Put in this form the two theories are compatible, for they answer different questions. They can be made into genuine rival theories: (a) if the first asserts that differential rewards are necessary for an industrial society and the second asserts that they are not; or, (b) if they both agree that some kind of differential rewards are necessary and the first theory asserts that this, in itself, will create social classes, while the second argues that this does not necessarily occur.

If we assume that these two theories can then be tested—and so far they have not been—and that the first is refuted, does it follow that functionalism itself is at fault? And does it prove that functionalism is ideologically tainted? The answer to the first question must be that it depends on what is meant by functionalism. The answer to the second question is that it does not matter very much whether theories are or are not ideologically tainted: what matters is whether they can be rationally appraised without reference to ideology.

The curious thing about this debate is that both theories of stratification can be interpreted as functionalist. Thus, the critics of the Davis-Moore theory explain how social class systems function to maintain themselves. Their conception is one of a set of interacting, mutually reinforcing processes. Of course, what these critics mean by functionalism is the assumption that some process, such as the persistence of class divisions, is beneficial to society as a whole. In this sense, their theory is not functionalist. But in this sense any theory is on dangerous ground: for it can always be shown that a feature of society is beneficial to it in one respect or another.

Another example that illustrates the ambiguity of so-called functionalist and anti-functionalist controversies is the discussion of power in society. The 'functionalist' view, which has been put forward by Talcott Parsons, is that power is a facility for operating a political system.[36] This means that unless some men have power to make certain kinds of decisions and to initiate actions to see that these are carried out, many other things would not get done; it also means that unless men are rewarded by power, they will not be attracted to perform certain tasks. The implication of this theory is that the existence of a structure of power in any society can be explained in terms of the functions which this performs for the social system. This is perhaps another way of saying that power is not a bad thing in itself, for without it certain generally desired things would never get done. The opposed theory states that power exists because certain social positions afford some men the opportunities to coerce or induce others to accept their domination and to comply with their demands; it also asserts that the institutions of political representation, where they exist, are so interlocked with other features of social structure, such as the distribution of resources and the links of patronage, that they become the instruments of certain social classes or dominant elites. The implication of this theory is that power serves those who have it and it also affords them the opportunity to hold on to it and to pass it on to others of their choosing. A further implication is that if decision-makers were truly responsible to their supporters, they would not really have power over them at all; nor would the exercise of power be necessary, for administrative decisions would reflect the demands of those on whose behalf they are administered. The ideological overtones in this debate are scarcely concealed.

In this example, as in the previous one, the so-called anti-functionalist theory is also, *in a sense*, functionalist: for it explains how structures of power persist by showing how they are part of a wider system of interdependent processes. The first theory is functionalist in the rather special sense of referring to the 'needs of society' as a whole.

The notion that society as a whole has certain needs is an old one in social theory and was in the past an undisguised appeal for certain forms of political organization. What it is trying to convey is something like this. There are some things which are necessary for the welfare of the majority of which they are not necessarily aware and which they cannot, therefore, achieve simply by acting on their individual desires; these things may therefore be called 'social needs', though they are not discovered by investigating the individual needs of the majority. For example, if all men are left to express their own selfish desires then they may so fight among themselves as to prevent any one or more of them from exercising power over the rest; but in the long run this may prevent them from realizing certain aims, such as that of military defence. Most versions of this doctrine refer *ultimately* to the benefits which certain forms of social organization bestow on the individual members of society; but some refer to the good of some collective entity in itself—such as the State, the Nation or Civilization—regardless of the benefit accruing to any individuals. This latter version is purely metaphysical, insofar as there is no way of discovering whether some abstract entity has or has not benefited from some social institution or another. In other words, it is always possible to show that the Nation or Society has benefited, for there is no way of checking this; at least individuals, whether in small or large numbers, can voice an opinion on such matters.

This digression is relevant to our discussion of the theories of power and the ideological imputations which affect such controversies. For if the so-called functionalists are simply stating that power is a necessary condition for the achievement of certain goals which are considered desirable by the members of society, then it is simply a question of whether they are right or wrong, not of whether they are ideologically biased. (Of course, it is possible that their ideological biases would influence their assessment of the evidence; but that is another matter.) And if they are stating that the manner in which power is exercised is determined more by the pressures from within the social system than by the selfish interests of a power elite, here again it is a question of empirical inquiry. Of course there are huge problems in conducting such an inquiry to the satisfaction of opponents or, indeed, of anyone else. For one thing, how is one to distinguish between the interests of the powerful and their own *interpretation* of the pressures of the social system? No doubt, since it *is* so difficult to test such a theory, there is considerable room for qualitative judgement; and, doubtless, this opens the way for bias in the assessment of evidence. And the same is true of the opposing theory. But the only way to take the debate out of the area of ideology—and there will be those on both sides who have no wish to do this—is, in fact, to scrutinize the assumption and evidence of both sides as rationally as possible.

In fact, it is clear that neither theory is necessarily true at the expense of the other. Each is an interpretation of political reality —a model, if one prefers—which emphasizes some aspects of reality at the expense of others. Clearly one model is more appropriate to some circumstances than to others. There are some societies in which political elites invent imaginary social needs in order to justify their exercise of power; but even they will, in the modern world, make many decisions which could be said to benefit the masses in some ways. On the other hand, there are societies in which the exercise of power is controlled to some extent by those on whose behalf it is exercised, and for whom it functions largely as a means of getting things done in a collective and coordinated manner; though even in these cases there is a tendency for those who wield power to define certain interests in terms of their own roles. Perhaps some functionalists have been guilty of assuming that because the exercise of power serves to main the structure of society, it therefore serves the interests of its members. All societies have self-perpetuating tendencies. But the fact that societies resist change does not mean that their members are content.

Conclusion

Functionalism has been heavily criticized, and much of the criticism is just: but it is as well to recognize what the criticism really amounts to. In the first place, theories which seek to explain the existence of social phenomena in terms of the contribution which they make to the preservation of a larger 'whole' *are* quite unacceptable.* But to concede this is not to invalidate the use of

* This point has been made somewhat differently by Kingsley Davis.[37] But his arguments are too cavalier in their readiness to accept that functional explanations are teleological while insisting that all sociological explanation and, indeed all scientific explanation is, in some senses, functional. The point is that functional explanation alone is unacceptable in sociology. If, as Davis thinks, sociological explanation cannot dispense with functional analysis— and for some sociological problems this is disputable—then the most one can say is that functional analysis can be a part, but never the whole, of sociological explanation.

functional analysis as *part* of genuine sociological explanation. For what functional analysis does is to demonstrate some degree of circularity—or 'feed-back', if one prefers the more fashionable term—in the casual processes of social life. It does this by creating models which abstract a number of features from the recurrent on-going flow of social reality and presenting these *as though* they constituted totalities. But such totalities—or 'boundary main-taining systems'—are not the totality of any real social phenomena; they are constructed totalities only. From the field of social reality many such totalities can be created. When this part of the analysis has been carried out it is then possible to use the model of interrelated processes in order to provide a true causal explan-ation of some social phenomenon. For example, if one wishes to explain the emergence of new religious movements in certain societies which have come under colonial domination or influence, one must show, among other things, how men are attracted to these religions by the kinds of salvation which they offer in circumstances of social and cultural breakdown; but one can only identify the nature of this breakdown by showing how the earlier sets of religious beliefs and practices affected and were affected by other conditions of social life. Or, to take another, rather different sort of example, one can only explain certain difficulties in overcoming obstacles to economic growth in modern Britain if one constructs a model showing how a number of factors of class structure, aspirations, values and forms of economic conduct mutually reinforce one another in a particular state.

No doubt it is also true, as so many critics have alleged, that functionalism cannot explain social change. But then it is doubtful whether functionalism, as such, can truly explain social per-sistence. For if a theory can *explain* why social structures tend to persist, then it must be able to explain why they change; for to do this latter requires only to assert that the conditions making for persistence are absent. If one takes functional arguments to absurd conclusions and asserts that every item in a social system is so interrelated with every other that the whole must persist in a given state, then, of course, such a theory can explain only persistence. But even if one were to take such a view of social systems seriously one could only do so by treating it as a model: that is, as an imaginary social world. Such a model could be useful—as I show in Chapter VI—in characterizing the difference between very simple and very complex societies; and it helps to explain why certain characteristics are associated with simple systems which are not found in more complex ones. But, it is, for all that, only a model. No real society is quite like that, and most are quite unlike it in many respects, though all are in *some* respects, like it. Thus, functionalism, as a doctrine, does not, in itself, explain social persistence any more than it explains social change. What it does is to suggest a range of models which enables one to look for the explanation of why some systems tend to resist change more than others, and why some are extremely prone to change.

And this brings one to a criticism of sociological functionalism or holism which is seldom made. It is that functionalism does not provide an explanation of its *own* assumptions: that is, functionalist ideas do not explain why it is that functional inter-relationships exist in all social life, and why the degree of functional interdependence in societies or in sectors of societies itself varies. If it could do this then there would be no difficulty in showing that the explanation of both social persistence and of social change makes use of the same theories and models of social life. This explanation must proceed by way of some notion of social action and interaction.

NOTES

1. Auguste Comte, *Cours de Philosophie Positive*, I, p. 29, IV, pp. 230–1.
2. F. A. Hayek, *The Counter-Revolution of Science*, Free Press, 1952, pp. 129–206.
3. See Donald G. MacRae, 'The Crisis of Sociology' in J. H. Plumb (ed.) *Crisis in the Humanities*, Penguin, 1964, p. 127.
4. See Jay Rumney, *Herbert Spencer's Sociology*, Atherton, New York, 1966, Chapters IX and X.
5. Emile Durkheim, *The Division of Labour in Society*.
6. Emile Durkheim, *The Rules of Sociological Method*, Chapter V.
7. Emile Durkheim, *The Division of Labour in Society*, Book Two, Chap. 2.
8. Emile Durkheim, *The Elementary Forms of Religious Life* (trans. J. W. Swain) Collier, N.Y., 1961. Book 2, Chs. 5–7.

9. Cf. I. C. Jarvie, *The Revolution in Anthropology*, Routledge, London, 1964.
10. See K. R. Popper. 'Science: Conjectures and Refutations', *Conjectures and Refutations*, Routledge, 1963, pp. 33–65.
11. B. Malinowski, 'Anthropology', *Encyclopaedia Britannica*, First Supplementary Volume, London and New York, 1962, pp. 132–3.
12. B. Malinowski, *A Scientific Theory of Culture*, University of Carolina Press, 1944.
13. Op. cit.
14. A. R. Radcliffe-Brown, 'On the Concept of Function in Social Science' in *Structure and Function in Primitive Societies*, Free Press, 1952.
15. A. R. Radcliffe-Brown, 'Religion and Society', op. cit.
16. A. R. Radcliffe-Brown, 'The Mother's Brother in South Africa', op. cit.
17. E. E. Evans-Pritchard, *The Nuer*, Oxford, 1940, pp. 160–1.
18. Talcott Parsons, 'Position and Prospects of Systematic Theory in Sociology', *Essays in Sociological Theory*, Free Press, 1949.
19. Talcott Parsons, *The Social System*, Free Press, 1951, pp. 450–2.
20. See for example, D. F. Aberle, *et al.*, 'The Functional Prerequisites of a Society', *Ethics*, 60, 1950, pp. 100–11.
21. Talcott Parsons, *Essays in Sociological Theory*, p. 224.
22. See for example, R. P. Dore, 'Function and Cause', *American Sociological Review*, December 1961, pp. 843–53.
    and, Carl G. Hempel, 'The Logic of Functional Analysis', in L. Gross, *Symposim on Sociological Theory*, pp. 271–302.
    and, Robert K. Merton, 'Manifest and Latent Functions', *Social Theory and Social Structure*, Free Press, 1949, pp. 21–81.
    and, Harry C. Bredemeier, 'The Methodology of Functionalism', *American Sociological Review*, Vol. X, 1945, pp. 242–9.
23. E. A. Gellner, 'Concepts and Society', *Transactions of the Fifth World Congress of Sociology*.
24. See Carl G. Hempel, ibid.
    and Ernest Nagel, 'A Formalization of Functionalism', *Logic Without Metaphysics*, Free Press, 1956.
25. I. Schapera, *Government and Politics in Tribal Societies*, Watts, London, 1956, pp. 175–6.
26. Carl G. Hempel, ibid.
27. E. R. Leach, *Rethinking Anthropology*, Athlone, London, 1961, pp. 1–27.
28. W. Goldschmidt, *Comparative Functionalism*, Cambridge University Press, 1966.
29. See Max Gluckman, *Custom and Conflict in Africa*, Oxford, 1959.

30. Robert K. Merton, ibid.
31. A. W. Gouldner, 'Reciprocity and Autonomy in Functional Theory' in L. Gross (ed) *Symposium on Sociological Theory*, Harper, New York, 1959, pp. 241–70.
32. Robert K. Merton, ibid.
33. Kingsley Davis and Wilbert E. Moore, 'Some Principles of Stratification', *American Sociological Review*, Vol. X, 1945, 2, pp. 242–9.
34. Talcott Parsons, 'An Analytical Approach to the Theory of Social Stratification' and 'A Revised Analytical Approach to the Theory of Stratification', *Essays in Sociological Theory*, Free Press, 1954, pp. 69–86 and 386–439.
35. See Melvin W. Tumin, 'Some Principles of Stratification: A Critical Analysis', *American Sociological Review*, Vol. 18, 1953, No. 4. and Walter Buckley, 'Social Stratification and the Functional Theory of Social Differentiation', *American Sociological Review*, Vol. 23, 1958, pp. 369–75.
36. Talcott Parsons, 'On the Concept of Political Power' in R. Bendix and S. M. Lipset (eds.) *Class, Status and Power*, Routledge, 1967, pp. 240–65.
37. Kingsley Davis, 'The Myth of Functional Analysis as a Special Method in Sociology and Anthropology', *American Sociological Review*, Vol. 24, 1959, pp. 757–73.

4.

The Action Approach

The Assumptions of the Theory of Action

THE THEORY of action consists of a number of assumptions, set out below, which prescribe a mode of analysis for explaining the action or conduct (for the time being the terms 'action' and 'conduct' are used interchangeably) of typical individuals in typical situations. These typical individuals are referred to as actors or social actors.*

(i) The actor has goals (or aims, or ends); his actions are carried out in pursuit of these.

(ii) Action often involves the selection of means to the attainment of goals; but even where it appears that it does not, it is still possible for an observer to distinguish analytically between means and goals.

(iii) An actor always has many goals; his actions in pursuit of any one affect and are affected by his actions in pursuit of others.

(iv) The pursuit of goals and the selection of means always occurs within situations which influence the course of action.

(v) The actor always makes certain assumptions concerning the nature of his goals and the possibility of their attainment.

(vi) Action is influenced not only by the situation but by the actor's knowledge of it.

(vii) The actor has certain ideas or modes of cognition which affect his selective perception of situations.

(viii) The actor has certain sentiments or affective dispositions which affect both his perception of situations and his choice of goals.

(ix) The actor has certain norms and values which govern his selection of goals and his ordering of them in some scheme of priorities.

* The statement and discussion of these assumptions owes a great deal to the writings of F. von Mises,[1] Talcott Parsons[2] and Max Weber[3] though not all of their views are necessarily accepted.

Some of these assumptions need little clarification, others more.

(i) *Goal-Orientation*

To say that all human action is directed to the attainment of goals seems obvious and indisputable; indeed, one could argue that goal-orientation is simply a defining quality of action: presumably, if one does not remain inactive, one must be motivated; to be motivated means to have a goal and to seek to reach it.

However, some types of action do seem to be without a goal: one describes certain types of behaviour, such as that of a man wandering about a room, as 'aimless'; one might even say that the smoking of a cigarette is without any discernible goal. But one could argue that such action only *seems* to be without a goal. A man may wander 'aimlessly' to relieve tension or in order not to have something specific to aim at; one may smoke a cigarette to achieve greater social poise and to 'handle' anxiety. One may say of such actions that they have no obvious, conscious goal and that whatever goal they have may be highly unspecific. But to say that a goal is not specific is only to suggest that there are many ways of achieving it, and that the moment of achievement may be very difficult to identify.

Many goals are highly specific and the attainment easily identified; an example is an increase in earnings. Furthermore, many goals are consciously recognized by all or some of the actors involved in them. It often happens that men do not consciously recognize their own goals—at least they do not readily admit to recognizing them—but they may easily recognize the same goals in others. A perfect example of this is the goal of increasing one's prestige or power. However, this goal is not necessarily very specific, nor is its attainment always easy to recognize.

For many sociological purposes, goals can be treated as fairly specific and as consciously recognizable, if not recognized. Men do not seek election simply in order to relieve personal tension; they may do so because they wish to participate in decision-making. However, the sociologist must never assume that all goals are equally recognizable by the actors concerned, nor that they are equally specific. Similarly, the identifiability of goal-attainment is also a variable; it is less easy to identify the attainment of spiritual salvation than to identify an increase in income.

(ii) *The Selection of Means*

To state that action involves the use of means for the attainment of goals is to assume that means and goals are empirically or analytically distinguishable. This assumes that the means are not defined in terms of the goals; where the goal is so specific that there is only one way to achieve it, there is almost no distinction between means and goals. It is easiest to distinguish between means and goals when there are many ways to achieve the goal —that is, when the goal is vague.

Where both means and goals are concretely identifiable objects or states they are also readily distinguishable; where, however, they are a complex flow of events the distinction can only be made with analytic effort. It is easy to recognize the planting of seed and the watering of plants as means to a goal, which is to produce crops. It is less easy to distinguish regular elections as a means to the end of preserving democratic freedoms, for in the final instance, regularity of elections is one such freedom. But even if one specifies other goals—such as not imprisoning political opponents—the difficulty is still there, since the clear connection between one state and another is not easy to recognize.

Human actions may involve the manipulation of physical objects for the attainment of goals which can be identified largely in physical terms. Here the distinction between means and ends is easy to make. But where human actions involve goals and means which are identified as phenomena only by virtue of the value and meaning given to them by men in society, then the distinctions are less easy to make. Yet, for many sociological purposes one must recognize that however specific goals may be for the actors involved, they can also be made less specific by them. Wage-earners who have the specific goal of increasing their income in particular firms or industries may appear to have few means at their disposal: they can demand higher rates of pay, or give increased labour time. But, if so specific a goal cannot be achieved, there is often a readiness to make it less specific; for example, to move from one industry to another. Some goals are, of their nature, highly specific: for example, men who are seeking to maintain their ethnic identity are unlikely to exchange this for the more general goal of any type of social identity.

(iii) *The Relationship Between Goals*

No man, however 'single-minded', has only one goal. Sometimes men pursue goals as though all others were subservient to them: some goals, such as 'self-respect', are ultimate, and many others are means to them; while other goals, such as the accumulation of wealth, either in the form of money or as assets realizing income, are strategically important for the attainment of a variety of other goals. It is because some goals are, in these respects, more important than others, that the relationship between goals has some stable structure.

There are three main reasons why some goals do have priority over others. The first, and most obvious reason, is that some goals are more highly valued than others: if men value an immediate increase in leisure more than an immediate increase in income, then they will not work longer hours though they may work harder in order to obtain the same earnings in a shorter period of labour-time; if, on the other hand, men value certain changes in the pattern of leisure activities more highly than an increase in immediate leisure time, then they may agree to work harder and longer hours in the immediate future. However, a rank order of goals may change with changing circumstances. For some men, as income increases, the value of immediate leisure may assume greater importance than the value of changes in the pattern of leisure activities.

The second reason, which is illustrated by the previous example, is that the attainment of some goals is a necessary means to the attainment of others. If men put work before leisure this is not because they necessarily value work more highly, but because their aspirations in terms of leisure activities may be high enough to require substantial increases in income.

The third reason is that the pursuit of some goals may not be feasible in certain circumstances, or the cost of pursuing them may be so great as to jeopardize the quality of the achievement or the possibility of pursuing many others. For example, political leaders may value revolution more than reform; but, in some circumstances they may recognize that the pursuit of revolution is unlikely to succeed, and may even jeopardize the achievement at some later date, while the pursuit of reform, though it may delay the ultimate success of revolution, might at least ensure some continued support for revolution. On the other hand, there may be circumstances in which leaders disavow the pursuit of particular reforms simply because this may weaken the chances of securing a great many more reforms by revolutionary action.

The strategies of action are not governed simply by the structure of relations between goals in this sense, but are also affected by the assessment of the effects which the adoption of particular means may have on the attainment of other goals. Devaluation may be an effective way of solving a particular economic problem; but its effects on the solution of other problems may lead to its exclusion.

To discuss the pursuit of goals in terms of a recognizable structure, or a conscious strategy, is not to suggest that most men acting in most social situations do use such strategies in these ways. In many, or most instances, a strategy has already been established for men, through the trial and error processes of past actions. But even where this is so, and often when it is not so, there is no strategy which neatly relates the goals into a structure of optimal attainment. In many respects, men learn to treat what they have, and what they do, as the optimal attainment. *To discuss the conscious, rational strategy of relating goals to one another is to create a polar conception of action, to which some cases approximate.*

(iv) *The Actor's Situation*

To explain an action is, for the most part, to understand the position of an actor in a particular situation or type of situation. Typical actions are those which occur when the conditions of the situation are to some extent or another facts of social relationships and culture.

To some extent men bring their goals to their situations: whatever the circumstances of the situation, the goal of survival may be constant. But goals are often, to some extent, created by situations. An actor may enter a situation in order to achieve some goal, and may be lead by it to pursue others in addition to, or in place of the original goal; but sometimes situations 'present' the actor with certain goals to pursue. For example, the members of primitive societies who are conquered by colonists may be influenced to increase their incomes because of the need to pay the costs of their new way of life.

An important aspect of any situation is the availability of means to pursue particular goals. Men who are colonized might wish to retain certain valued items of their culture. But if circumstances rob them of the means of doing so, they may devise substitutes for the same valued goals. For example, if men are barred from head-hunting in order to compete for prestige, they may substitute other goals, such as defeating other groups in competitive games in which the individual may win prestige.

The actions of men are governed not simply by the circumstances of situations which are external to them, but also by the subjective manner in which these situations are experienced. The subjective elements in situations are the actor's ideas, feelings and state of knowledge. These elements are very often culturally shared. Thus a situation is fully social when the external elements in it are other social actors, and the internal or subjective elements are the culturally shared dispositions of the actor.

(v) *The Actor's Assumptions*

If an actor assumes that there is a possibility of pursuing a particular goal in a particular manner, or if he assumes that a goal can be realized at all, or if he assumes that a particular course of action will produce certain consequences, then he may act in terms of these assumptions whether or not they are correct, or whether or not they can be shown to be correct. These assumptions are of two main types: those that are empirically testable and those that are not. Empirically testable assumptions are those for which evidence can be adduced and which can, in principle, be refuted by empirical evidence. Assumptions may be untestable for several reasons: they may posit the existence of ends and means which are both 'empirical entities', but may assert a connection between them which is not amenable to empirical testing; or, they may state the conditions for achieving goals which are not empirical entities. A magical belief—for example, that the sprinkling of water brings rain—deals with empirical entities; anyone can witness both phenomena; but it asserts a connection between them which is untestable. A religious belief—for example that prayer brings spiritual salvation

—is untestable not only because the connection between prayer and salvation cannot be tested, but because salvation itself is a non-empirical entity.*

Strictly, a magical assumption is testable; one can show that sticking pins in effigies does not hurt some men. But those who accept such assumptions need not treat them as testable. However, religious assumptions are not, in any sense, testable; it is never possible to produce instances of men who have not been saved by prayer, since one never knows whether or not someone has been saved; the ways of all gods are mysterious.

Empirical assumptions may refer to the manipulation of nature, or to the manipulation of men; non-empirical assumptions may refer also to the manipulation of supernatural beings and powers.

(vi) The Actor's Knowledge of the Situation

The conduct of an actor may not be explained simply in terms of the situation as it appears to the observer, for the actor's knowledge of the situation may be different from the observer's. It is the actor's knowledge which governs his reaction to a situation. If a general is informed that an enemy's forces are smaller than his own, he may be led to attack. However his information may be correct, but partial—the foe may be small in number but well equipped to withstand a particular type of attack—or incorrect. In either case, it is the general's knowledge of the situation that matters; the outcome of the battle, of the war and of much else, may turn on what he thinks the situation is.

(vii) Ideas and Modes of Cognition

The actor's selection of information, his perception of his condition and hence, his conduct, may be influenced not simply by his assumptions concerning the feasibility of achieving certain goals in particular ways, but also by certain modes of thought of which he may be largely unaware. The tendencies to classify men

---

* I am aware that the use of the terms empirical and non-empirical to refer to entities is problematic, since many abstract, scientific concepts such as gravitation and entropy, may be considered as non-empirical in that they are not themselves observable. However, every scientist recognizes, at least intuitively, that there is a difference between the status of concepts like entropy and spiritual salvation.

as good or bad, tall or short, valiant or cowardly, or to classify objects as spherical, angular, smooth, rough, heavy or soft, all reflect modes of thought which are built into the language which one uses; and many cognitive orientations which are relevant for sociological inquiry are far more complex than these.

In most societies there are a host of social category systems which coexist, overlap or intersect, and whose existence influences the perception of situations in subliminal but significant ways. An example of this is the categorization of men into ethnic or racial groups. If this, or similar modes of discrimination are used, there is a tendency for the observer to select certain characteristics to represent these social units. Such cognitive modes may themselves be influenced by, or even produced by, recurrent social situations; but once they exist they influence the perception of social situations and the conduct which occurs in them. It is common for a mode of cognition which has emerged in one type of situation to be carried over into others.

(viii) *Affects and Sentiments*

The perception of situations and the selection of goals are influenced also by affective needs or sentiments.

Affects, such as hostility, love, envy, loyalty or the need for protection, may be simple or may be compounded of a number of different elements; thus the expression of loyalty to one party may necessarily entail one of hostility to another. Affects or sentiments may be expressed directly towards certain objects, or they may imbue them with affective significance by complex processes whereby the actor and the objects are interrelated: the chief processes of this sort, are those of identification, incorporation, projection and displacement. The first involves the actor in seeking gratification by treating the characteristics of some object as though they were his own: men identify with leaders by attributing to themselves certain characteristics of the leader. Incorporation consists in acquiring those characteristics which are taken from another object; when this occurs the actor need no longer be in the situation in which the other object is found in order for its characteristics to influence his conduct. Projection involves the attribution of characteristics of the actor to some other object: a man who accuses another of hostility is often asserting his own, and thereby provoking that of another.

Displacement consists in attributing characteristics to one object which may belong to another.

These mechanisms are often intermingled: for example, a racial minority might be imbued with characteristics which define them as hostile or nefarious. This may involve displacement in that the true source of hostility is beyond the grasp of the actor; but it may also involve projection in that the minority is imbued with characteristics which the actor possesses.

It is not always easy to distinguish between affects and modes of cognition; they intermingle to structure the perception of social situations; though often they are created or, at least, mobilized by the situation itself. Categorization of social units, for example, may be linked with feelings of solidarity, hostility, etc.; and these may be expressed through the complex mechanisms of identification, projection, etc. In some conditions the readiness to express an affective attitude may be influenced by the existence of categories; in other conditions the connection may be the reverse one. For most purposes the readiness both to 'cathect' and to categorize in certain ways is influenced by the qualities of the objects in situations as they are experienced by the actors.

(ix) *The Significance of Norms and Values*

The actor's choice of goals and, in particular, his ranking of goals, is strongly influenced by norms and values. Norms are specific prescriptions and proscriptions of standardized practice. Values, on the other, express preferences, priorities or desirable states of affairs, but not specific forms of conduct.

Norms may be cultural but not necessarily social. What one eats on specific occasions is a cultural norm; the fact that one must share what one eats on specific occasions with specific categories of others, is a social norm. Cultural norms are all those prescriptions or proscriptions of practice which are shared with others and adopted by participating in a particular social unit; social norms are all of those cultural norms which relate to other objects as actors.

Norms may or may not be fully underpinned by values. Slaves may normally act according to certain prescriptions enforced by their masters; but they may do this simply because the only choice is between obedience and punishment, which may be death; they may reject the norms if, and when, the opportunity arises. But even if they fail to reject the norms in favourable circumstances, this may be not because they desire to conform to them, but because they have been conditioned into total submission. It could be argued that in one case they value life, under submission, and without punishment, more than a show of rebellion accompanied by punishment, and that in the other case they value continuity more than freedom. In this sense, the conformity to these norms *is* underpinned by values. But it is not underpinned by values which slaves and masters share, and which define such norms as preferable to others. It is in this last sense that one might say that values underpin norms: for example, if serfs carry out their obligations to their lords, and lords to their serfs, and both parties are bound by a moral commitment to maintain the relationship, then it can clearly be said that values underpin these norms. But it should not be assumed that because men do not opt out of relationships or rebel against them or complain of them, that they necessarily feel committed to them by the acceptance of common values; the choice may be between obedience and minimal security, on the one hand, and freedom and uncertainty on the other. However, there is little doubt that men do evolve values which limit the range of norms which they are willing to adopt or reject.

Norms may prescribe the use of certain means, or they may only set wide limits to the kind of means that are used; but the precise prescription of means usually suggests that there are, theoretically, certain alternatives. Thus, barter as such, as a means to the acquisition of certain goods, is a norm in those societies in which there is no recognized currency or no call for its use. But the detailed norms of conduct in barter situations, which are culturally prescribed, may exclude certain practices, such as bargaining.

Norms do not prescribe goals as such, unless these are means to the pursuit of other goals, or unless these norms are also underpinned by values. To be rich, as such, is not a norm unless it is also valued, or unless it is a means to prestige.

The degree to which actions are influenced by norms and values varies from one type of conduct to another and from one type of society to another. In all societies norms and values are more likely to influence conduct when such conduct regularly involves the actions of others. But there is a wide gap between mere influence of norms and determination of conduct by norms. Where societies institutionalize the notion of privacy, then, in certain spheres, normative influence may be weak. However, the possibility of freedom from norms depends not only on permissiveness but on the range of possible choices which are permitted by technical, aesthetic and moral conditions.

Where there is choice there is a greater possibility of, and need for, a strategy of action. Where there is little choice, either because of the structure of society or because of the limits of technical possibility, then strategies of action are less relevant. This suggests that actions can be classified in terms of the possibility of choice and in terms of the conditions which permit or limit this. In the sociological literature this issue has been discussed in terms of the problems of rationality or non-rationality of conduct.

Types of Social Action

Three authors have, in my judgement, raised most of the fundamental questions concerning the degree of rationality of social conduct. They are Marx, Weber and Pareto.

(i) Marx's Model of Action

Marx used a highly simplified model of what may be called instrumental rationalism; that is, he assumed that men have certain goals and that, if circumstances permit, they will use any means available in the pursuit of these. He tended to treat the social actor as a living calculator of tactics and strategies.[4] He did this, not because of his contempt for man, but because he considered that the analysis of all or most social systems, particularly the analysis of capitalism, calls for this approach.* Capitalism according to Marx, more than any other system, encourages instrumentality.

* I am well aware that the views of the early, 'romantic', Marx were rather different. But I hold to the opinion expressed by Raymond Aron in his unrivalled discussion of Marx that there is little in the early Marx of value to sociology as such.[5]

Marx did not deny that men have emotional needs, and that they have values. But he considered that the direction of emotional expression was, for social purposes, governed by the practical considerations of those who were in the position to influence social sentiments. And values were largely the expression of the same class whose interests were dominant in society.

Marx's conception of social action was derived largely from the end-means schema used by the classical economists. What he did was to extend this mode of analysis from the economic sphere to the analysis of the social system in general. He assumes that men have certain fundamental goals which compel them to interact with the material world and which also derive from this interaction. This process creates the need for social relationships. But out of these relationships and the needs of technology there emerge certain forms of the control of resources which Marx calls the relations of production. Once these forces and relations of production are assumed to exist, the conduct of men can be explained in terms of the logic of each situation which they face and of the problems which they are compelled to solve. The development of any social system results from the development of one type of situation into another, each link in the chain being forged by the solution which results from the previous situation.

This use of a simple idea of instrumental rationality enables Marx to view the characteristics of each part of a social system as necessarily resulting from those of the basic parts: the logic of economic situations compels a certain logic of political, judicial and other situations. The same simple idea enables Marx to construct a model of the development of each system and of its transformation into another type.

Marx departs from the assumption of instrumental rationality chiefly in his use of the idea of 'false consciousness'. He suggests that while those who own and control the forces of production and, therefore, the labour of others, do have a rational perception of the relationships between their various goals and the means to their attainment, those who are subordinate to them may not have this. The exploited class may fail, for some time, to comprehend the true logic of its situation; for it is the victim of a 'false consciousness' which leads it to accept its situation as unchangeable and the rights of those who dominate them as unchallengeable.[6] When this 'false consciousness' is dispelled, there is a recognition that certain goals are attainable and that certain opportunities can be seized. Those who manipulate ideology so that it sustains a 'false consciousness' for others, may not, themselves, be victims of it; quite the contrary, their manipulation may itself, be highly rational; ideology is an instrument for the maintenance of privilege.

Marx's application of instrumental rationality is too simplified to be acceptable as a basis of all sociological inquiry. But its great merit lies in its emphasis on the structure of situations and on the interconnected 'logic' of related situations. If this encouraged a form of sociological determinism it was, at least, of the right kind. Marx, unlike vulgar Marxists, saw that all men, regardless of their position, act according to the demands of their situations and are, in this sense, victims of them. But his view of the nature of these situations, and of the forms of conduct within them, was too limited.

(ii) *Max Weber's Typology of Social Action*

Weber, unlike Marx, formulated an explicit theory or scheme of social action. Action or conduct must be subjectively meaningful. To understand the conduct of others one must observe not only what they do but know what meaning they attach to their actions. This may not be obvious in one's own society, where one presumes the nature of actions by observing them in their contexts: one knows that a man touching his toes in his bedroom at 7 a.m. is exercising his limbs only, not praying. But in a foreign society one cannot distinguish calisthenic acts from ritual ones unless one has some knowledge of certain key ideas which give meaning to certain observable motions.

Weber distinguishes four main types of action: *Zweckrational, Wertrational,* traditional, and affectual.[7] Action is rational if it involves some assumption that the use of certain means is necessary to the attainment of particular ends. The purest form of rational action is the *Zweckrational,* a term which may be translated as 'instrumental rationality'. In this type of action the actor may assess the costs of pursuing a certain goal in a certain way and may also assess the value of the goal itself; Weber presumably meant that the goal can be treated as a means to some other goal.

The second type of rational action is the *Wertrational,* or value-oriented rationality. Here there is no way of assessing the efficacy of the means; furthermore, the goal is an end which is valued in itself, and not a means to a further end. An example is the performance of a ritual to achieve a state of mystical union with some spirit or god. The action is considered rational by Weber because there is an assumption that the means will produce the desired goal. But to distinguish the means from the goal is almost impossible; the achievement of mystical union may be defined in terms of a state of mind associated with the ritual act.

This is an example of an extreme form of *Wertrational* action. But one can think of cases where, even though the goal is an ultimate end, valued in itself, there are still alternatives in the choice of means. Furthermore, unlike the case of ritual means and mystical goals, there are types of *Wertrational* action in which the beliefs which guide them are empirically testable assumptions. For example, if one person wishes to win the love of another, the goal might be considered an ultimate value; and there is no reason why the actor should not assess the efficacy of different means, for the achievement of the end is something which can be empirically recognized. Of course, if the goal is to *express* love, rather than win it, then the action is rather similar to that of performing a ritual to achieve a mystical state; for the end is a subjective state which only the actor can recognize; he can always decide that it has been reached; there is, therefore, no easy way of assessing the efficacity of means.

In using the term *Wertrational* to describe one type of conduct, Weber is not implying that values do not influence *Zweckrational* conduct. In the latter, values may influence the choice of means as well as the ranking of goals; but the achievement of a goal is not valued in itself.

On the whole, Weber used the term 'rational' to refer to conduct; but occasionally he applied it also to the beliefs of the actor. The actor's beliefs are rational if some reason can be given for holding them. The man who performs a religious ritual to achieve a mystical state, like the man who performs a magical ritual to bring rain, is not usually able to provide a reason for this assumption; thus, his actions are rational, in terms of his belief, but his belief is not rational.*

* This problem has been recognized and thoroughly discussed in a recent article by Agassi and Jarvie.[8]

Weber's discussions of the different role of values, in the two types of rational conduct, and of the difference between rational and non-rational beliefs, is highly relevant to an appraisal of his distinction between rational and traditional conduct; it is, therefore, also relevant to an appraisal of his whole scheme. For Weber, traditional conduct consists in doing what has been done in the past without considering alternatives. This type of conduct is not rational, because both means and goals are accepted by the actor; a course of action is not chosen in order to achieve certain goals; indeed it is not chosen at all. An example of traditional conduct is the payment of tribute by a commoner to a chief. The commoner makes the payment because he has learned that this is customary. If the commoner can give no reason for making the payment, other than to say 'it has always been so', then there may be good grounds for stating that his conduct is not rational. But if he gives as his reason 'the chief is father of his people, and is entitled to receive what he asks', then his conduct may well be treated as rational. It may be *Wertrational*: the goal of pleasing the chief, who is father of his people, is a valued end; the means adopted, the payment of tribute, produces the desired result. Or, alternatively, the conduct may be *Zweck-rational*: the tribute has always been paid because it pleases the chief and enables one to obtain favours from him, and failure of payment displeases the chief and induces him to inflict punishment on the offender. To this Weber might reply that whether the commoner can give a reason for payment or not, he will make it because he has considered no alternative. The conduct would only become rational if the commoner did consider non-payment and then opted for payment as the more convenient choice. But anthropologists would argue that when one unravels forms of conduct which appear to be nothing more than traditional in Weber's sense, one discovers a concealed rationality: for example, Trobriand men make payments to their sisters' husbands because their sisters provide them with heirs; or men ceremonially exchange gifts because this creates ties between them which are politically and economically useful. To all of this one could reply that ethnographic analysis shows that certain rational solutions have been arrived at over time and then embodied in traditional precept; the conduct prescribed by these precepts is subsequently performed because it is prescribed.

Traditional conduct may, of course, be classed as rational on the grounds that the goal of such conduct is the preservation of tradition itself. If an objection is raised to this that there is little or no distinction between the means and the goal of conduct, it could be said that much traditional conduct is no less rational than conduct which Weber terms *Wertrational*, since in both cases there is no way of giving a reason for the assumption which underlies conduct.

All of this has led some writers to argue that all conduct, with the possible exception of affectual conduct, is rational; and that all social conduct is rational because it is almost never purely or even predominantly affectual.[9] The gist of this argument is that conduct in social situations is always the product of the situation, the ideas which men have within it and about it, and the goals which they pursue; since actions always follow from these things, they must always be rational. An added assumption is that affect is scarcely relevant, on the grounds that it is idiosyncratic to the individual actor, and not typical of the situation of many actors. If this view is accepted, then there is no point in talking of non-rational social action, since all of it is rational. This raises more difficulties than it solves, and the way out of these is to discard the very broad categories and to distinguish types of action in terms of a large number of elements which may be combined in very different ways. But before doing that one must consider Weber's category of affectual conduct, as well as Pareto's attempt to deal with the problem.

Conduct, according to Weber, is affectual if it is governed largely by a need to express some emotion. At one extreme, affectual conduct is reflexive: to express fear as a reaction to some threat, is of this type; the conduct has no goal other than the expression of the emotion. At the other extreme, where some means are chosen, almost deliberately, to achieve some emotional state, affectual conduct comes close to the rational.[10]

This seems to make sense. But the difficulty arises when one considers acts which appear to be affectual and non-rational but which can be explained in terms of an *unconscious* rationality.[11] Consider the following example: a man, in a fit of rage at being wrongly accused of some misconduct by his superior, instead of accepting the criticism, or attempting to prove his innocence of the charge, strikes his accuser, and is dismissed from his job.

This conduct appears to be irrational or non-rational even to intimates of the man concerned. But a psychoanalyst may show that the so-called loss of control brought on by an emotional state has a meaning. His interpretation is this. The man who is accused in fact wishes, unconsciously, to be punished for a display of violence and uses the accusation as a means to this end. If the psychoanalytic interpretation of this and similar acts is accepted, then it may well be that many forms of affectual conduct are, at some deep level, rational. Once again, this suggests that the term rational may cover almost every type of action, thereby reducing its value.

Weber did consider affectual conduct relevant to sociological inquiry. For example, he explained the origin of religious movements largely in terms of the emotional appeal exercised by some men over their followers; he called this appeal charisma, suggesting that these men possess a certain quality of grace which makes them attractive to others. But, on the whole, Weber did not grant to affectual conduct a place of primary importance. He considered that most forms of social conduct which were not traditional could best be explained as an approximation to rationality, and that such factors as sentiment and emotion should be introduced only to explain deviations from the rational ideal. But it should be stressed that Weber used the concept of rationality partly as an heuristic device to establish norms of typical conduct.

Rationality was also, for Weber, an empirical ideal. With the breakdown of traditional structures of society there occurred a development towards increasing rationalization. This is connected with the individual's freedom of manoeuvre, particularly in market relations.

(iii) *Pareto on Logical and Non-logical Conduct*

Pareto, like Weber, constructed a highly elaborate scheme of social action.[12] Also, like Weber, he distinguishes between logical and non-logical conduct. But here the similarity ends; for Pareto placed far greater emphasis on the category of non-logical action than did Weber. Indeed, for Pareto, logical action is scarcely relevant to social inquiry. In some other respects Pareto's views are rather similar to those of Marx; for both pay little attention to the avowed assumptions of action and seek motives which are concealed behind the stated reasons of actors. But whereas, in Marx's view, the motives are to be inferred largely from the conditions of action itself, in Pareto's view they are not; indeed Pareto considers that the true motives may be concealed from the actor himself.

Logical action, for Pareto, consists in applying the logico-experimental method. This consists in using empirical knowledge and valid inference in choosing means to the attainment of ends. Some forms of social conduct do approximate to this ideal—the obvious one is economic conduct in a market economy—but most forms of conduct are remote from it.

Conduct can be non-logical, according to Pareto, for several reasons: if the assumptions of conduct are false or not empirical; if the consequences of action are not considered; if the motives of action are not recognized by the actor; and, if the actions taken do not follow from the assumptions. Underlying the explanation of why these various conditions of non-logicality should occur, is Pareto's theory of instincts, residues, interests, sentiments and derivations.

Pareto recognizes that pure instinct, which is the fundamental source of human conduct, cannot account for most of the particular features of social life; he therefore makes greater use of the categories of residues and interests. Residues are modifications and refinements of instinct which are formed by experience: thus sexuality is an instinct, but incest prohibitions and sexual asceticism are residues. Interests are particular types of residue; they are motives for the attainment of wealth, prestige and power. Pareto also makes great use of the concept of sentiments, which may be close to being instinctual but may also be elaborate refinements of instinct, and which are, therefore, a type of residue.

Almost all social actions are governed by sentiments and interests, or else by other residues. Actions may *appear* to be governed by certain ideas or theories which men put forward to explain their conduct. But to accept these theories or derivations, as Pareto calls them, at their face value, is a grave error. Derivations are theories which men use to give an account of themselves, for they have a need to do this; but they only conceal the true motives of conduct, which lie elsewhere. In fact, says Pareto, the same residues may give rise to a variety of derivations to rationalize them: the sociologist's task is to probe beyond the superficial differences to reveal the similarities. Thus, the totemic feast and the Eucharist may express the same residue; but they are associated with very different derivations in the form of religious belief; behind these differences is the common element: the morally binding significance of ritual commensality.

Pareto does not, in fact, deny the importance of ideas. For he recognizes that there is a complex process of interaction between ideas, feelings and motives. But the ideational element which has causal significance for social conduct tends to be subliminal.

For many sociological purposes, Pareto makes great use of two particular sets of residues, which he calls the 'instincts of combinations' and the 'instincts of aggregate persistence'. The first produce a tendency to combine things in different ways which leads to innovation; and the second produce a tendency to maintain things in the same relations in which they have existed, which leads to conservatism or opposition to innovation. The trouble with these concepts is that they are used *ad hoc* and *ex post facto* and have little true explanatory value. If things change then one refers to the first type of residue and if they do not, one refers to the second type. Indeed, this is the trouble with the whole use of residues to explain conduct.

Sometimes Pareto comes very close to conceding that much conduct is logical even though the motives may be concealed, because the state aimed at is empirically 'verifiable'; thus, conduct governed by interests is more logical than that governed by a moral ideal.

Pareto's scheme raises numerous difficulties. Firstly, to call action non-logical because the assumptions of the actor are false, is absurd. Many scientific theories turn out to be false though they have been assumed to be true for centuries. And if one allows some false assumptions then one can also admit others that would not be considered scientific according to Pareto's cultural standards—for example, the assumptions of magic. These may indeed be false, but are they any more false than many scientific theories? One could argue that magical assumptions are not empirical. But why are they not? To state the sprinkling of water accompanied by the recitation of a spell will be followed by rain is, indeed quite empirical; there is ample evidence to show that the effect does not usually follow. Of course the mechanism whereby the one set of events produces the other is not stated and cannot be investigated. But is the same not true of Archimedes principle as originally formulated? Pareto would say that Archimedes principle is believed because it is supported by evidence, whereas the assumptions of magic are believed because of some deeper need. There may be something to this view; but it itself has never been established by evidence.

In the case of other assumptions, such as those of religion, one could say that they are not testable at all, for they refer to states which cannot be observed; at least they are empirically irrefutable. One cannot dispute that God is angered by man's misdemeanours. Pareto does not distinguish assumptions which are irrefutable, like those of religion, from those of magic and popular science, which may be refutable, but are still adhered to because countless refutations are explained away.

The second difficulty lies in Pareto's assertion that action is non-logical if its consequences are not thought out. In this sense no action *can* be logical, for no one can ever think of more than a small number of consequences of his actions. What Pareto clearly means is that some actions are taken in a state of wishful thinking; no attempt is made to calculate or anticipate the consequences. But sometimes this type of conduct turns out to be rational. In conditions of imminent danger the man who painfully calculates the consequences of his actions may be lost, whereas the man who acts on faith in his intuition might just succeed.

The third difficulty is Pareto's assertion that action is not logical if the motives are not recognized by the actor. This seems very plausible. For if one is not conscious of one's motives how can one plan one's actions? For example, if one of the motives of violent action is revenge, the actor may fail to achieve any other goals because his actions are precipitate and uncontrolled. But Pareto does not consider that many actions are rationally performed even though the actor is not fully conscious of what he is doing; a great many skills consist in not thinking about what one has to do, but in acting with quick reflexes.

Pareto's assertion that action is not logical if it does not follow from the assumptions of the actor is unassailable. Unfortunately, however, it is often impossible to know all the assumptions of action in advance, and one can always introduce an assumption, *ex post facto,* to make any action appear logical.

But Pareto's general intention is laudable. He is aware that much action is not logical in the conventional sense of that term. This is because sentiments, affects and blind faith play a great part in determining the course of action and in inhibiting the use of empirically testable assumptions and logical calculations. He is also aware that men may blind themselves to reality because this is more tolerable than accepting it, and that they may pursue imaginary goals—that is, goals which can only be achieved if the actor alone asserts that they are achieved—because they cannot achieve those which are more 'real'.

(iv) *Aspects and Components of Action*

The model of purely rational action is inadequate, and the attempts of Weber and Pareto to rectify this simple model are both remarkable achievements. But neither Weber nor Pareto avoids certain difficulties in trying to distinguish rational from non-rational action, though both raise a number of problems and discuss a number of different elements or aspects of action. This enables one to progress beyond their achievement. The way to do this is to start by listing the various possible elements which can be found in any type of action.

The first element is the strategic significance of a goal: is the goal a means to another end or is it not? And if it is, is it used as a means to many other ends or to a few, or to one only?

The second element is the availability of alternatives: are there many means to an end or few or only one? and is the number determined by the definition of the goal or by the limitations of knowledge?

The third element is the epistemological status of the goal: is it a condition which can be described by a statement which is empirically testable or is it not?

The fourth element is the epistemological status of the connection between means and ends: is this connection described by a statement which is empirically testable, or is it not?

The fifth element is the efficacity of means: can the use of means be assessed in terms of the costs involved, and can the degree of success of the action be measured?

The sixth element is the relevance of affects: is the choice of means or ends influenced by affects and to what extent? Or, is the goal itself an affective state?

The seventh element is the part played by norms: Is the goal defined in normative terms? Or is its choice influenced or governed by norms? And to what extent are the means influenced by norms?

The eighth element is the part played by values: are the norms governing or influencing conduct underpinned by values or not?

The ninth element is the attitude towards the assumptions of conduct: are the assumptions accepted dogmatically or are they subject to critical evaluation in the light of argument or evidence?

The tenth element is the overall orientation: is the action considered strategically in relation to a number of other actions, or is it not?

The eleventh and final element refers to the consciousness of the actor of the features of the situation: is he conscious of his assumptions and motives or is he not?

All of these elements are considered by Weber and Pareto. But both seem to assume that the possible combinations of them are very limited: for Weber has four types of action and Pareto only two. It may well be that the logically possible combinations are not all found. But it is certain that the number of possible combinations is greater than Pareto and Weber recognized.

It should also be emphasized that the alternatives are not clear-cut, but are polar types and that most actions are affected in varying degrees by each element. Of course, it is much easier to classify a type of action in terms of the combination of elements which it contains than to measure on a scale the degree to which any element is found in it.

An Evaluation of Action Theory

A number of criticisms can be levelled at the action approach. The first is that it commits the fallacy of psychologism. The second is that it is not sufficiently psychological. The third is that it is in some forms inadequate. The fourth is that it is not an explanatory theory at all.

Psychologism, or psychological reductionism, is a doctrine

which asserts that all sociological questions are ultimately explicable in psychological terms, since all social phenomena are ultimately reducible to the properties of the human mind. A trivial and naive example of this would be to explain the existence of the human family in terms of the need for affection. Such an explanation would be rejected on the grounds that the form of family sentiment is the product of family life, not its cause. A less trivial example would be to explain the existence of religion as a projection of the unconscious fantasies of parental figures which are retained by adults from their infancy. This might be rejected on the grounds that it does not explain why such a projection takes the form of religion, rather than something else, nor does it explain why some men are less prone to believe and practise a religion than others. On the whole, psychologism is rejected on the grounds that the mental characteristics which it adduces to explain social phenomena are thought to result from the very social forms which are to be explained.

But whether psychologism is acceptable in any form or not, is it true that action theory is necessarily psychologistic? Some critics of the action approach argue that it is committed to the assumption that the characteristics and conditions of action exist independently of the particular forms of society and culture, and that, if this assumption is to be upheld, it must be wedded to the view that such characteristics are derived from the human mind; for if they do not derive from the particular forms of social life, from where else can they derive? It may, of course be true that some action theorists have committed the psychologistic fallacy. Pareto does treat the residues as explanatory factors and this would seem to imply a form of psychologism.

Whether or not the type of explanation suggested by Pareto can be defended, it is not necessarily typical of the action approach. Other action theories are specifically *opposed* to psychological reductionism. *Indeed the whole intention of their authors is to exclude psychology from sociological explanation.*[*][13] Their fundamental argument is that social action is governed by two sets of factors: those conditions in social situations which are external to the individual

* It is also curious that some of the opponents of the action approach favour the use of psychology in sociological inquiry, while some of the holists, who are most criticized by action theorists, can be said to commit a rather interesting form of psychologism themselves.

actor(s); and those conditions within the actor which affect his reactions to and perceptions of situations. Both sets of conditions are given to the actor by his society. For while it is true that the actor's subjective characteristics may be, to a large extent, individually idiosyncratic, these can hardly account for the social typicality of his conduct.

It is at this point that the second type of criticism becomes relevant. The gist of it is that if action theory is to use concepts such as 'motivation', 'cognitive orientation', 'sentiments', 'affective dispositions', etc., then it must also use theories which explain how these mechanisms operate: it is because most types of action are not purely instrumental, and do involve perceptions, feelings and values, that the mode of influence of these must be accounted for. The counter-argument is that such mechanisms are not ruled out of existence, but are deliberately ignored because their investigation would not necessarily illuminate sociological analysis. The influence of socially shared motivations, values and ideas is taken for granted; and this is sufficient for the analysis of the structure of social situations.[14]

Psychology may or may not be relevant to some sociological explanations but this does not affect action theory as such; for it can incorporate psychology if this is desired; this has been shown by Talcott Parsons.[15]

The third criticism is rather different from the first two and has been made recently in a rather interesting and trenchant form by Alain Touraine who is, himself, a defendant of the action approach.[16] This argument follows Gurvitch in drawing a distinction between conduct and action. The first is behaviour which is in conformity with established norms; the second is creative or innovative. Touraine seems to prefer, in effect, the popular usage of the term 'action', in which the man of action conforms to norms only when he chooses to; for the rest, he is his own normative master. Touraine's argument is that the theory of action which regards conformity to norms as an indispensable element, cannot explain social change, nor can it explain, therefore, how the norms themselves come to be established; it takes as given much that requires explanation. Touraine's own theory is the neo-Marxist one that it is in the creative act of work and in the relations of work that men establish the fundamental norms of society, and that changes in these are promoted by the constant interaction of man with his man-made material and social environment. His assumptions of action, which are strongly influenced by the early Marx, are far from being those of instrumental rationalism.

Touraine's criticisms of much action theory are interesting, powerful but not necessarily persuasive. He overlooks the possibility, suggested earlier in this chapter, that no action theory need assert that norms and values *determine* the course of action: both Weber and Pareto allow for motivational elements and for structures of situations in which norms and values may *influence* the course of action, *but not fully govern it*. Furthermore, as I show in the following chapter, one can explain, in general, why norms exist, in terms of models of interaction. It is true that such models do not explain the emergence of a *particular* set of norms; neither the action approach of Touraine nor that of anyone else can explain the particular characteristics of social norms; nor can any such approach, by itself, explain why the norms of some societies change more slowly than the norms of others.

The final criticism of the action approach is that if it disavows psychologism, then it does not explain anything at all. The argument is as follows. If the theory explains social phenomena in terms of the motivations and other psychological characteristics of actors, then it is at least a genuine explanatory theory, even if it is rejected for other reasons. But if it explains social phenomena in terms of the structure of social situations, including the actor's subjective view of these, then it is assuming what is to be explained! (This is similar to Touraine's argument.) In other words, the explanation is circular or tautological; the social situation is the product of action and action is governed by the situation, and by the culturally accepted modes of perceiving and reacting to these situations.

In all sociological inquiry it *is* assumed that some features of social structure and culture are strategically important and enduring and that they provide limits within which particular social situations can occur. On this assumption, the action approach can help to explain the nature of these situations and how they affect conduct. It does not explain the social structure and culture as such, except by lending itself to a developmental inquiry which must start from some previous point at which structural and cultural elements are taken as given.

The criticism that action theory, in itself, explains very little, is valid. Action theory, as such, is a method. It is a set of near-tautological assumptions which structure the mode of cognition of social inquiry, which is, on the whole, concerned with the conditions and the products of social interaction.

NOTES

1. I. L. von Mises, *Human Action*, Regnery, Chicago, 1966.
2. Talcott Parsons, *The Structure of Social Action*, Free Press, 1949.
3. Max Weber, *The Theory of Social and Economic Organization*, (trans. A. R. Henderson and Talcott Parsons), William Hodge, 1947, pp. 79–112, 145–56, 170–1.
4. See Karl Marx and Frederick Engels, *Selected Works In Two Volumes*, Foreign Languages Publishing House, Moscow, 1951.
5. Raymond Aron, *Main Currents in Sociological Thought*, (trans. Richard Howard and Helen Weavers), London, 1965, pp. 109–80.
6. Raymond Aron, op. cit., p. 175.
7. Max Weber, ibid., pp. 104–7.
8. See also I. C. Jarvie and Joseph Agassi, 'The Problem of the Rationality of Magic', *British Journal of Sociology*, Vol. XVIII, No. 1, March 1967, pp. 55–74.
9. See J. Agassi, 'Methodological Individualism', *British Journal of Sociology*, Vol. IX, 3, Sept. 1960, p. 244–68.
10. Max Weber, loc. cit.
11. Von Mises, op. cit., p. 12.
12. Vilfredo Pareto, *Sociological Writings* (Selected and Introduced by S. E. Finer, trans. Derek Mirfin), Pall Mall, 1966, pp. 13–87 and 183–250.
13. John Rex, *Key Problems of Sociological Theory*, Routledge, 1961, pp. 87–8.
14. Ely Devons and Max Gluckman, 'Conclusion: Modes and Consequences of Limiting a Field of Study', in Max Gluckman (ed.) Closed Systems and Open Minds: *The Limits of Naivety in Social Anthropology*, Oliver and Boyd, Edinburgh, 1964, esp. pp. 158–68 and 213–18, 222–61.
15. Talcott Parsons, Edward Shils (eds), *Toward a General Theory of Social Action*, Harvard, 1951, esp, pp. 3–30, 47–158.
16. Alain Touraine, *Sociologie de l'action*, Paris, 1965, p. 9.

5.

Social Action, Interaction, Structure and System

Introduction

An ACTION is social when one or more of three conditions are fulfilled: first, the situation of the actor includes other actors whose presence is taken into account when the action is performed; second, the situation is such that these others possess facilities, objects or characteristics which enable them in some way to influence the conduct of the actor; third, the actor shares with these others certain sets of expectations and, possibly certain values, beliefs and symbols. These conditions can be present in varying degrees and in varying proportions. If all three conditions are well met, then two aspects of social life are found: the actions of different actors, sharing common social situations, will tend to be the same or similar; the actions of the same actors in the same types of situation will tend on different occasions to be the same. These two aspects together constitute social structure.

Where there is structure—that is, where the two characteristics of lateral and temporal standardization and recurrence are found —then the interactions between different actors will tend to produce some degree of interrelatedness between the different standardized sets of actions: this aspect of social life can be called system.

To differentiate between the terms 'social structure' and 'social system' is not to imply that these separate terms exist because they necessarily denote different things, or readily distinguishable areas of social reality. How and why both terms came to exist is of little interest or concern here. This is simply a proposal to make use of an existing linguistic distinction to call attention to two aspects of social order. When one states that action is structured one implies that it is somehow hemmed in by constraints which ensure that it will take a certain course, and that these constraints endure. When one asserts that action is part of a wider system one implies that the effects of one type of action —which can be analytically separated from another—spill over into another type. Clearly, structure and system are inseparable concepts. For actions are structured 'laterally' as a consequence of the interrelatedness of a wider collectivity; they are structured temporally as a consequence of the reinforcing effect which one set of activities has upon another. Similarly, a system of interaction can only operate if standardization occurs within a collectivity over time.

It is for these reasons that some writers—especially Weber, Pareto, Simmel and George Herbert Meade—have, in their different ways, attempted to found a science of sociology (in the case of Meade, a science of social psychology) on the study of social action and interaction. Whether they have succeeded or, if they have succeeded, in what ways they have done so, is a much discussed issue. But before attempting to deal with it, something must be said about the content of such attempts.

Much of what has been said by a number of different authors on this subject has been brought together in an original and remarkable synthesis by Talcott Parsons. The Parsonian synthesis does reject many of the less tenable proposals of previous authors —for example, Pareto's attempts to reduce sociological explanation to psychological assumptions—and includes some others, particularly from psychoanalysis.

The Parsonian System

The starting point for Parsons is the nature of action itself.[1] All action is directed to the attainment of goals. There are three aspects of this process (of motivation): they are cognitive, cathectic and evaluative. An actor, striving to reach a particular goal, must have some ideas and information about the objects which are relevant to goal-attainment; he must have some feelings about them in relation to his needs; and, thirdly, he must make choices. In addition, he must have certain standards of evaluation and selection: these are cognitive, appreciative and moral. All of these elements, or aspects of motivation and evaluation become, or are made social through the process of interaction.

Interaction occurs when any one actor, 'ego', needs or wishes to take account of the actions of another actor 'alter'. If the interaction between 'ego' and 'alter' is regular—that is, if both 'ego' and 'alter' regularly need to achieve certain goals and, in doing so, are obliged to take account of one another's conduct —then certain mutual expectations will emerge: each party will seek to predict what the other will do, and, at the same time, each will be obliged to adjust his conduct somewhat in order to meet with the other's expectations; in short, 'ego' will modify his expectations of 'alter's' conduct in order to predict it successfully, while 'alter' will modify his conduct in order to meet with 'ego' expectations. The pattern of mutual expectations which gradually emerges becomes a norm, or set of norms, which both 'ego' and 'alter' accept as binding upon themselves and as defining the particular conditions of their interactions.[2] The specific privileges, rights, duties, obligations and disabilities which are imposed upon each party to the interaction by their acceptance of norms define their *roles* in relation to one another. For example, if 'ego' and 'alter' interact solely to exchange goods, then the mutual expectations which they have of one another's conduct—which may or may *not* include the rate at which the goods or services are to be exchanged—will characterize the role of 'trader'; if 'ego' and 'alter' interact in order that 'ego' should receive from 'alter' the right to use land which 'alter' controls, and for which 'ego' provides certain services to 'alter', or makes certain payments, then the norms which emerge prescribe the roles of landowner and tenant, or patron and client as the case may be.

Parsons argues that the emergence and acceptance of norms is not usually a mere *ad hoc* affair in which each party minutely weighs the advantages and disadvantages of any particular set of norms. For, he insists, each party enjoys a number of secondary benefits from the relationship, or the circumstances of it, which motivate him to maintain it in its ongoing form. Firstly, each party develops a vested interest in the stability of the relationship as such: in other words, rather than 'shop about' incessantly for the most advantageous arrangements—where this is possible, and often it is not—each party will settle for the relationship which exists, for it is at least predictable. Secondly, each party develops a desire or even a 'need', according to Parsons, to please the other and to obtain recognition from the other for meeting his expectations: in other words, each party tries to obtain some kind of gratification from the interaction process as such, and also seeks to provide this gratification for the other; this often leads to symbolic expressions of faith, mutual interdependence, and so on. Thus the process of interaction creates, nourishes, and sustains in each actor the need to continue to participate in the relationship. Interaction provides and sustains the motivation in each actor to adhere to the norms. It also provides a mechanism of control for deterring or limiting deviation from the norms; for each participant needs both reciprocation in kind as well as approval for conformity.

The process of interaction between 'ego' and 'alter' can, Parsons thinks, be used as a microcosm of social systems; for all such interaction contains the elements of which social systems consist. These elements are shared systems of belief, sentiment and values; and culturally standardized criteria of technical, aesthetic and moral evaluation. Thus, different elements in the system of values and other ideas in society are seen to be derived from the conditions of social action and interaction.[3] Parsons actually goes further in linking the nature of social action to the characteristics of social systems: he does this by listing five pairs of dilemmas which confront any actor in a social situation, and suggests that social systems may be largely characterized by the solutions which they provide to each of the dilemmas and, even more, by the combination of solutions to be found in any one type of social system. These pairs of dilemmas are known as 'pattern variables'.[4]

The first dilemma which faces an actor is whether he should try to obtain immediate satisfaction in a social situation or whether he should be willing to defer this. This is the choice between *affectivity* and *affective neutrality*.

The second dilemma is between basing a relationship on a single interest or on a number of interests: this is the choice between *specificity* and *diffuseness*. For example, a customer may be interested in his greengrocer solely as a supplier of fruit and vegetables, while the tradesman may be interested in the customer solely as a supplier of income for himself. But in some societies men may only trade with one another if they are kinsmen or friends, and in other societies men may only consume their produce with those with whom they also produce and with whom they also participate in common rituals. The relationship between greengrocer and customer in modern urban society is usually highly specific while that between members of the same family is more diffuse.

The third dilemma is between *universalism* and *particularism:* should one actor treat another, for certain purposes, in terms of certain criteria or rules which would apply to anyone, regardless of any other characteristics which he may have, or should he treat him first and foremost as a member of a special category which is related to him in a certain way? The most obvious example of universalism is that of judicial procedure in most advanced, industrial societies: an officer of the court should treat every accused person or proved offender in terms of the same laws—making allowances for the circumstances of the offence and the previous record of the offender—and should not be influenced by his likes or dislikes or particular relationship to the offender. But in feudal society a magnate would not apply the same laws to his peers as he applies to his serfs; legal conceptions would be particularistic.

The fourth dilemma is between treating another person in terms of what, or who he is, rather than in terms of what he can be expected to do: this is the dilemma of *quality* v. *performance.* For example, should one reward someone for being white, rather than black, or should one reward him only if he is thought to perform certain tasks with a minimum degree of efficiency, regardless of his skin-colour?

The fifth and final dilemma is that of *self-orientation* v. *collectivity-orientation:* does one give primary emphasis to one's own interests or to those of a collectivity? For example, should a worker or group of workers accept wage restraint in the interests of the wider society (collectivity orientation) or should they press for higher wages for themselves and their families (self-orientation)?

It is arguable that few of these pairs of alternatives are true dilemmas for any social actors since, insofar as there are solutions to them, they are provided for the actor by the norms of society, and are not freely chosen: this is not *necessarily* true of the choice between affectivity and affective neutrality, and between self- and collectivity-orientation, though it is true of the other three pairs. To this objection Parsons would doubtless reply that in the imaginary world of 'ego' and 'alter', such a dilemma would have to be resolved, one way or another, and that an understanding of this enables one to explain why it is that all social systems have had to find such solutions.

A second objection to the 'pattern-variable' scheme is that even if particular dilemmas are solved by the actor, rather than the solution being presented to him by society, they are not necessarily solved in one way or the other according to the alternatives presented by Parsons. For example, workers may reject a particular form of agreement with managers, such as a scheme for payment by piece-rates, even though it benefits both the firm and themselves, on the grounds that it is rejected by the union or by their fellow-workers, some of whom may suffer as a result of it. Is this a case of self-orientation, or collectivity-orientation? It is difficult to say.

Then again, a particular solution may be partly of one sort and partly of another. The magistrate may apply the law equally to everyone; but in passing sentence he may be influenced, even quite consciously, by the character of the offender, which may in some way fail to appeal to him. The magistrate may justify his repugnance by arguing that the law itself permits him to consider the character of the offender and the nature of his motives. Or to take a parallel but different sort of example, consider the selection of appointments to certain types of office, such as the diplomatic corps in Britain or some other similar society. It may be found that successful applicants are those from particular schools, families, status groups and from a particular social class. This may be due to the fact that those who make such appointments are themselves from these schools, families, etc. But they may easily justify their selection in terms of criteria of performance, as against quality, and universalism as against particularism; for this justification may take the form of asserting that only applicants with those particular characteristics are likely to succeed in diplomatic circles. Turner has drawn a distinction between systems of achievement which are based on true contests and those which are based on sponsorship.[5] The latter may well exhibit the characteristics of a spurious application of criteria of universalism and performance.

To this Parsons could reply that in some social systems or situations *no* attempt is made to justify conduct in terms of universalistic criteria, and that these cases actually prove the rule. What they prove is that universalism may be established in some societies and not in others, and that where it is upheld some means may have to be found to sabotage its operation.

A third objection is that Parsons gives no good reason for his certainty that these pairs of dilemmas—if they are true dilemmas— exhaust the possibilities of orientation in social interaction.[6]

A further objection is levelled not just at the pattern variables, but at the whole method of basing a theory of society on certain principles which are derived from the exigencies of interaction between 'ego' and 'alter'. This asserts that actors do not interact in a void and construct their social world, but that they approach interaction already influenced by past social experience and that their choices are limited, if not governed, by the existing structure of society which even decrees what kinds of interaction are possible within it.

This objection is not quite in order, though what it states is entirely true. Parsons does not claim to be able to explain why societies possess particular characteristics simply by deriving statements of these from certain higher-level laws of interaction. He, of all people, is fully aware that concrete social structures have 'emergent' properties. His position on this particular matter can be summed up in three statements. First, social systems are, in fact, systems of interaction: therefore, whatever properties they have must be found in the simplest forms of interaction. Second, the simplest forms of regular interaction between two actors— and these can be two individuals or two collectivities— demand the establishment of norms, and all of the other elementary characteristics of social life. Third, the analysis of the processes of interaction between two 'pre-social' actors is purely a thought-experiment. In fact, what Parsons states concerning the nature of simple, dyadic interaction is by way of an argument *a fortiori*. What he is in effect, asserting is that if imaginary pre-social actors will, when they interact, establish norms, then it is even more likely that socialized individuals will do this. Parsons recognizes that when two or more actors interact—even if they are total strangers to one another, or are members of cultures which are totally strange to one another—they do so as participants in a social system and culture, and that they do not come 'raw' to the situation of interaction. But this recognition does not vitiate his method: for essentially, what he is trying to explain is why there can be no social life without a normative system, shared beliefs and criteria of evaluation, and values which rank goals hierarchically. All of these elements, he claims, can be observed in the microcosmic social system. Given that all actions take place *within* a social system, one can then understand how such systems maintain themselves. This argument is powerful, but it seems to have one important weakness; it underestimates the element of domination which may play a large part in structuring a particular type of social relationship. This point is elaborated and discussed in a later part of this chapter.

The Parsonian model of dyadic interaction is indeed used solely to explain why norms and other features of social systems exist. It explains the establishment of these only for particular individuals or incumbents of social roles; it does not, by itself, explain the process of standardization which occurs throughout a social system. To do this, one has only to add that the processes of such interaction will be repeated within a given collectivity because the conditions and exigencies of interaction are similar, if not the same, for all or a great number of members of the collectivity. Thus the interaction model can be used to explain the *two* fundamental aspects of social structures and social systems; the first is explained in terms of the requirements and consequences of the interaction process itself, and of the needs which it establishes; the second is explained in terms of the typicality of such types of interaction. This last must necessarily make use of the assumption that it is the social structure and culture which in large part create typical situations and exigencies; so the explanation tends to be circular.

From his examination of interaction, Parsons goes on to the social system itself. To do this he distinguishes between three levels of abstraction, all of which relate to the nature of social action; they are the social system, the culture and the personality.[7] The first is the system of interrelated roles which are prescribed by shared norms and underpinned by fundamental values. The second is the interrelated system of shared values, beliefs and symbols which is found in any collectivity. The third is the system of motives, affects and ideas as internalized in each individual. These three systems overlap and interact.

The social system then, is the set of roles, some of which form constellations called institutions.[8] But not all roles are equally institutionalized: for example, the role of peace-maker between quarrelling friends is not nearly as institutionalized as that of arbitrator in industrial disputes; and this last is not as well institutionalized as the role of magistrate. The degree of institutionalization depends partly on time and on the nature of the activity. Clearly the longer a set of normative prescriptions has been in existence, the more institutionalized it may become. And if activities demand very precise congruence of role expectations, then they too must become highly institutionalized. A high degree of institutionalization implies that little in the performance or definition of the role is left to chance or to individual or collective interpretation. But there may be considerable variance in the form of institutionalization. For example, bureaucratic structures are usually highly institutionalized, simply because there are so many roles whose performance is geared to one another; while parental roles in modern, urban society are, in some respects, less institutionalized because their performance is dependent only on a small number of other roles. However, efficient bureaucracies are those in which only the organizational prescription of roles is strongly institutionalized, while the prescription of solutions to problems raised within the bureacracy or between bureacrats and clients is left open, at least to some extent. On the other hand, within the family, some of the solutions to everyday problems are provided by legal definition of responsibilities, duties, privileges, rights, etc.

One of the important tasks in the analysis of social systems is to show how certain regularities of conduct in the less institutionalized areas of social life are affected by the constrains and limitations imposed by the more institutionalized sector: thus, neither law nor professional code prescribes in detail how the physician should approach his patient, the lawyer his client, or the teacher his pupil; but in all these spheres there are regularities which are due to the subtle interaction between the highly institutionalized structure, certain cultural elements, and the demands of the personalities of the actors. When such regularities of conduct endure, they may themselves become highly institutionalized.

Although Parsons considers that the study of the social system is the main focus of sociological inquiry, he does not consider such study possible without reference to the cultural and personality systems as such. He advances several reasons for this. First, cultural factors, such as religious beliefs, influence the motivations and perceptions of the actors, and their choice of means for goal-attainment. Second, the 'gearing' of actors' motivations and perceptions to the performance of social roles must be compatible with the general 'needs' of the personality. For, although cultural and personality items are themselves parts of relatively autonomous systems, they do enter into the social systems provided this does not do too much violence to their integrity. In this respect, Parsons realizes that there is considerable flexibility in all three systems.

The fundamental elements of the social system are those values which set limits to the range of norms which can exist and coexist. These values can, in turn, be characterized in terms of the 'pattern variables'. For example, the fundamental value system can be characterized by universalism, performance, specificity and affective-neutrality, such as in a modern, industrial, bureaucratized society, or it can have all of the opposite characteristics, such as are found in a small, tribal society. But these are not the only two possibilities: in principle, there are thirty-two possible combinations, though in reality the number of types of real system is much smaller, since not all combinations create viable systems.[9]

Every social system must cope with four sets of problems: that of allocating its material, human and cultural resources in certain ways; that of defining and sustaining the pursuit of certain fundamental goals; that of maintaining solidarity; and that of sustaining the motivations of the actors and of repairing any damage to these which arises out of the performance of required social roles. These are known as the problems of adaptation, goal-orientation, integration and pattern-maintenance.[10]   In complex social systems each set of problems is the 'task' of special institutional sectors: but within each sub-system of society—the economy, the polity, etc.—or even within an organization, all four sets of problems have to be dealt with. The way in which each of these four sets of problems is dealt with depends, of course, on the particular fundamental values of the system or sub-system.

The emphasis on fundamental values is the cornerstone of Parsonian theory. The argument behind this, elaborated in Parsons' first major work, is as follows: Men's actions are neither random nor simply governed by impulse; quite the contrary, they are orderly in the two senses that they do not result in a war of all against all, nor do they vary unpredictably. These two characteristics of order can only exist if all or most members of a society share certain ultimate values which define their goals and prescribe the permitted means for their attainment. These values introduce order and meaning into the conduct of the individual and restrict conflict and chaos in a society.

None of this leads Parsons to assume that the fundamental value system so affects all aspects of social life as to ensure that they are completely consistent or compatible with one another. Quite the contrary, he fully concedes that there must be inherent 'strains' in every social system because the requirements of different parts of it are *not* necessarily compatible with one another. For example, Parsons, following Weber, recognizes that the occupational structure of modern industrial societies is highly bureaucratic, and rests on universalism, performance, affective neutrality and specificity, but he is also aware that each individual is socialized, in his early years, within the small, conjugal family, which embodies the values of particularism, diffuseness, affectivity and quality. It is clear that the values of the family are opposed to those of bureaucracy; thus, in effect, Parsons concedes that the different requirements of a complex modern society must, of necessity, promote tension within the personality and within the social system itself. However, he seems to have abiding faith in the capacity of social systems and personality to provide compensating mechanisms to cope with these problems.

Further Criticisms of Parsonian Theory

The work of Parsons has evoked much sympathy and has created an important following; but it has also provoked much criticism. The critics are of various kinds: some denounce Parsons for asking the wrong questions and, therefore, for producing the wrong answers; others propose different ways of answering the same or similar questions; while a third group tries to criticize from within—to find fault with Parsons while conceding some of his fundamental arguments.

About the first type of criticism little or nothing useful can be said. Parsons does not set out either to diagnose 'the totality of Man's condition' or to suggest ways of 'reconstructing Man and Society'. This may condemn him, but it leaves his ideas intact. Of course, some of the assumptions which are used by such critics are truly sociological and deserve to be treated as such; others are purely ideological.

The critics in the second category tend all, in their different ways, to favour certain ideas which Parsons has himself obtained from Max Weber, but to combine these with other ideas of Weber, and those of Marx, to form a very different synthesis. Their favourite criticisms are that Parsons emphasizes consensus and value commitment at the expense of conflict, coercion and domination. These points are taken up in Chapter 6, but one general remark can be made here. Neither Parsons, who is fully aware of the objections raised by his critics, nor, for that matter, his critics themselves, has attempted to treat the two opposing sets of ideas as genuine rivals in the examination of a particular problem or set of problems. In view of this, it may well be that the rival claims are not always mutually exclusive. Dahrendorf has considered the possibility that the 'rival' theories apply to different types of case, but the examples he cites are rather jejune: he says, for example, that the consensus model of society is scarcely applicable to the case of the East German uprising, while it may be applicable to some other situation.[12] This is tantamount to asserting that where there is violent opposition to a regime there is little reason to postulate a state of consensus and good reason to postulate one of coercion; one would scarcely have thought otherwise. Parsons himself could retort that his theories and models of society are meant to explain why many social systems persist with relatively little violent opposition and how they manage this.

But Dahrendorf must be fully credited with having recognized the strengths as well as the weaknesses of the Parsonian theory. And his own discussion of the nature and operations of power and authority have done much to stimulate a reappraisal of both Parsonian ideas and the Marxian ideas which are opposed to those of Parsons.

Rex's criticism of Parsonian theory applies particularly to modern industrial societies whose stability, he would argue, owes more to the *ad hoc* character of class conflict, than it does to any deep commitment to ultimate values. Rex himself starts out from the assumptions of an action approach, but sees interaction as more likely to create conflict than value consensus. Such consensus as there is in industrial societies exists within social classes which have collective goals and a common culture. The fundamental characteristic of the social system is that of structured conflict.[13]

The Nature of Social Constraints

As a critic of Parsons Dahrendorf seems to fall into the second category: he accepts the Parsonian problems but rejects most of the solutions. Rex appears to be on the borderline between second and third categories, though more in the second than in the third: he accepts some of the Parsonian solutions as partly acceptable or as leading in a direction from which to deviate. Lockwood seems to fall into the third category: what he has in fact done is to turn some of the Parsonian arguments back on to the author of them. In some respects he has achieved a notable success; but he has also fallen into a trap of his own making.[14]

Lockwood starts out from the Parsonian solution to the 'Hobbesian problem of order'. Parsons, he argues, is quite committed to the Hobbesian view that without certain constraints men would engage in a war of all against all; or at least they would engage in a great deal of conflict and would scarcely be able to depend on one another. Parsons explains the containment of conflict and chaos in terms of the operation of norms and values. He then, according to Lockwood, ignores this dark world of conflicting interests and confines his sociological attention to the world of institutionalized norms and values which have been erected upon it. Insofar as he pays attention to conflict, disharmony, etc., he locates these as strains within the normative system! This, Lockwood thinks, is the fatal Parsonian error. For it fails to recognize that the structure of conflicting interests is not demolished by the erection of a normative system upon it, but continues to function. In fact, Lockwood argues that the best evidence in favour of this is the operation of the normative system itself! This operates in the way it does *because* it must function to contain, limit and direct the pursuit of interests. These interests derive primarily from the conditions of the distribution of real resources. Lockwood's model of the social system is heavily influenced by that of Marx.* In effect, what Lockwood is saying is this: if there were no fundamental conflicts of interest in society there would be no need for a normative system to control and contain them; therefore, the persistence of the normative system indicates the enduring significance of conflicting interests. Lockwood's final criticism of Parsons is that he must, of necessity, ignore or misunderstand the true nature and influence of power in the social system, since this stems from the infra-structural processes.

Lockwood insists that he does not treat the two sets of factors —the structure of interests and the normative system—in terms of historical or causal primacy: he is not suggesting that the infra-structure arises first and is then followed by the erection of a super-structure. Nor does he deny for a moment that the two sets interact; he insists, however, that they be kept separate for analytical purposes; the one *underlies* the other in an analytical sense only.

Before attempting an evaluation of these views there is one weak point which should be dealt with initially: this is Lockwood's

---

* It is also reminiscent of the Freudian model of the personality. The Freudian ego and super-ego, particularly the conscious parts of them, conceal the workings of the id and other unconscious elements. But their operations testify to the constant pressures exercised by the lower levels to express themselves.

assertion that the persistence of the normative system itself indicates the persistence of conflicting interests. This argument rests on the belief that if A comes into being to control B, then the continued presence of A implies the continued presence of B. Such an assumption is indefensible: men may build city walls to defend themselves, but the fact that they have never destroyed these walls does not mean that the need for defence still exists. Similarly, one could argue that if a normative system does arise to contain conflicting interests, it may persist despite the disappearance of those forces which originally produced it. And one might explain such persistence by showing that a normative system provides the conditions of its own survival. And even the recognition of significant, structured conflicts within the society would not necessarily support Lockwood's position, for it might be argued that these *result* from the normative system itself. This criticism does not necessarily signify major disagreement with Lockwood's fundamental position. In fact, one may agree with the general tenor of much of Lockwood's argument without accepting his formulation in all respects. Essentially, it contains four separate, but interrelated propositions, which should be assessed separately. First, the distribution of resources in society, which constitutes a real factor, can be analytically separated from the normative factor. Second, the real factor, of interests, constitutes an infra-structure, while the normative system constitutes a super-structure. Third, conflicts, which means conflict of interests, stem from the infra-structure, but are contained, moulded, and otherwise influenced by the normative super-structure. Fourth, the structure and processes of power derive from the infra-structure.

To deal with these arguments I propose a different type of scheme which, I hope, will help to present the gist of Lockwood's case without committing the same errors. This alternative scheme is presented before returning to the merits and weaknesses of Lockwood's argument.

In any process of social action and interaction there are two sets of factors which can be analytically separated: those which are external and those which are internal to the actor. That is to say, the social constraints which produce socially standardized conduct are one or other or both of two sets of factors: those which inhibit or encourage the actor from without, and those which inhibit, activate or direct him from within. The external factors may be other actors or they may be mere physical objects, including animate ones. The internal forces may be pre-cultural or non-cultural, and for want of a better term I propose to call them 'natural' dispositions: for example, the need to reduce hunger or thirst, or to avoid excessive pain or seek comfort, or to obtain certain libidinal gratifications, together with the ability to make certain types of discrimination between desirable or favourable or unfavourable objects, are all included under the term 'natural' dispositions, though they may not all be innate or genetically inherited characteristics. Such 'natural' dispositions may not, in all circumstances, be obeyed. The internal forces are also culturally standardized motives, beliefs, modes of cognition and standards of evaluation which all influence attitudes towards other objects, including other actors.

To simplify theoretical discussion, one might divide the external forces into social actors and physical objects, which last may include complexes of physical objects which constitute a physical situation. (This would cover 'objects' such as earthquakes.) And one might similarly divide the internal forces into natural dispositions and cultural dispositions. Further, one can divide the social actors, as external objects, according to whether or not they act as participants of or representatives of an institutional structure; and one may divide the physical objects into those which are culturally fashioned and those which are not. (Lévi-Strauss's distinction between the 'cooked' and the 'raw' is but one instance of this 'opposition', as he himself has pointed out.[15])

These distinctions must in all cases be treated as ideal polar types. The distinction between actor and physical object sometimes breaks down: slaves may be treated as though they were objects. The distinction between institutionalized and other actors is sometimes difficult to make: for example, the members of a queue are, in some respects, participants in an institution, but in others they are not. The distinction between natural and cultural dispositions is often difficult to define: for example, maternal possessiveness towards offspring is probably not instinctive, but it may be 'natural' in the sense that most mothers will have it because of their sense of identification with the child. The distinction between fashioned and unfashioned physical objects is not always clear-cut; for example an area of land becomes a culturally fashioned object when its boundaries are recognized, even though the boundaries as such may be there as part of nature. Bearing in mind these reservations, the following three diagrams can be used to portray the possible combinations which can exist:

DIAGRAM I

EXTERNAL FACTORS

	SOCIAL ACTORS	PHYSICAL OBJECTS
NATURAL DISPOSITIONS	A	B
CULTURAL DISPOSITIONS	D	C

INTERNAL FACTORS

In the first diagram, there are four possible combinations: the external object may be a social actor and the internal disposition towards him may be natural (A); the external object may be purely physical and the attitude towards it may be largely natural (B); the external object may be physical and the attitude towards it may be culturally acquired (C); and, finally, the external object may be social and the attitude towards it cultural (D). An example of A would be the attitude of two strangers towards one another in time of famine, each of whom considers the other a rival for scarce food. An example of B would be the attitude of any man to the occurrence of a drought. An example of C would be the attitude of a Jew or a Muslim to a pig, of a Hindu to a cow, or of men in most primitive societies to any natural disaster which is explained in terms of magical or religious theories. An example of D would be the attitude of two or more friends or ritual 'blood-brothers' to one another, or of two or more company directors to one another, and so on. What clearly distinguishes A from D is that in the first case there is no need for social or cultural definition of the actors' rights or obligations in order that the actors should recognize the relationship between themselves and act upon it—

though the absence of such norms might well be an important factor in influencing the actors to define the relationship immediately as one of hostility—whereas in the second case the relationship simply could not exist unless there were such a cultural definition. The distinction between B and C is equally clear. Thus, for certain purposes it could be argued that cases of type A and B have as much (if not more) in common with one another, as have cases of type A and D. The implication of this is that social actors may, for certain purposes, constitute the same type of external object as mere physical objects or conditions.

Some cases would be in certain respects like A and in other respects like D. For example, a master might treat a slave as a mere instrument or, at best, as a draft animal, but his *ownership* of the slave would be defined in terms of legal norms, and these would affect his rights in relation to others of a slave-owning status, or of a potential slave-owning status. The slave might accept the condition of domination more or less as a physical condition in which rebellion is punished; on the other hand, he might come to accept the norms of his status, particularly if he is born into slavery and learns that he has certain rights as well as disabilities. An important point is that cases of type A may develop into those of type D, and those of type D might 'degenerate' into those of type A. Similarly those of type B might change into those of type C—a recognition that drought causes widespread death and disease may lead to a belief that this condition is a form of supernatural punishment—while the reverse process may also occur.

In the second diagram a distinction is made between actors who act as participants in an institution and those who are simply present as individuals or collectivities, regardless of their institutional membership. An example of II A would be difficult to find: an actor could not really recognize an external force as an institution unless he internalized some cultural dispositions which enabled him to do this. If, for example, one speaks of someone as being 'crushed' or 'destroyed' by an organization, one must imply that the relationships and activities of an organization so affect one of its members, or even a non-member, as to undermine his well-being; but this can only come about if the 'victim' is aware that there is an organization. If a man is crushed or even frightened by a crowd leaving a football stadium, then

DIAGRAM II

SOCIAL FACTORS

	Non- INSTITUTIONAL INSTITUTIONAL

INTERNAL DISPOSITIONS

	INSTITUTIONAL	Non-INSTITUTIONAL
NATURAL	A	B
CULTURAL	D	C

he need only have a 'natural' attitude towards the object; this last example would be a clear case of type II B. However, one might argue that some cases, though they are not *strictly* of type A, do come near to it. Thus, a slave may recognize that his master's right to keep him in servitude is supported by authority, but he may not internalize a *moral* commitment to this authority; thus his attitude to the institutional structure is simply that it traps him physically; it is not in his interests to try to escape because he may suffer punishment on recapture or fail to obtain any other source of livelihood if he succeeds in remaining free. In classifying this type of case under II A, or as borderline to II A, one recognizes that there is a *fundamental difference between the recognition of a normative expectation and a commitment to uphold the norm*. This is of utmost importance in reviewing Lockwood's argument.

No great difficulty arises in finding cases of type II C. If individuals internalize certain norms of politeness and/or fairness, then, as members of crowds in a public place, they treat one another in certain ways: for example, they avoid pushing, or they even form queues. For each individual the crowd is a non-institutional external force to which he reacts in accordance with cultural norms.

Cases of type II D are those most commonly dealt with by social scientists who are primarily interested in the institutional structures of social life. For example, if one is a member of a political party, one's political conduct is influenced by the institution of the party as if it were a force external to oneself; but one can only recognize this force if one also internalizes the norms of political activity and party membership.*

But, while recognizing that the analysis of institutional structures requires the assumption that those who participate in, or are affected by, such institutions, do internalize certain cultural dispositions towards them, one must also heed the warning given above: there is a considerable difference between an actor's merely having an appropriate expectation which is elicited by other actors, and his having a commitment to the institution which may require little external pressure to elicit. This is, perhaps, another way of saying that *the proportion of*

---

* It has sometimes been suggested that the analysis of certain institutions is incomplete if one does not take into account the natural dispositions of the actors as well as their cultural dispositions. Those who hold this view tend to choose the case of family and kinship relations.[16] The argument they advance is that the recognition of family and kinship ties is a cultural elaboration of biological ties which may take many forms, depending upon social and other circumstances. It is, of course, perfectly true that family and kinship ties have a biological or physical basis, which is less obvious in the case of other types of relationship. But if one wishes to explain (a) why kinship ties are important in all human societies, (b) why remote kinship ties outside of the elementary, conjugal family unit are more important in primitive and other non-industrial societies than they are in urban, industrial societies, and (c) why the types of structure of kinship relationships vary in different types of society, one gets very little help from the facts of biology (that is, from natural dispositions) except, possibly, in answering (a). One might say that in primitive societies men cooperate with their kinsmen because they trust them more than strangers, and that this trust is based, if not on instinct proper, at least on the primordial tie between mother and child in which a sense of trust is established by virtue of the tactile and other satisfactions which both parties get from the relationship. But this does not help one very much. It is, perhaps, simpler to say that in primitive societies men cooperate with their kinsmen because all those with whom they interact as members of their society, and are not complete strangers to them, *are* their kinsmen. All of these people who are related by descent and affinity recognize something called a tie of kinship only because they incorporate the physical facts of procreation and parturition into a cultural system of norms and other ideas; and they recognize *categories* of kinsmen almost purely as a function of normative definition. Of course, it must be admitted that there are certain physical facts of kinship which limit the range of institutional formations. But it is doubtful whether these physical facts operate by way of pure natural dispositions.

internal to external pressures within an institutional structure can vary from one type to another.

DIAGRAM III

PHYSICAL OBJECTS

FASHIONED   UNFASHIONED

	FASHIONED	UNFASHIONED
NATURAL	A	B
CULTURAL	D	C

(left vertical axis label: INTERNAL DISPOSITIONS)

In the third diagram a distinction is made between physical objects which are culturally fashioned and those which are not. (There is, of course, great variation in the degree of such cultural fashioning.) Both types of object are external to the actor and both can be treated either in terms of natural or cultural dispositions. An example of type III A is the attitude to cooked food on the part of a starving man—it satisfies his hunger. An example of III B is the attitude to raw food in order to satisfy hunger. An example of III C is the refusal to eat certain types of raw food which are deemed culturally unacceptable. A different type of example of III C is to treat a mountain or a wood as sacred. An example of type III D is the treatment of food cooked in certain ways as impure or unclean. A very different sort of example of III D is to revere an icon.

The purpose of this digression has been to appraise Lockwood's argument concerning the relationship between the infra-structure of interests and the super-structure of norms in social systems. To do this one must clarify two further matters: first, the meaning of the terms 'interests' and 'norms'; second, the meaning of the terms 'infra-structure' and 'super-structure'.

To say that action is partly or wholly governed by interests is to say that one of the aims of action is to ensure that certain means are kept or made available for the pursuit of particular goals, whatever these may be. If one says that the Church has an interest in property, one implies that the Church as an organization will lose some of its power if it does not have resources to finance itself, and that these resources are in the form of property. If one says that a state has an interest in provoking hostilities with its neighbours one implies that one state benefits, perhaps in terms of internal political stability, by the continued creation of military or other political incidents in its relations with some other state. Conflicts of interest occur when two or more actors, who may be individuals or collectivities, can only seek to achieve and to preserve certain advantages if they do so at one another's expense. Structured conflicts of interest exist when two conditions are fulfilled: a number of actors seek to secure certain advantages at the expense of a number of other actors; and this state of affairs endures by virtue of the relationship which exists between the two sets of actors.

The term 'norm' can have at least two meanings. First, it can mean 'that which regularly occurs'. In this sense it is the norm for people to marry at a particular age and for a certain proportion of the population to commit suicide. The second meaning of the term refers to what members of a society have the right to expect. They do not have a right to expect most marriages to occur at a certain age, though they do have a right to expect marriage to be allowed at a certain age without parental permission; nor do they have a right to expect a certain rate of suicide, though the relatives of those attempting suicide do have a right to call upon the agents of the law to prevent the act. The first may be called the statistical meaning of the term, and the second the cultural meaning. Not all norms, in the cultural sense, are in fact norms in the statistical sense: for norms may be ideal but not in fact realized. Lockwood, following Parsons and others, is using the term in the second sense.

What exactly is meant by the terms 'infra-structure' and 'super-structure' it is difficult to say. If one simply means that a social structure or system should be analysed in such a way that some aspects are referred to as basic or fundamental, then it is possible to refer to almost any part or aspect of social life in these terms. It is often stated that the family is still the basis of social life in modern, industrial societies. This may simply mean that everyone is a member of a family though not necessarily of a political party, an industrial organization or a church. But it is equally arguable that the political system, the system of industrial organization, social class, etc., are *all* basic features of society. To refer to some set of factors of variables as fundamental to social life can have one or more of the following useful meanings. The strongest meaning is as follows: A constitutes an infra-structure and B a super-structure if the character of B is fully determined by the character of A. The second, weaker, meaning is that A has more effect on B than B has on A. This allows some interaction between A and B. The third meaning is that the characteristics of A are often highly concealed and overlaid by those of B, but that they continue to operate, somewhat independently of the operations of B. Lockwood, like all sociologists, rejects the first formulation, but he seems to accept both the second and the third.

The first weakness in these ideas is the extreme difficulty of defining social interests independently of a normative system. In short, to oppose norms and interests, as though an emphasis on one excludes an emphasis on the other, is possibly to commit a category mistake. Consider the following example. It is in the interest of many whites in Southern Africa to maintain a system of racial domination. The advantages conferred on whites by this arrangement are as follows: it provides some, if not all, with higher incomes and other material benefits which they would otherwise not enjoy; it provides them with the political means of preventing opposition to the system and, therefore, blocks attempts to reform it; it provides some lower-class whites with status privileges which they would lose if coloureds, Asians, or blacks could compete more favourably for educational and occupational mobility; it protects whites from the demand to include non-whites in most social relationships, particularly that of marriage, but excluding those of employment and of commercial transactions; it protects whites from the possibility of political disruption—or chaos, as they would say—which would allegedly result from a grant of universal franchise.

Why do non-whites participate in this system? Why do they perform certain roles in ways expected of them? Why do they not withdraw from it, turning the tables on the whites and demanding separate states, however poor? Why do they not overthrow the system? A true Parsonian, according to Lockwood and others, would answer all of these questions in the following way. Both whites and non-whites internalize certain norms which prescribe the roles permitted to different racial groups, and share certain values and beliefs which emphasise the inherent inequality of different racial groups. The hypothetical Parsonian might also add that all groups also internalize certain norms and values concerning the acquisition of money-income in exchange for services of one sort or another, so that they are induced to participate in the economy.

If this would be the Parsonian reply, then the critics would be right to reject the first part of it; though it is very doubtful whether any sociologist would venture this particular answer. Whites in Southern Africa protect the advantages which they have in the way in which they do, for several reasons: first, if they adopted any other policy they might lose these advantages and fail to gain any others which they value; second, even if the long-term advantages (to many of them) of abandoning policies of white domination were explained to many whites, they would scarcely be influenced by them because they would consider that the immediate and long-term disadvantages outweighed any advantages; and they would think, feel and react in this way because they could not tolerate the notion of racial equality and all that it implies. Third, most whites believe that only repressive measures can prevent their cultural, and possibly physical, destruction.

Blacks, Asians and Coloureds in Southern Africa participate in the system because they can only satisfy their wants by doing so; these wants are to some extent culturally determined, but not altogether; some would come near to starvation if they did not participate. Insofar as they do not revolt against the system this is largely because they are ill-organized to do so, do not see the possibility of doing so without great harm to themselves, and with much chance of success; finally, they accept the system because it conditions them to accept it. Of course, in participating in a variety of roles they necessarily internalize expectations concerning the roles of others; in this sense, their actions are governed by norms. Their actions are also governed by values insofar as they aspire to certain goals which are not simply given by nature: they wish to increase income to satisfy a variety of wants, such as the purchase of objects which give them status in certain sections of the society and, possibly, to preserve ancestral lands which are valued in themselves. It is unnecessary to assume that most non-whites adhere to certain norms because they share certain values with whites which underpin these norms. But it might also be mistaken not to recognize that some non-whites may also internalize certain diffuse moral values which encourage them to accept certain laws because they are laws. However, this may be rare and even on the decline.

It would probably be more fruitful to characterize a social system of this sort in a different way. First, one could say that many blacks and whites interact as though the other were simply part of an external environment which had to be coped with: this is probably the attitude of many blacks to white institutions; these are almost like physical objects to be encountered in a certain way. But this would be only one aspect of the system. In some types of relationship—for example between white employers and black domestic servants—there may be a tendency for mutual indentification of the other as a social person, to whom certain positive values apply. In other situations—those involving relations between the police and offenders or suspects, the relationship is also charged with affects and values, but of a highly negative kind: the parties do not treat one another as mere objects in the environment, but in fact attribute to another objectionable but very human qualities; it could be argued that these are predominantly 'natural' rather than cultural attitudes.

Even this case, which would seem to lend itself best to a Marxian or neo-Marxian model, cannot be adequately interpreted in the terms suggested by Lockwood. And if one turns from this to others, such as those of caste or feudalism, the difficulties increase. It is not that Parsons is right, but that the counter-model to Parsons is inadequate. I suggest that as a start, it might be profitable to explain certain aspects of social structure and social systems in terms of the degrees to which different types of internal and external constraints operate. This leaves much room for a recognition of the fact that in some social system the institutional structure and cultural dispositions towards them may be of overriding importance—for example in the Hindu caste system, and in the Balinese political system—while in others the interaction between actors as objects and as 'natural' reactors may have greater relevance. No social system is without all components.

Turning to the next question, can one, in fact, denote certain features of a social system as an infra-structure? Clearly not in Lockwood's terms. For if interests are often defined in terms of cultural norms then there is no sense in considering one as underlying the other. One could defend the view that the satisfaction of certain wants is a primary concern in all human societies and that the institutions which are more closely concerned with this are, in a sense, the infra-structure of society. But what does this mean? The term infra-structure then becomes synonymous with 'those institutions which are concerned with satisfying certain primary wants'. But primary wants are not always placed above others: so clearly they do not determine them, though they may affect them more than they are affected by them. But what is important about the structures of political and economic power is that those who dominate them are in a position to satisfy any wants of their own—be they primary or not—and to determine the degree to which others are in a position to do the same. It is in this sense that these institutions are basic to social life. Thus, it is not the structure of interests which is basic to the social system, but the institutions which control any resources or facilities (which may be symbolic) to which others need access to satisfy whatever wants they may have.

The third question concerns the source and nature of conflict. Does this stem from the nature of social interaction itself and is it, in this respect, different from other features of social life such as reciprocity, role-performance and cooperation? On the face of it the answer seems to be 'yes'. Insofar as pre-social men interact, they may either ignore one another or they may struggle with one another; but they are unlikely to engage in reciprocal conduct, and certainly most unlikely to cooperate, unless they establish some norms to which they adhere. There is a counter to this which suggests that men need reciprocity and even cooperation no less than they need to struggle with opponents, and that this need derives from the personality which, in turn, is fashioned by the nurturant relationship between mother and child.

It may be that men inherently engage in conflict; it may also be that they inherently need allies or social partners with whom to interact; it may also be that men have both of these needs. But all of this is largely irrelevant to the study of social systems. For in these both conflict and reciprocity, cooperation, etc., are produced by the conditions of cultural and social life. And conflicts over religious disagreements can be as violent, if not more violent, than conflicts over the distribution of resources. Of course, there is an important point to Lockwood's argument. It is that participation in institutions does not prevent social actors from pressing the advantages which are presented to them in the process of participation; nor does it necessarily inhibit them from rebelling against those who have dominant roles within these institutions.

This brings us to the problem of power. Parsons does not necessarily neglect this problem within his system, as Lockwood indicates. But he tends to view power as a resource for maintaining a system or guiding changes within it, rather than as a device for imposing certain characteristics on the system. Lockwood tends to the view that power consists in controlling whatever it is that others consider valuable or desirable and that it can be used to determine the nature of the normative system.

If one reverts to the Parsonian model of dyadic interaction it is fairly clear that power need not be excluded as a variable. An attempt to deal with just this problem has been made by P. Blau.

On Power and Exchange[17]

Blau starts out from the nature of interaction, and the model of interaction which he employs is known as the exchange model. His purpose is to show that the nature of power can be explained in terms of the characteristics of interactive exchange. But his ultimate concern is to move from the level of micro-sociological analysis to an explanation of how power operates in real social systems. Exchange occurs when some goods, services, or other benefits are given in the expectation that their equivalent will be returned. The benefits of exchange can be extrinsic or intrinsic; that is, they can consist of things or services which are separate from the process of interaction and from the particular characteristics of those involved in it, or they can relate directly to interaction as such, and to the nature of those involved. Visiting others because one enjoys food and drink which one cannot supply for oneself, is a case of enjoying extrinsic benefits; visiting for the sake of interpersonal contact with the particular individuals concerned, is a case of enjoying intrinsic benefits.

In many cases, says Blau, each party to a potential exchange has something which others want. But in some cases one party may have nothing immediate to offer. In order to obtain what he needs he may have to take it by force or engage in indirect exchange. But if neither of these solutions is possible, he can only offer the other a lien on future services and on a form of submission; this is an acceptance of power. Power exists when one party can regularly use a threat of punishment or withdrawal of facilities from another in order to gain compliance. Power is distinguished from sheer physical coercion in the following way: in the case of pure coercion the powerless party cannot opt for punishment or withdrawal of facilities in return for non-compliance. For example, a man who literally is thrown into prison is subject to pure physical coercion. A man who gives up his freedom rather than lose his life submits to power. Power involves exchange; pure physical coercion does not.

Blau shows that power results from certain conditions of exchange or lack of them. He then traces the consequence of this for social structures. His argument, in effect, is this. Wherever human collectivities exist there will always be a need for some men to offer a potential lien on services etc., in return for immediate or foreseeable concrete benefits. This creates a need for power. Those who get power may have personal abilities or they may control resources or inspire loyalty which makes them desired. One of the things they can give is approval, so that personal qualities may be a condition for obtaining power. But in seeking power men run risks of differentiating themselves from others and presenting themselves as enviable. Some men—the majority—will prefer the benefits of approval by those who have power, and of their satraps who have less of it to the possible benefits of power itself. This is all highly ingenious. It is certainly valuable in that it shows that the emergence of power as a feature of social life is inevitable even if some circumstances do not favour it. But the question remains: how much power is actually created in this way. Blau is rather fond of using as paradigms relationships of friendship, love and those which occur in small groups whose structure is left to the spontaneous process of interaction. However, power structures are not always established in this way; they resemble the paradigm of conquest more often than that of the free market. It is not simply that men wait to be given power by those who need them to perform a necessary role. These possibilities certainly exist: men with charisma are needed by others who enjoy their favour in its own right; and men of ability are needed to perform tasks of leadership, coordination, etc. But in many cases men are only too ready to create the conditions in which they or others like them, are 'needed'. And they establish a structure of power which constantly generates the conditions for its perpetuation; among these conditions is a set of so-called 'needs'.

Blau would scarcely dispute this. But he could respond to this criticism in three ways. First, he could argue that what he is explaining is the autonomous and inevitable emergence of power as a function of exchange, regardless of the conquest factor: in short, he could claim to furnish a theory of the sufficient, though not necessary conditions, for the emergence of power. Second, he could argue that this process is more common than the conquest process. Third, he could argue that even where the conquest or domination theory applies, it is still possible to explain the *persistence* of power structures in terms of an exchange theory. The first of these arguments is unassailable. The two theories are not mutually exclusive. The second argument is almost overwhelmingly difficult to test; how does one show that one social process of this kind is more common than another? And even if it is demonstrably more common, this does not make it more significant. Processes which are rare may have more far-reaching consequences than those which are common. The third argument is largely acceptable: once a given structure of power exists it does provide conditions in which the holders of power can provide facilities which others need so badly that they will call on these holders to exchange services for a potential demand on their own. But what Blau seems to under-emphasise is the degree to which power constitutes a condition for determining the rate of immediate exchange of goods, services or instrinsic benefits. In some societies gangsters have power insofar as they possess the means of creating immediate fear—of destruction of life or property or both—unless certain tribute is paid. They can decide not only the payment of tribute, but the terms of payment; and this is the predominant element in many structures of power. They may give benefits of protection from others like themselves —rather in the way that armed men can establish feudal power over villagers by protecting them against predators like themselves—in return for immediate gain. This creates an expectation which makes the relationship stable. If such a relationship persists it can lead to the creation of generalized power. Those who have power in one area may gradually control the means of meeting a number of wants and can also create them: and they can increasingly make use of a greater variety of services—for example, the exercise of subordinate tasks of administration— which requires a general lien on compliance.

Blau readily admits that in the study of power and of other features of social systems, the exchange model has its limitations. He concedes that social systems have emergent properties, and that in examining any particular aspect of social life these must be taken for granted. But, like Parsons, he assumes that the micro-sociological paradigms of interaction can be used to explain certain general properties of social systems. He also assumes —and acts on his assumption, which is more, I think, than Parsons does—that one can apply the exchange model, whether in the study of power or of some aspect of social life, to the processes which go on within a given system. The advantage that Blau's approach has over that of Parsons is that it need never assume that a stable form of compliance must rest on the shared internalization of values which makes all parties to a social relationship morally committed to its norms.

Of course, there is one great weakness in exchange theory: it can be abused in such a way as to render many of its explanations tautological. Any interaction can be treated as an exchange in which all parties receive something in return for what they have given. For example, if a slave permits himself to be taken into captivity, rather than fight to the death, one can explain his conduct by saying that he has exchanged freedom for physical survival. Or again, one may say that men are dominated by religious leaders because they are willing to submit in exchange for religious certainty. Sometimes this might be the case. But when men are raised in a society in which the Church dominates they are offered little choice in the matter. Exchange theory seems most profitably applied where there are real options which men recognize. For example, in the traditional system of Hindu castes and *jajmani* clientship, the members of dependent castes accept a certain fixed return for their services from their patrons. It might be shown that there is an underlying pattern of exchange here: the fixed return gives security, and the stable relationship includes political protection and, possibly, ritual services. But to analyse this pattern of exchange is one thing; to use the analysis to explain why the relationship endures is quite another. For, in all probability, the relationships of caste and clientship are part of a larger system of factors, including religious belief, domination, internal caste cohesion, and a sense of caste privilege in relation to other castes, which reinforce one another. However, when some aspects of traditional social structure are weakened or undermined by economic and other developments, men may be partly freed from their caste and clientship obligations: yet, despite this, they may continue to accept the conditions of these relations, rather than offer their services in wider market, because of the security which they obtain from them. Here one may be entitled to introduce the exchange model to *explain* the persistence of the system. For here the costs of alternative actions are possibly reckoned.[18]

Finally, when exchange theory is applied to the intrinsic benefits which men obtain from adherence to an ideology, religious faith or ritual activity, the results are unenlightening or even absurd. To use the notion of exchange is, necessarily, to assume that various alternatives may be measured against the other. As Homans rightly says, the notion of exchange implies some idea of opportunity cost.[19]

The Value of Interaction Theories and Models

One point has been strongly emphasized throughout this chapter: theories or models of interaction do not permit one to derive from them very much about the nature of social structures and social systems. The obvious reason for this is that the content of interaction is governed by the social structure or system in which it occurs. Even Simmel, who pioneered the micro-sociology of interaction, was fully aware of this. He hoped to treat these models of the dyad and the triad, of superordination and submission, rather as a physical scientist treats geometry: as a set of ideal descriptions of the nature of the real world which enable one to portray its general characteristics with greater simplicity and elegance.

The great value of the interaction approach is fourfold. First, it enables the sociologist to show how far the conditions of social life result from the unintended consequences of action; for action alone emphasizes individual or collective intention; interaction emphasizes the unfeasibility of carrying out most intentions without creating consequences which were not intended; for as soon as one actor must take into account the actions of another, he is no longer master of his own destination; even if he eliminates the other actor he has produced an event to be coped with which will have consequences beyond his control.*

The second merit of interactionism is that it avoids reification and teleology in the explanation of how social structures and systems operate. For, though not all interaction is structured or part of a system, all social structures and systems are the products and the conditions of interaction.

The third merit is that it does provide the analytical and explanatory link for showing how different features or parts of a social system are interrelated. This is demonstrated in the next chapter.

Finally, the interaction approach, linked with the flexible notion of social action outlined in the previous chapter, does provide the basis of a theory of social change. If social systems are systems of interaction then change must result—usually without intention—from the conditions and processes of interaction itself.

In any real society each actor enters into relationships influenced

---

* Much of the discussion of freedom or liberty seems to miss this point completely. An ideal society is supposed to make men free to do as they will provided they do not interfere with the freedom of others. But can such interference be avoided? Unless all men become completely self-sufficient, or unless they devise a superb consensus which spells out the minutiae of social conduct, their actions, no matter how free, will have consequences which they could not have intended because they will affect the actions of others and be affected by them.

by a whole host of cultural assumptions and constrained by an existing network of relationships and institutions which is usually far beyond his ken. Furthermore, interaction is often not immediate or interpersonal, but mediated or impersonal. Such interactions, which may occur over wide physical, cultural or social distances, requires established norms which can not be fashioned *ad hoc*, as in many close, interpersonal relations. This requires linguistic communication and the use of other symbolic devices which are part of a shared culture or, possibly, part of a civilization which extends beyond the borders of particular societies. How such systems of interaction maintain themselves is one of the most important questions in sociology.

NOTES

1. Talcott Parsons, *The Social System*, The Free Press, 1951, pp. 3–23.
2. Loc. cit.
3. Loc. cit.
4. Op. cit., pp. 58–67.
5. R. H. Turner, *The Social Context of Ambition*, San Francisco, 1964.
6. See Max Black, 'Some Questions about Parsons' Theories' in Max Black (ed) *The Social Theories of Talcott Parsons*, Prentice-Hall, New Jersey, 1961, p. 288.
7. Talcott Parsons, *The Social System*, pp. 3–24.
8. Ibid, pp. 24–88.
9. Ibid, pp. 180–200.
10. See Chandler Morse, 'The Functional Imperatives' in Max Black (ed), *The Social Theories of Talcott Parsons*, esp. pp. 113–52.
11. Talcott Parsons, *The Structure of Social Action*, The Free Press, 1949.
12. Ralf Dahrendorf, *Class and Class Conflict in an Industrial Society*, Routledge, 1959, pp. 161–2.
13. John Rex, *Key Problems of Sociological Theory*, pp. 96–155.
14. David Lockwood, 'Some Remarks on "The Social System"', *British Journal of Sociology*, Vol. VII, 2, 1956.
15. Claude Levi-Strauss, 'Le Triangle Culinaire', *L'Arc*, 26.
16. See E. A. Gellner, 'Nature and Society in Social Anthropology', *Philosophy of Science*, Vol. XXX, 3, 1963. and J. H. M. Beattie, 'Kinship and Social Anthropology', *Man*, Vol. LXIV, July-August, 1964.
17. Peter M. Blau, *Exchange and Power in Social Life*, New York, 1964, pp. 1–32.

18. See Scarlett Epstein, 'Productive Efficiency and Customary Systems of Rewards in Rural South India' in Raymond Firth (ed), *Themes in Economic Anthropology*, Tavistock, 1967.
19. George C. Homans, 'Social Behaviour As Exchange', *American Journal of Sociology*, 63, 1958, pp. 597–606.

6.

Social Structures and Social Systems

Introduction

SOCIOLOGISTS commonly ask the question: 'What is it that holds a society together?' This question could be interpreted as meaningless: for if society exists, then it is, by definition held together by the relations between its members; and if these do not exist, then there is no society. On the other hand, the question could be interpreted as meaningful, but as having several meanings, not one:*

(i) Why do members of social groups and systems continue to participate in them? For example, why do the citizens of one state, or the members of one tribe, clan or lineage, or the office-holders of one organization not leave it for another?

(ii) Why do the sections or segments of a social unit, or collectivity, hold together? Why do they not secede from the whole of which they are parts? Why do lineages not split off from tribes, and tribes from states? Why do sects not become separate churches, or factions become different parties? Why do conjugal family units remain part of joint family units? This is the problem of *cohesion*.

(iii) Why do members of a social group, quasi-group or collectivity continue to recognize themselves as an entity, distinct from other such entities, and why are they prepared, under some conditions, to act as an entity? This is the problem of *solidarity*.

(iv) Why do the participants in a social system or sub-system of a society adhere to or conform to its norms? These are the problems of *compliance, commitment, conformity* and *consensus*.

(v) Why do the different acts of men in social systems continue to complement, reciprocate, support or correspond to one another? This is the problem of *mutuality*. A subsidary problem in this category is that of *cooperation*.

* What follows in this chapter is largely an elaboration of the discussion in Chapter 2.

(vi) How is it that different sets of activities which occur within a society or sub-system of a society do not obstruct one another, and may even lend support to one another? And how do the different sets of beliefs, symbols, values and sentiments coexist? This may be called the problem of *functional interdependence* or, as it is sometimes called, the problem of '*system integration*'.*

(vii) The final problem is that of social *persistence*.

The Problem of Participation

Continued participation of individuals in social groups or social systems can be due to one or more of a number of factors: the absence of, or ignorance of, alternatives, unwillingness to risk change, moral commitment, a fatalistic acceptance of conditions, coercion, or the threat of it, the perception of present or future advantages in continued participation, involvement in a network of social relations, the need for a familiar culture or subculture, the need for strong and familiar social ties, and so on. Commonly, it is due to the sheer weight or pressure of some or all of these factors combined in a given social structure: men pursue their interests in a particular social group or social system because the possibilities of doing so are presented to them in their immediate social environment and also because the very nature of their interests is defined for them within a given system. These interests may involve control over or access to material resources or the attainment of esteem, prestige or power; and they may also include certain culturally defined goals with which the individual is identified, such as the maintenance of certain types of social relationship.

Sometimes men do move from one social group to another, as they may opt out of a system or sub-system of a society. Even in some primitive societies men can detach themselves from one social unit and attach themselves to another; whether this is possible depends on the nature of the political structure and the

---

* This term is used by D. Lockwood[1] who distinguishes between 'system integration' and 'social integration'; this second term subsumes those which are here distinguished as cohesion, solidarity and consensus.

possibility of enforcing, encouraging or binding men to particular units.[2] In general, whether men can move out of social groups or opt out of social systems—for example, from participation in religious or political institutions—depends on what is permitted. But even where physical movement or disengagement is permitted, it does not necessarily occur. On the whole, men move most easily from those groups or systems where effective affective commitment, and identification with common symbols which evoke and sustain such commitment, is low.

However, even the strongest ties and deepest commitments are sometimes broken when the opportunities arise and the advantages are thought to be great. But even then, there may be reluctance to pursue or recognize advantages and opportunities; what men have is more secure than what they *may* have. Deliberately to create a change in one's circumstances requires great motivation: men who migrate from one society to another must be attracted by the expectation of powerful advantages. Even when there is a breakdown in a social system, and men lose their commitment and sense of social and symbolic attachment, there may still be powerful forces opposing total disengagement. In parts of Africa, tribesmen who have become townsmen have often continued to participate partially in the tribal system; in fact, there has been a tendency in the past to use the resources of one social sector to shore up some vestigial and shrunken version of a traditional system.[3]

Clearly the conditions which affect continued participation in a group system are related to others, such as commitment, cohesion, and solidarity.

The Problem of Cohesion

The cohesion of a social unit such as a group, quasi-group or collectivity, is the resistance to division or secession. This condition may be due to one or more of a number of factors: allegiance to a larger unit; overall coordination; mutual interest or interdependence; intersection of ties; and the quality and strength of ties.

Allegiance to a larger unit may be based either on opposition to some external group, or on some internal consensus or identification.

Opposition to a foe, who may exist or who may have to be created, or to an imaginary foe, is usually a poor basis of long-term cohesion, unless it is supported by other conditions; for continued external threat may, itself, serve to drive wedges between units which comprise a larger collectivity.

Allegiance to a larger unit is more likely to persist if there is some set of values and symbols which can evoke and sustain it. One of the most important forces of allegiance is the use of a common language: this encourages or permits interaction, which in turn facilitates the establishment of common values and symbols of identification; secondly, a common language, which is different from other languages, may itself become a symbol of identification.

Language is not the only source of identification with a social unit. In fact, a common language often fails to prevent division and permanent secession. Religion also may make for unity, but not necessarily: sectarian divisions are inherent in the organizational and belief structures of certain religions.[4] Where the members of a social unit share a great many cultural items—religion, language, moral and aesthetic values and other behavioural norms—they are more likely to recognize a common allegiance. But for a common culture to exist there must be continued social interaction over a long period; and this, in turn implies cohesion.

One of the surest bases of common allegiance is the recognition of a coordinating agency which has persisted over time and gained legitimacy. An agency, such as the State, may contribute to cohesion in several ways: first, it provides joint facilities for the members of the various component units which they would otherwise not have; second, it provides the means for compelling the continued allegiance of component units, or preventing deep division or secession; and thirdly, it provides a symbol of identification for these units. These three functions are interrelated. Clearly, the provision of facilities increases the recognition of legitimacy, and vice versa. The use of compulsion in preventing secession may, however, increase or reduce legitimacy, and the need for its use may result from the absence of legitimacy. The use of centralized force to limit internal division and prevent secession is a poor basis for continued cohesion; it provokes opposition to its own power, and encourages competition between the component units to gain power; and this, in itself, may encourage further strife and secession.

The existence of mutual interests or, better still, of interdependence, particularly through the division of labour, is one of the most powerful forces of cohesion. Interdependence can occur in various forms. There can be political or military alliances between regions, feudal domains, lineages, clans, tribes or nations. There can be ritual interdependence such as exists between castes or the segments or sections of a simple society. And, finally, there can be economic interdependence of many kinds: for example, men may require one another's assistance in the performance of tasks which require the pooling of labour or material resources; men may participate in systems of differentiated tasks; or they may exchange facilities, resources or services which have become increasingly necessary to one another.

Interdependence, of whatever kind, does not necessarily prevent deep division or even secession. Societies may have civil wars, states may divide, trading partners may become hostile to one another, military allies may break their alliances and form new ones, and even units which participate interdependently in common ritual performances may certainly be divided in other spheres.[5]

The degree of cohesion between interdependent units depends partly on whether the same or similar advantages obtained by the constituent units from their relationship can or cannot be obtained by forming such relations with other units. Mutual indispensability is likely to increase when the different constituent units of a collectivity have been interrelated over a long period as part of a complex economic system involving a high degree of internal differentiation. One important reason for this is that the pursuit of goals by any members of any constituent section or segment is dependent upon the pursuit of goals by others in a variety of other sections. The second reason, closely linked to the first, is that differentiation creates divisions, such as those of class and status, which cut across segmental divisions, thereby weakening them.

To say that the intersection of ties is a basis of cohesion means, in effect, that the cohesiveness of a unit is likely to be high when the divisions within it intersect, and low when the divisions are overlapping or congruent with one another.* But there is an important qualification to this line of argument: even if there are cross-cutting ties within a group or collectivity, some ties may be so much stronger than any others as to withstand the effect which these others may have on them: for example, class loyalties are often not weakened by local loyalties, while national loyalties are seldom weakened by those of class.

However, when due consideration is given to this qualification, the truth of the general proposition can scarcely be denied. One of the chief reasons for the fear of secession in many contemporary new nations, such as India and Nigeria, is the lack of an inter-secting network of relationships to weaken the forces of region-alism and ethnicism: in fact, such networks may exist *within* each region, thereby strengthening their own internal unity. Of course, it is not enough to recommend the extension of extra-ethnic ties in order to inhibit secessionist tendencies and divisions between regional units; for the main difficulty lies in creating the conditions which promote new types of relationship; the creation of such conditions, particularly through industrialization and bureaucratization, is itself inhibited by the existence of segmental networks of relationship; there is a vicious circle of causes and effects.

If ties do not cut across one another but overlap there is a high degree of cohesion within the unit which contains these overlapping ties. In small traditional communities and societies, relationships tend to be 'diffuse'—the same individuals who are related to one another by one set of interests are also related by a number of others. When such units are then incorporated into a larger one to form a modern federal state, they retain their cohesiveness until new ties emerge which reduce the cohesivness of the 'old' unit. Clearly, if relationships within a segment are diffuse, while those outside of it are 'specific', each segment is bound to be far more cohesive than the wider political unit of which they are a part.†

* This point has been emphasized by Simmel[6] and elaborated by Cosen[7] and Gluckman.[8]

† The terms 'diffuse' and 'specific' are used here in the Parsonian sense:

The different factors which make for cohesion may or may not be mutually supporting. If relationships are diffuse within any segment of a larger unit, then there will be a dearth of cross-cutting ties between segments. If there is a strong coordinating agency, this is likely to create ties between units or to establish administrative statuses which cut across segmental divisions, and this may also foster loyalty to the wider unit by creating some object with which to identify. And if there is interaction between segments, this is likely to produce some elements of a common culture.

Clearly then the degree of cohesion in a society or group is also affected by the nature and degree, of solidarity, consensus and functional integration.

The Problem of Solidarity

The solidarity of a group, quasi-group or collectivity is a readiness to act in concert for certain purposes; however it is not simply a psychological state, for if a collectivity never does act in concert its solidarity may be spurious. But the term refers to the shared disposition of the members of a collectivity, not to the structure of its relationships. This last is covered by the term 'cohesion'. In principle, a group may be cohesive without its members recognizing this; but it has no solidarity without some tacit or conscious recognition of this.

Solidarity in any social system may derive from interests which stem from internal social relations, or it may result from external pressures, or as is common, it may result from both. But even internal bases of solidarity exist only because certain interests are opposed to those of outsiders; and external pressures can only create solidarity if they activate internal interests.

While solidarity does not exist without common interests, these alone do not create it unless they are recognized and given some importance. The solidarity of the international working

---

'diffuse' ties are those in which many interests are compounded in the same relationship; 'specific' ties are those in which one or a few interests are contained in the same relationship. See chapter 5, pp. 98–9.

class has never been realized; and even the intra-national solidarity of industrial workers may be weak when ethnic and religious solidarities are strong. On the other hand, there may sometimes be an interest in solidarity as such; and where this exists it may take little in the way of 'objective' common interests to establish and maintain it, at least for a short while. For example the expression of national or ethnic solidarity is, under some conditions, an end in itself: where this is the case, groups may create external enemies, or, indeed, internal ones, who may become real, or who may remain in the realm of phantasy.

In some cases solidarity results from group participation in common activities, and the sharing of common ideas and values, and this may then create for the group concerned, certain common interests as against others; thus, a local community may develop a solidarity if an attempt is made to incorporate it into a wider community. In other cases, solidarity must be created to defend common interests: thus if members of an ethnic minority are exploited or suffer discrimination, they may form organizations to combat this; to maintain commitment to these organizations they may create solidarity through the establishment of ideas, symbols and values which define them as an entity; thus, one form of ethnic particularism must give rise to another, and a struggle to end ethnic discrimination may intensify ethnic solidarity, and hence ethnic hostility.

Solidarity implies some degree of consensus: if a group recognizes itself as such, its members must at least be agreed on one thing—the defining quality of group membership. If there is a great degree of consensus within a group—if there is a number of common interests, and if the agreement between the members is of a morally binding nature—then an intense solidarity is likely. But solidarity can also exist if the activity performed by a group demands a high degree of personal cooperation in the face of difficulties or danger.

Some forms of solidarity are associated with strong emotional bonds between individuals who are intimately related to one another. Such solidarity can easily be transformed into explosive hostility. There are two reasons for this. The first is that, under such conditions, any failure in the fulfilment of obligations is treated with deadly seriousness so that there is a constant possibility of friction. The second reason is that intimate, affective solidarity in a group requires the constant control of hostile sentiments; resentments develop which have little opportunity for expression; the result is that when differences do occur, they may take highly disruptive or even violent forms. It is not that unexpressed hostility accumulates as unreleased energy, but that grievances are compounded. Highly charged, affective solidarity often occurs when groups are on the defensive, or when they are treated with contempt, suspicion or envy by others. Under these conditions, solidarity may have practical functions—the sense of unity promotes a readiness to protect rights or to obtain them—but it may also be an end in itself, offering psychological protection to the individual. Where such solidarity exists among a group which suffers inferior status, the members may internalize this sense of inferiority and treat other members of their group with potential hostility. Such groups are demonstrative in the expression of their solidarity, but beneath the surface they may be riven by interpersonal or factional disputes.

The creation and maintenance of solidarity can occur spontaneously through collective action, or as the unintended consequence of the actions of many individuals and groups. But frequently it is due, in no small part, to the existence of focal institutions around which it crystallizes. Of particular significance in this respect is the institution of leadership or of authority. Freud believed that all group solidarity necessarily results from the identification of members of a group with a particular leader.[9] His theory is that individuals project onto leaders the qualities which they esteem and which they would like to possess—the leader is the idealized image of themselves—while at the same time, they 'introject' the image of the leader—that is, they imagine that the leader, with his many admirable qualities, is part of themselves; this collective identification with the leader creates an effective bond between the members of the group and the leader, and between the members themselves; they share the leader and their attitudes towards him; they are 'brothers'. This theory has much in common with Max Weber's theory of charismatic leadership and legitimation[10]—though Freud's theory explains what Weber's takes for granted—and it may account for a particular kind of solidarity which is associated with a particular kind of leadership. There *are* groups in which the members are 'brothers'; and some of these—not all—are founded by leaders with special personal qualities. Furthermore, the theory may explain some of the symbolic functions of traditional forms of leadership. But solidarity commonly rests on identification with an institutional structure whose present leader or leaders are not necessarily imbued with very special qualities. The Freudian theory is not a general explanation of the social forms of solidarity; and it does not account for the boundaries of social identification.

The Problem of Compliance, Commitment, Conformity and Consensus

It has repeatedly been emphasized that one of the conditions of solidarity, and of continued individual participation in social systems, is the readiness of individuals to act in conformity with the norms of society. This can be called compliance. One form of compliance, which has been much discussed by social theorists, is commitment which, in turn, involves the notion of consensus. But there are various forms of compliance, of which commitment is only one.

As Etzioni has recently emphasized [11], compliance has two aspects: the internal motivation of the actor, and the external pressure exercised by other actors, and by the system in which the actors participate. In different forms of compliance these two aspects assume different kinds and degrees of importance. In some cases, such as compliance with the norms of certain religious organizations, the internal motivation may be paramount; here, the key mechanism is possibly that of guilt or, more specifically, a sense of sin. In other extreme, but by no means unusual cases, such as those of slave labour, external pressures may be dominant. But no external pressure can operate without an internal motivation or disposition to respond, even if this internal state is simply that of a fear of loss of life, liberty, property, or some privilege. And no internal motivation can produce conformity to a norm unless the actor has internalized the disposition to conform to some system outside of himself; often the disappearance or collapse of such a system is accompanied by a weakening of the internal disposition; but this need not be the case—many motives, ideas and attitudes die hard.

There are four main types of conformity. First, one may conform because it is convenient to pursue one's goals in a particular way, or because this is the way to ensure the reciprocal conduct of others, which is a necessary condition of success in achieving one's own goals; these goals may be the pursuit of wealth, material security, power, prestige, social acceptance, love, and so on. Second, one may conform because one habitually pursues certain goals in certain ways in response to external stimuli. Third, one may conform because of a sense of obligation which may or may not be related to a perceived interest. Fourth, one may conform because of the fear of the consequences of nonconformity, which may produce punitive deprivations or inflictions, including the deprivation of honour or self-esteem.

The first type needs little further discussion. Norms and values have developed partly to cope with the exigencies of human action and interaction; and conformity is maintained, in part, by the expectation that some exigencies will continue to be met. The fundamental assumption of exchange theory is that conformity can in some senses, be seen as regular conduct in which some of the gains and costs of interaction have been calculated and discovered in the past, and the 'solution' accepted. But even the most instrumental attitude to norms is influenced by some degree of commitment and habit-formation. Goals are not chosen randomly, but in terms of a value-laden hierarchy; the choice of a certain means to them must meet certain criteria of efficiency, or aesthetic or moral preference.

The second type also needs little further discussion. To use the norms of language, as everyone does, is neither to weigh the cost of deviance, nor to obtain some inner satisfaction from conformity. But language is not peculiar in this respect; men adhere to a great many norms habitually, not because they value them as part of a tradition but because they have learned to use them and have seldom entered situations in which the possibilities of their rejection or modification have arisen. Such situations do sometimes occur; writers question the rules of language to meet certain requirements of style and structure; and such deviations may become a cause for aesthetic or even moral commitment.

Commitment comes into its own strictly when there is considerable possibility of deviation, and when certain perceived short-run disadvantages of conformity are thought to outweigh the advantages. This does not mean that all those that are morally committed are necessarily aware of the possibilities of deviation or of the attractions of it; but it does mean that such commitment may be weakened or otherwise altered when the recognition of other courses of action occurs.

Moral commitment may be associated with a recognition of long-term advantages for oneself, or of advantages for a wider collectivity. But this is not a necessary characteristic of it. One may renounce, ignore or withstand the demands of a wider collectivity in the name of some moral principle—for example, one may refuse to fulfil certain military obligations which are an 'offence to one's conscience'—even though one is not being called upon by another recognized collectivity to do this. However, moral commitments do often have this 'altruistic' form. To renounce personal gratifications, or the gratifications of those who are intimately associated with one through strong affective ties, requires some strong motive, and this may take the form of moral justification. But all moral justification consists in obtaining satisfaction from the knowledge that one's conduct is right as judged by some standards other than those of personal need. In the final instance, one can only experience moral commitment if the failure to act in conformity with certain standards creates a conscious sense of guilt.*

Commitment may not, of course, be moral in the full sense: men may be commited to scientific or aesthetic goals or principles, and may be prepared to defy certain socially accepted moral principles in the name of these. But, insofar as commitment is a factor in creating or maintaining the operation of social

---

* The term 'conscious' is deliberately used here. Unconscious guilt is a powerful force in the human personality; and Freudians may be right to argue that it is the source of the moral faculty in the individual, deriving from the processes of identification of the child with the parent. (According to one such theory, the unconscious basis of the 'super-ego' is the fear of reprisal experienced by the infant in relation to its parents. The infant harbours hostile feelings and fears retaliation.) But, though this explains how the personality is able to cope with moral injunctions, it does not explain the nature of these in social relationships; for the infant experiences a very narrow range of these, and must later acquire a knowledge of the moral standards which apply to a good many areas of social life.

institutions, it must be moral in addition to anything else. A commitment to science or to artistic freedom can become a matter of conscience.

The fourth and final form of compliance or conformity is that which results from the fear of reprisal or punishment. This is close to the first form, in which the motive for conformity is to ensure certain advantages. But in general, men do distinguish between being induced to do something, and between being compelled, on pain of suffering, to do it. In the one case conditions are provided or established within which the actor may choose to pursue certain goals; if he does not wish to conform then he may opt out of the situation; it is only if he declines to conform *without* opting out that punitive sanctions are applied. In the other case the *only* choice is between compliance and deprivation. The most obvious forms of punitive sanction are deprivation of livelihood, property and the freedom of movement, or the infliction of pain.

It is often argued that it is not the fear of punishment that deters men from nonconformity, but the sense of moral obligation. This argument rests on two hypotheses: first, that some offenders against moral, legal and other norms obtain satisfaction from the prospect of punishment, and unconsciously seek to be punished; second, that punishment often encourages further acts of nonconformity. Both these hypotheses may be true; but their truth is not inconsistent with the assumption that externally imposed sanctions do deter deviance. Some men may desire to be punished; but only a small percentage of men in any society suffer from this in a pathologically extreme form. And while punishment may provoke hostile reactions in some, it does not necessarily do this for all men; in any case it is the *prospect* of punishment which deters, not just the punishment itself. One of the most important deterrents is the shame which attaches to any public knowledge of an offence and to the publicity given to official or unofficial punishments. In fact, one of the most effective punishments for certain types of offence in some societies is public shaming which brings dishonour, or loss of self-respect, to the offender.

Some writers suggest that the use of shame, as an external mechanism of social control, is common to primitive societies and small, traditional, rural communities, while the use of guilt, an internal mechanism of control, is found largely in advanced, urban societies. This, like many other plausible theories, is not without some supporting evidence, but needs correction. The underlying argument is that social relationships in small-scale societies and closed communities are characterized by familiarity and immediacy, and that this enables the community to control deviance by the exertion of public pressure in the form of disapproval or even disgrace. An associated argument is that a strong sense of guilt is usually absent from such societies because this requires a particular form of child-rearing based on the intense identification of the child with the parent. The weaknesses of this view are twofold; in the first place, there is considerable evidence that a sense of guilt is strong in some non-industrial or primitive societies; secondly, the sense of shame, like the sense of guilt, can only be elicited by the group if the psychological mechanism is internalized. This has been argued powerfully by Gerhart Piers, a psychoanalyst, and Milton Singer, an anthropologist.[12] They point out that men can experience shame without being detected in a misdemeanour, while guilt may not, in some cases, be aroused without the presence of some 'others'. They suggest that some forms of shame and guilt are dependent largely on external sanctions while others are not. It may then be true that in simple societies great reliance is placed on the fear of public dishonour simply because this form of social control is easily mobilized in such societies. But there is more to it than that. In societies in which men participate in social relationships with their 'total' personalities there is a greater likelihood that they will have a developed sense of honour; after all, their self-esteem is at stake in so many spheres; if a man fails in some sphere this is known to his fellows in every other sphere in which he participates.

The use, or threatened use, of external sanctions which arouse guilt or shame seem rather different from those which demand compliance through physical coercion, threat of material deprivation, and so on; the one requires some degree of internalization of moral norms and values, whereas the other requires only some disposition to fear or resent an assault on the self or some other deprivation. But the real difference between the types of sanction may be slight: physical punishment may, in some conditions, be more degrading than painful; and the deprivation of material resources or privileges may similarly involve a loss of honour either directly or indirectly. Whether physical and economic and other such forms of coercion also involve moral and symbolic coercion, depends on the degree to which those who are coerced share some moral and other values with those who coerce them. The extreme case in which there is little or no sharing is that of industrial or plantation slavery, especially where the slaves are obtained by conquest, belong to cultures different from those of the conquering society, and are treated as totally outside the moral community. Insofar as these slaves are not born and reared in the society of their servitude, they have little or no opportunity to identify with their masters and to internalize symbols and values which can be 'manipulated' so as to produce a sense of duty or responsibility or even honour, and reactions of shame and guilt. In such conditions slaves are not entirely unlike draft animals in their status, or lack of status, though they may not consider themselves as such*; their lack of rights reduces their humanity in a very real sense. But even slaves may come to be treated increasingly in terms of a stable system of norms which accord them rights and thereby incorporate them to some extent into a moral and symbolic system.

This raises the vexed question of consensus about which much theoretical debate in sociology has recently centred. The term itself is distressingly vague. Clearly if there is conformity to norms and this is not based purely on coercion—in the extreme case of industrial slavery it might be—there must be some consensus on norms; in fact, even a highly coercive system is not purely arbitrary and makes use of norms which become mutually predictable and upon which there is, therefore, consensus. Indeed there must always be some consensus on linguistic and other norms involving symbolic communication; and coercive systems may use a whole apparatus of visual symbols which structure the perception of those who are commanded. In this and other senses, every stable system of social interaction involves some degree of cultural consensus, even if the culture is highly specific to a particular system of interaction; *even concentration camps have their internal culture.* All discussion of consensus, in this minimal sense, has little explanatory value. What is usually meant by consensus is something more than this: it implies

* For this insight I am indebted to Professor D. G. MacRae.

that adherence to norms is not based purely on inducement and coercion, but also on an acceptance of certain values and on the psychological need to conform which is itself, a fundamental value.

In this sense also, there is consensus in all societies and certainly in particular sectors of all societies. Even in social systems which most resemble the despotic model, communal, vicinal and kinship relationships are always governed to some extent by moral norms and values, even if large-scale economic and political organizations rely greatly on coercive measures and some element of inducement. Inducement is, of course, a significant factor in such relations; but it does not work on a simple *quid pro quo* basis: goods and services are provided to others (with whom there is common participation in a number of activities) though not necessarily in the expectation of an immediate return. The moral attitude consists in the assumption of good faith.

But the implication of the theory of shared value commitments is that even in those spheres in which inducement and coercion seem to dominate, there is an underlying moral and symbolic system on which all else rests. The intention of this theory is that the structure of command and obedience is necessarily founded on obligation, and it is here that it is weakest. First, it overlooks the opportunities for compelling obedience through the combined use of force and inducement. Second, it does not recognize that it is just in those areas of social activity in which obligation to a higher authority is lacking that the combination of inducement and coercion is necessary if a particular type of organization is to be maintained. Third, the consensus theory fails to explain how some degree of commitment to authority is initially established.

All systems rely on coercion, inducement and some element of commitment. For at least three reasons total despotism seldom, if ever, works; there are always rivalries within a dominant class, and those with greatest power must offer inducements to different factions to win and maintain their support; there are always possibilities of rebellion or *coup d'état* from within the élites, so that concessions are made to those in lower statuses to maintain their support; finally, it may be technically difficult to police a large-scale society, so that there is constant pressure to rely on symbolic rather than physical coercion. The question is why some systems require a greater emphasis on consensus, while others depend more on coercion or inducement.

It has commonly been assumed that simple, small-scale societies enjoy a fairly high degree of consensus of moral, aesthetic and other values, and that all non-industrial societies approximate to this condition in varying degrees. It *is* true that in these societies there is a considerable uniformity of beliefs, norms values and practices, and in this sense there is a high degree of consensus. But this consensus does not explain uniformity or conformity; it is an aspect of it.

But in complex societies there is also a need for some consensus; for without this there would be no basis to legality. The opponents of this view point to the pronounced sectional differences in modern industrial societies as evidence of the lack of consensus. For one thing, they say, there is no fundamental agreement on how wealth should be shared between every contending sectional interest; and even where there is no 'free-for-all', this is not due to any consensus, but to State decisions which can scarcely be challenged. It is this seemingly limited choice between endless sectional conflicts, on the other hand, and totalitarian decision-making, on the other, which argues against the existence of consensus in industrial societies. Of course there is no total consensus. If workers accept the privileges of employers and managers, this is scarcely due to moral commitment. But there is a consensus on some things; at least both employers and managers speak the same language of pecuniary incentives. In fact, it is because all sections of industrial societies share certain common values—the desire for higher incomes to acquire an increasingly wide range of goods and services—that there is so much conflict over the distribution of rewards. And, as Durkheim pointed out more than fifty years ago, there is some basis of consensus on rather broad moral assumptions. And this moral sense that social obligations are binding must be directed specifically to the legal norms of the society.[13] This does not mean of course that there is widespread agreement on certain 'official' ideologies and sets of values which are often mistakenly thought of as the moral props of society.

Role Congruence, Reciprocity and Cooperation

Roles are made congruent or reciprocal insofar as the normative expectations of each role complement those of other roles. The type of relationship which is most bound by role expectations is co-operation, which is the polar opposite of conflict. Cooperation is a deliberate and voluntary effort to facilitate the performance of tasks by others in return for similar services. There are various forms of it. In the simplest, the cooperation inheres in the specific activity itself: for example, if two or more men farm land which they own jointly. In more complex forms of cooperation the return for services may be delayed: one farmer may assist another to clear a field in the expectation that reciprocal assistance will be given at some other time. In some cases cooperation can be contractual and its obligations specified, in others the arrangement may be diffuse and open.

Cooperation is a form of reciprocity; but not all reciprocity is cooperation: to buy goods or to barter them, is a form of reciprocity but it is not necessarily cooperation. Cooperation is also a form of interdependence; but many forms of interdependence are not strictly cooperative: industrial managers and workers are interdependent, but they do not cooperate. Both reciprocity and interdependence are compatible with conflict; but to cooperate is to renounce conflict. This does not mean that those who co-operate cannot also be in conflict with one another; they can indeed, but the issues of conflict must be separate from that of co-operation. Two brothers may cooperate in work, but may be rivals for the favours of the same woman. But they cannot work together and, at the same time, aim to prevent one another from succeeding in the goals of the work activity; this is obvious. But reciprocity may involve conflict: one may exchange goods for other goods, services or money and seek, in doing so, to gain at the expense of another; this is clearly not cooperation.

Conflict involves deliberate attempts to prevent the attainment of goals by others. At its most extreme it takes the form of struggle. Conflict itself involves a relatively low degree of normative definition of role performance between the conflicting parties; when men seek to outwit one another, to eliminate one another from a contest, or to interfere directly with one another's attempts to attain particular goals, they gain advantages by adopting courses of action which are not expected, and which cannot therefore be prescribed within roles. This does not mean that conflict necessarily occurs without any normative constraint. Usually, the opposite is the case; in most forms there are very specific normative constraints within which conflict occurs: when spouses quarrel, there are some things which are not said and done; when entrepreneurs compete, certain practices are not adopted; when managers and workers bargain over wages they may use the strike and lock-out, but they try to avoid destruction of property and physical violence; when combatants go to war, they adhere to certain rules in the use of weapons, in the treatment of prisoners, and so on. In the first example, the restraints are built into the moral character of the relationship: usually spouses experience guilt when resorting to certain practices in their quarrels. But in the other examples the adherence to norms is clearly in the interests of the conflicting parties; neither side may wish the conflict to spread or take forms which become unmanageable. When the advantages of adhering to such norms are no longer weighed against the disadvantages the norms may come to have morally binding significance. But whether this occurs or not, the adherence to norms necessarily sets limits to the relationship of conflict; it is therefore, correct to say that conflict, *in its most extreme forms*, involves the renunciation or absence of normative constraint.

Cooperation, in its most extreme form, and when it is not sporadic or purely spontaneous, must involve a high degree of commitment to norms and, usually, to certain moral values. There are several reasons for this. Firstly, regular and successful forms of cooperation demand a high degree of predictability of conduct. Secondly, cooperation demands that those involved should renounce certain goals or defer certain gratifications. Neither of these conditions can be met without a high degree of normative prescription which must, in the long run, be buttressed by moral values.

Societies or social systems may contain a considerable degree of harmony, in the sense that the performance of roles is reciprocated without a great deal of obstruction; but this does not mean that such systems are highly cooperative; between the poles of cooperation and unrestrained conflict lie most forms of social relationship. Within these relationships there is a constant tension between reciprocation and non-reciprocation. Most of the forms of structured conflict in all societies are constrained by norms which prescribe the limits and modalities of opposition: these prescriptions, however, are signs of reciprocation, or, indeed, of the absence of conflict in certain areas. The acceptance of such restraints may be explained in terms of interest and convenience; but their institutionalization does also result in the adoption of a moral attitude to them.*

The lack of role reciprocation or mutuality may be due not simply to direct conflict of interest; it may also be due to, or be associated with, the lack of compatibility between different social sectors or sets of norms.

System Integration, or Functional Interdependence

The concept of system integration or of functional interdependence refers to the way in which different sets of norms, values,

---

* It is sometimes said that, for these reasons, much structured conflict and competition in society, even when it takes the form of struggle, can be understood on the analogy of ritual contests and competitive games. In these last, there are elaborate rules which prescribe the limits within which players or teams of players can adopt the strategies of outwitting and defeating their opponents. There may be an element of truth in this, but the paradigmatic demonstration breaks down on an important point. Players in a game may abide by the rules to avoid penalties or because of moral commitment; but without the rules there would be no point to the game or contest: the aim is to devise strategies which will enable one to win within the rules. In 'real' social situations, the rules are also adhered to in order to avoid punishment or because of a moral commitment; but adherence may also result from mutual convenience; if one 'side' becomes more powerful than another it can prevent the other from continuing to play the game according to the previous rules or indeed, according to any rules. A team that scores a goal must agree to permit the other side to try to do the same *from a position of equal strength*; for example, both teams return to the centre of the field. But in war, if one side wins a battle it pursues its enemy from a position of strength; in collective bargaining, if workers succeed in winning some concession from managers they use this to strengthen their future bargaining position. Games, tournaments and ritual contests may resemble other conflict situations in *certain* respects; but they cannot be treated as models in which most forms of social conflict are simulated.

role-structures, institutions, beliefs and symbols, which are characteristic of a social system, are interrelated.

There are three aspects to this. Firstly, there is the degree to which one social or cultural process contributes to the operation of another, or of others. An example of this is the way in which educational differentials tend to buttress those of wealth, power, and prestige, by maintaining the cultural gap between élites and masses; needless to add, this is also an example of how the contribution of one part of a system to another is 'reciprocated' —status differentials also contribute to the maintenance of cultural differentials.

The second aspect can be more negatively defined as the manner in which, and degree to which, different features of social life can coexist without actually obstructing one another's operations. For example, certain features of Japanese family life have persisted from pre-industrial to industrial conditions; these may not actually contribute to the preservation of the industrial system, nor is their persistence necessarily dependent upon the industrializing process; but, on the other hand, neither of the two structural features seems to obstruct the working of the other. (Of course, it might be said that the traditional survivals do contribute to the working of the peculiar, *Japanese* form of industrial society, which in turn contributes to the survival of traditional family forms.)

The third aspect of functional integration is that of psychological correspondence between different ideas, norms and symbols of a culture, so that they constitute a consistent pattern. An example of this would be an emphasis on hierarchy in all sectors of the social structure; another example would be the tendency or readiness to compromise in all forms of social conflict.

The various forms of functional interrelation are commonly taken for granted, though it is recognized that the degree to which they are found does vary from one system to another; but there have been few satisfactory attempts to explain either the phenomena or their variations. One theory asserts that those who man certain key or dominant institutions ensure that other institutions, ideas, etc., play their part in supporting the system as a whole. Marx's theory of social systems is a variant of this; for Marx argues that the character of most institutions is governed either by the needs or the ideological modes of those who control the economic relations of production. The principal objection to this theory is that it explains far too much of social life as the direct product of human will or intention; it fails to explain the high degree of integration which exists in many simple societies in which men seem least able to manipulate their social systems in this deliberate way.* Indeed the degree of integration of social systems may be in *inverse* relation to the possibility of deliberate design. This is not to deny that *attempts* are made in certain complex societies, with varying degrees of success, to fashion a highly integrated system by deliberate design.

A second explanation of this phenomenon is a variant of the value-consensus theory: it states that there is a core value-complex in each society which tends to govern the character of its key institutions, dominant ideology, etc.; since all parts of a system reflect common principles, they must, of course, be integregated with one another. This theory is scarcely an improvement on the first. Insofar as institutions do reflect common core values they may, in this sense be said to be integrated with one another. But institutions may be compatible with one another, or may even support one another, *without* reflecting the same values. The Kshatriya castes in Hindu society may uphold military values while the Brahman castes uphold values which oppose any form of destruction of life; yet the two may not only coexist, but even lend support to one another; the military castes may preserve a structure of authority in which the priestly castes enjoy a high level of prestige, while the Brahmans legitimize the whole structure of caste relations.

But even if a whole range of institutions in a society did both reflect common values and provide mutual support for one another, it would not necessarily follow that value-consensus was a necessary or sufficient condition for system integration. For the existence of core values, which are embodied in a number of institutions, might well be the *consequence* of functional interdependence; values do not necessarily give rise to the institutions which embody them. It may sometimes occur that new

---

* Professor Claude Lévi-Strauss would argue that even in the simplest societies men do consciously or deliberately fashion their institutions in this way. There is some truth in this; but it is doubtful whether all functional integration is created in this way.[14]

values, as part of an ideology, give rise to the formation of a set of institutions which reflect them. If this happens, the new institutions will be integrated in the sense that there is a strain towards consistency at the ideational level; but this does not mean that the institutions are either compatible with one another or mutually reinforcing. Some of the key institutions established in the Soviet Union after the revolution may well have reflected the core values inherent in Bolshevik ideology; but this did not make them highly compatible with one another.

A third theory explains system integration as resulting from the internal adaptation of parts to one another. The argument is that parts which are incompatible with one another, or which do not reinforce one another, will gradually change until they are mutually compatible or reinforcing. This theory explains nothing, but merely assumes the process which is to be explained. And it can certainly not account for variations in the degrees and forms of functional interdependence and for the relative lack of it in some cases. A variant of this theory asserts that all systems must adapt to an external environment and that integrated systems are more adapted or adaptable than malintegrated systems. This theory is no better than the others: it does not show why more integrated systems *are* necessarily better adapted or adaptable to external environments; and, it does not explain how the process of internal integration occurs.

The only theory that is in any way satisfactory is that which explains functional integration as the largely unintended product of social interaction occurring over time. This not only goes some way to explaining the *existence* of functional integration, *but it also helps to explain variations in the nature and degree of it.*

One assumes, at the outset, that it is possible to distinguish a number of different sets of activities in a social group which are governed by different norms or sets of norms. One also assumes that those who interact in one activity will also interact, directly or indirectly in other activities. There are at least three possibilities here: those who interact in one sphere are the same people who interact in others; those who interact in one sphere interact with some others in some spheres but not in all; those who never interact directly, may interact indirectly through the mediation of others. Given that the participants in different social spheres will interact with one another directly or indirectly, it follows that the norms which govern action in different spheres will, to some extent influence one another. Normative influence can be of three kinds: first, if the different sets of norms regularly call for conflicting obligations or promote conflicting interests, then there will be some pressure to resolve these conflicts, or to devise some compromise between them, or to establish some bridging norms which make them less incompatible with one another; second, if one set of activities is necessary or useful for another, then there will be some pressure to make the norms mutually reinforcing; thirdly, if the different norms have some meaningful connection for the participants then there will be a psychological tendency to produce some consistency or correspondence between them.

Clearly, conflict between norms is only real if the different norms affect the same persons. Similarly, the mutual reinforcement of norms is only likely if those activities which are found necessary or useful to one another affect the same persons, or affect persons who interact with one another. And, finally, some degree of consistency or correspondence between social and cultural phenomena can only occur if these phenomena are internalized by the same persons who commonly interact. Whether the different parts of a system will affect one another, and the degree to which different parts will affect one another, depend on two important conditions: the frequency with which interactions occur between actors who are involved in the different institutional spheres; and the interactive 'distance' between the different institutional spheres. Clearly, if there is no frequent and regular contact between the participants in different institutional spheres—for example, if bureaucrats seldom interact with merchants—then there is less chance that the norms of each sphere will influence one another. And further, if interaction is mediated by a long chain of other interactions, rather than occurring directly, there is less chance of mutual influence.

With these assumptions the interaction theory can explain what none of the other theories can: why it is that there is a higher degree of structural and cultural integration in simpler societies than in more complex ones.* In very simple societies, most of the members participate, jointly, in a variety of institutional contexts —political, economic, ritual, etc.—and almost every (adult) member participates in almost all of these. This is another way

* This argument owes much to Eisenstadt,[15] Gluckman,[16] and Nadel.[17]

of saying that all relationships are 'multiplex'—they are governed by a number of obligations and interests—and that there is a low degree of differentiation in the society, so that all members of it are members of all institutions. Furthermore, most relationships are immediate, rather than mediated—that is, most members interact with one another directly—and where they are mediated, the span of mediation is fairly narrow, or, to put it another way, the 'interactive distance' is not great. Finally, interactions are frequent. In these circumstances the different sets of norms, beliefs etc., are likely to be brought into close relationship with one another. Any incompatibilities between norms will be readily experienced by those who are beset by them. And because the different norms are embedded in the same concrete relationships, particularly those of kinship, each set tends to reinforce the others: for example the norms of property ownership and usage will be affected by those of religious ritual and belief, and vice versa, because those who participate in common ritual activities may also have common interests in property.

Finally, because each member of society tends to participate in the whole round of activities, and therefore internalizes all or most of the norms, ideas and symbols of the culture, these will be contained within the individual minds of each member of society; and since each member will be in constant interaction with each other, there will be constant reinforcement and standardization of the different cultural items. These two conditions —'total'* internalization and constant interaction—favour the creation of a consistent or patterned relation between the different items of culture at the ideational level.

Each of the variables of functional interdependence—compatibility, mutual support and psychological consistency— affects the other. Insofar as items are compatible they tend to be used in support of one another; insofar as they are used or need to be used in support of one another, there is pressure to make them mutually compatible; insofar as they are closely integrated in these two ways they will be internalized by most participants as integrated items; and insofar as this occurs, the items will continue to coexist and to support one another.

This is the picture—or model—of functional integration in a simple social system. In a complex system—or in a model of a

* The word 'total' is not to be interpreted literally.

complex system—one finds all the opposite characteristics. First, relationships are highly specific—the personnel with whom one interacts in one institutional sphere may be totally different from those with whom one interacts in other spheres—so that the norms of different types of relationship can be kept fairly separate from one another. This being the case, if different norms are potentially in conflict with one another, the actors may not, for the most part, necessarily experience conflict with any regularity, so that the pressure for compatibility is not great. The second important characteristic of complex systems is the high degree of specialization of roles and of institutional 'segregation'; because of these, the norms of each sphere tend to be relatively autonomous; and this autonomy is facilitated by the fact that one interacts with different personnel in different contexts: if one does not interact with one's kinsmen in industrial organizations it is relatively simpler to keep the norms of kinship and organizational management separate from one another. Thirdly, each individual interacts with only a small proportion of the 'total society', and many or most interactions are mediated through a long chain of relationships; this means that there is less pressure for uniformity of norms and ideas. This difference may be partly off-set by the existence of bureaucratic structures and media of mass communication which tend to standardize many practices over a wide social field; but this standardization does not necessarily affect the 'private' sectors of life, or those sections in which some degree of choice, initiative or creativity are considered desirable. Fourth, each person participates in only a fairly small part of the total number of available activities, so that only a small part of the existing culture is internalized in any one mind; this means that there is little or no psychological possibility of creating some pattern-consistency between different ideas, norms, symbols, etc. And even if the individual mind does tend to create some consistency between the different cultural items which it internalizes, the set of items internalized by any one mind will be different from that internalized by another. Furthermore, because the individual is, to some extent, drawn into different sectors of activity which are segregated from one another, the different parts of the self are possibly compartmentalized, so that the internal strain to consistency may, for this reason, be low. This does not mean that in highly complex social systems there is little function integration. What it does mean is that *particular* parts of complex systems may be tightly integrated, but that these 'tight systems' may be only loosely related to one another. Putting this another way, one might say that in simple systems there is a greater degree of *'functional economy'* than in complex ones: if some cultural item exists in a simple system, then it will be used as much as possible by other items; in complex systems, there is not only more choice in the formation of 'functional alliances'—which may, therefore, be relatively weak—there is also greater functional independence. A clear example of this is the double functional significance of religious or mythical beliefs in simpler societies: these not only provide an upper limit to the explanation of the nature of the world, but they also provide an upper limit to the legitimation of a whole set of moral ideas and social norms. In complex societies religious ideas may provide an upper limit to intellectual curiosity and they may be used to justify some moral standards; but they are also kept quite separate from a whole host of moral values even when they are still used to explain the nature of the world or to give it meaning. In complex societies men may be torn between their moral obligations to Church and State, to God and Caesar; not so in simpler ones.

Of course, in all social systems the degree of functional integration, or of 'functional economy', varies from one part of the system to another. Even in the simplest systems there are some areas which are relatively autonomous with respect to others; and there are also many possibilities of conflict between institutional parts or between different norms. For example, in one Australian Aboriginal society—and these are, in certain respects, amongst the least differentiated social systems known to us—there is a fundamental conflict between the norms of gerontocratic control of younger females and other norms of sexual relationships and marriage.[18] In fact, one could argue that where functional incompatibilities do occur in simple systems they are less avoidable than in complex ones. It is for this reason that simpler systems are under greater pressure to create compatibilities between parts; *but it cannot be assumed that such pressure will necessarily be altogether effective.*

Of course, some complex systems display a far greater degree of functional integration than others: this is particularly the case where the goal of functional integration is part of an ideology which influences policy. An important feature of highly developed technologies is that they facilitate control by the State or other organizations over a wide range of social activities: these facilities include not only the means of communication but also those of coercion. Clearly, there are limits to the extent to which this is made possible: State interference with the autonomy of art or the organization of recreational facilities is less likely to rebound than interference with the autonomy of science. But attempts at integration of this kind always set up great strains in complex systems; even the efforts to coordinate different sectors of the economy may prove relatively unsuccessful when measured against the hopes of ideology—despite the use of computers.

There is one final aspect of this which should be mentioned; it is what Gouldner calls the problem of functional reciprocity. Gouldner asserts that, although different parts of a system can be said to be functionally related, this does not mean that the mutual effect of each on the other is of the same magnitude.[19] This is another way of saying that item X may influence item Y more than Y influences X. Gouldner's discussion is largely in terms of groups or social classes. He rightly states that some social groups have greater freedom of manoeuvre than others who are highly dependent upon them: what group A does, influences or determines what group B does; but what B does scarcely influences what A does because B tends to comply with the commands of A. But the problem of reciprocity also arises in examining the relationship between normative systems or institutional sections. For example, certain forms of pure scientific research may have little or no effect on other social processes, though the choice of such problems for research may be considerably influenced by other social and cultural conditions.

Gouldner's formulation of the problems of reciprocity and autonomy is doubtless influenced by Marx who was not unaware of the relevance of these issues for the analysis of social systems. For Marx recognized a process of interaction between different system parts, but nevertheless insisted that some parts affect others more than they are affected by them.

Persistence or Continuity in Social Systems

The final feature of social systems to be considered here is that of persistence. Obviously, one cannot conceive of social structure or system unless one assumes that social life has continuity. It may well be that all societies are constantly undergoing change; but it is important to recognize that social change is only conceivable in relation to persistence. What one studies is change in social structures and systems; which is another way of saying that the study of social change is the study of the disruption of social persistence, and the study of social persistence is the study of the processes which inhibit or fail to produce change.

Social systems or structures persist for a number of reasons. The first, and most obvious is that infants become social by identifying with their elders and by learning norms, values and beliefs from them. This does not mean that they retain or continue to accept everything that they have culturally inherited; nor does it mean that what they learn in this way is adequate for all social roles which they are to perform. But since all men need some stable points of reference, some anchor in the past, it is probably true, as Comte said, that they are in some respects and to some extent, conservative.

The second reason for social persistence is that norms prescribe what is typical or predictable and that some men, at least, develop a vested interest in this. Even when attempts are successfully made to change norms, or when norms change unintentionally —as they commonly do—there is never complete change in all aspects of a normative structure. Even after a successful revolution, one of the first exigencies to be met is that of establishing order, or preventing counter-revolution, and, indeed, of preventing revolutionary excess which might spread to the extent of threatening a new regime; in these circumstances the imposition of order commonly makes use of some existing institutional structures.

The third reason for social persistence is the force of legitimacy. This is linked with the first two reasons; for it is not simply that men prefer the familiar but that they come to accept it as right, and that they must be highly motivated to oppose it. The degree and extent of legitimation of institutions in a society depends greatly on how much benefit men obtain from these institutions and the extent to which they effectively participate in a moral community; sometimes, however, the members of a society may not, in fact, accept its institutions but may nevertheless identify with some symbol or representative of the society and, in this way, accept a status quo without considering many of the actual institutions as legitimate.

The fourth reason for persistence is the 'deadweight' effect of integration between institutions, beliefs, etc. Any pressure for change in one area of social life may be resisted because of the 'reinforcement effect' of different parts of social systems on one another. The present resistance of the Hindu caste system to the many pressures for change clearly illustrates this process: for it is not simply that members of dominant or honoured castes preserve the whole structure in their own interests—they scarcely have the power to do this in many cases—but that there are so many castes and that almost all of them have many interests in, and mechanisms for, preserving internal caste cohesion, which in turn serves to maintain caste differences. One explanation of all this is the low degree of industrialization in Indian society: for the assumption is that rural society is innately conservative in a psychological as well as a sociological sense. But this answer is inadequate: there is much evidence to show that caste cohesion and segregation persist to a considerable extent even in Indian urban areas; and there is also a suggestion that the slow growth of industrialization and of other forms of modernization are actually due, in part, to the persistence of caste.

Whatever may be true of large complex civilizations such as contemporary India (or Britain), in which there are great resistances to change, it is doubtless the case that small-scale, primitive societies have great powers of persistence; indeed it is arguable that they do not so much resist change but lack the conditions which encourage it, though they are not so highly resistant to certain forms of change once these impinge upon them from the outside. In fact, we have relatively little evidence concerning the tendencies for change in most primitive societies. All that is known is that they have remained primitive and that in *certain* respects some of them have not changed very much over centuries or millenia. One explanation for this is that they have not experienced

certain technological changes which are necessary for the development of highly differentiated structures and elaborate and varied
systems of belief. But why have they not experienced such technological changes? The answer might be that they do not have the
social and cultural conditions which are necessary for technological
innovation and discovery, so that there is a vicious circle of
causes and effects which is characteristic of highly integrated
social and cultural systems. This is strengthened by the argument
that simple, highly integrated systems, provide fewer 'openings'
for change and are, therefore, more self-perpetuating than
complex ones. The counter-argument to this is that simple
societies do change, as a result of internal and external pressures,
but that their changes may be imperceptible to both the outside
observer and to the members of these societies themselves,
over short periods of time; and since these are non-literate
cultures long-term changes cannot easily be recorded. A further
addition to this argument is that it is not that simple societies are
resistant to all change, but that our perception of their tendencies
to change is highly coloured by the expectations which are part
of our *own* social system. We have, in fact, an historical consciousness which is in part due to literacy and in part due to the preoccupation with progress or the failure to achieve it.

The final and, some would say, the most important reason for
social persistence, is vested interest; there are always some groups
in a society who either have an interest in preserving a particular
system or who prefer the status quo to the uncertainties of
particular types of change. But a vested interest is not sufficient
to explain persistence; a group with a vested interest in opposing
changes must also have the power to prevent them. Certainly a
combination of power and vested interest does account for a lack
of change in some societies; or at least, it is one factor in accounting for persistence. But this theory does not account for all
cases in which persistence is associated with a vested interest.
It does sometimes happen that there is widespread interest in
the status quo. This does not mean that all groups obtain equal
benefits from a system, but that many or all may prefer the known
benefits of a particular system to the unknown or doubtful
benefits of change, which may be feared in itself.

A system might also persist not because any one powerful
group has a vested interest in this, nor because all groups have

an interest in it, but because different sectional interests are opposed to one another so as to obstruct any pressure for change, even when some changes are highly desired by all or many social groups. In primitive, segmentary societies any attempt on the part of one segment to dominate others and to establish a centralized authority will meet with resistance and alliances to prevent this. In modern industrial societies conflicts of interest often help to preserve a status quo, and nowhere is this more obvious than in the attempts to promote economic growth and to control incomes in modern Britain.

All social and cultural systems have, by definition, a *tendency* to persist. The question is: how and why do some systems or system parts endure longer than others? To answer this type of question, and to explore the nature of social change involves seeing all societies as a field of tension in which a number of opposing and different kinds of force are at work.

Antinomies and Oppositions

The purpose of this chapter has been, so far, to survey certain problems concerning the nature of social systems. It might be argued, at this point, that to pose the questions in these particular ways is to commit the theoretical and ideological error of emphasizing one side of social life at the expense of the other. But this criticism is misdirected. The intention of this chapter has been to analyse the broad question—'What makes society work?'—into a number of component questions. Having done this one can now show the relevance of this analysis for further problems. But this analysis is at no point influenced by the assumptions that societies are inherently harmonious, consensual, efficiently working, or, indeed, so satisfactory that they tend to persist rather than to change. The questions are posed in this way for the obvious reason that it is impossible to conceive of society without some of those fundamental characteristics which have been discussed here. The point of the discussion is to show that these characteristics have been confused with one another and that some are far more necessary to social life than others.

But at no point is it implied that these characteristics are more significant than their opposites.

The first question dealt with is: 'Why do men continue to participate in social systems?' Clearly the implication of posing a question in this way is obvious: men *can* opt out of social systems, and if they do not, this may be because they have little or no choice in the matter. Yet, for all this, they do not, on the whole, opt out of certain areas of social life or shift from one society to another except under very rare circumstances, though there is always the *possibility* of their doing this.

The second aspect of social systems which has been analysed here is that of cohesion. Cohesion is a defining quality of social life. But some social groups or 'total societies' are far more cohesive than others. Furthermore, the forms and conditions of social cohesion vary. To say that a society or collectivity is cohesive is to say only that its component units do not separate from one another. But there are many possible positions which lie between the extreme state of fragmentation, on the one hand, and a high degree of cohesiveness on the other. Segments or units of a society may strain towards some degree of autonomy which is the price they demand for continued participation in a larger unit. But every form of cohesion is under strain. Sometimes, as in the case of certain segmentary societies, the only true source of cohesion of a large collectivity is the existence of intersecting ties; this may mean that the system is also one of *opposed forms* of conflict. In such cases conflict may be the very stuff of cohesion. But in all cases, cohesion is strained by division or the attractions of secession. This, as Simmel might have said, is as true of joint families as it is of federal states.

The third aspect of social systems is that of solidarity. The question that is posed is this: 'Why do social groups or collectivities continue to recognize themselves as such and to differentiate themselves from others like them?' In discussing this, three points have been emphasized. First, that there may be relatively little solidarity in large-scale societies—yet these societies may continue to exist. Second, the most effectively powerful forms of solidarity may often be the most 'fissionable'. Third, all forms of solidarity are strained by hostility or undermined by apathy; it is all a matter of degree.

The fourth aspect is that of commitment and conformity.

The points to be emphasized here are: first, that social life involves some degree of conformity to norms; second, that in the absence of moral commitment, normative conformity may be created or maintained by inducement or coercion; third, that neither inducement nor coercion are as effective, in the long-run, as moral commitment. Nowhere in this discussion is it denied that men conform in varying degrees to different norms and that the degree of commitment may be minimal in some cases and even non-existent in others. Various forms of so-called deviant conduct are, for certain groups, the norm. And when the norms are largely maintained by inducement or coercion they will readily be threatened or rejected if inducement or coercion fail.

The fifth aspect is that of consensus. In this discussion it is recognized that while there is no social life without some degree of consensus on a variety of social and other cultured norms, such as those of language, this does not mean that societies normally possess a broad and deep consensus on goals and the means to their attainment which serve to limit or prevent conflict. On the contrary, it is assumed that this condition is rarely found; however, some forms of conflict would not occur unless the members of society pursued the same goals, while the pursuit of different but compatible goals on the part of different social sectors might reduce the likelihood of conflict. Differences of interest are dominant characteristics of all societies but the structuring of interests between different groups signifies the existence of some convergence of interests as well. However, even in highly complex societies the expression of conflict may be kept within certain limits set by some degree of moral consensus.

The sixth aspect of social systems is that of reciprocity, of which one form is cooperation. The reciprocation of conduct is a defining quality of social systems, and it may be governed by a specific interest—including the interest of minimizing the coercive force of others—or by moral commitment, or by a mixture of these ingredients. But to analyse the reciprocative aspects of conduct is to abstract a system of roles from the broader reality of action and interaction. Within that broader reality much occurs which involves interaction without reciprocation: when armies face one another, when industrialists negotiate with workers, when pupils and teachers attempt to avoid or impose discipline in the classroom, when members of families quarrel, there is always a strain against the norms of conduct, against conformity to expectation. Sometimes this strain results in a total or partial disregard of these norms in the attempts to defeat or outwit an opponent, humiliate a rival, gain an advantage over a competitor, and so on. Often enough men can reciprocate the conduct of some only by not reciprocating the conduct of others; and frequently the reciprocation of conduct according to norms is, in any case, against the interests of some of the parties. When the 'terms' of interaction change—when those who have enjoyed power to influence the 'terms' in their own favour are no longer able to do this—there is commonly a disregard for the norms which have prescribed reciprocal conduct.

Under some circumstances—when the threat to security is great, when the expected returns are high, or when the dedication to certain values is powerful—men renounce the right to alter the terms of their reciprocity in response to shifts in their fortunes or in the balance of power between them; in these cases they are said to cooperate. Some degree of cooperation is to be found at least in some sectors of all societies. But the amount of cooperation that exists varies greatly from one society to another or from one sector to another. Even where there is a high degree of cooperation—for example, in certain types of rural community, in which the rules of cooperation may be highly institutionalized—this does not rule out the existence of conflict, hostility or indifference, which may all be contained within the very same interpersonal relations in which cooperation exists. In fact, where cooperation is bureaucratized and no longer depends largely on the social controls and goodwill which inhere in interpersonal relations, it permits a high degree of conflict, hostility, interpersonal tension, factional alignment, and so on. But there is a limit to the extent to which this can be tolerated: for even bureaucratized cooperative organization requires from the participants some degree of commitment to the norms of the system. The reason for this is that many cooperative organizations cannot permit formal punitive sanctions or civil suits. Insofar as cooperation excludes conflict it does so only, by definition, in certain areas of moral obligation.

Perhaps one of the most difficult aspects of social systems to discuss in these terms, is that of functional interdependence or system integration. The difficulty lies in the highly abstract nature of the concept. To discuss the integration of a cultural and social system is to single out those features of it which display some type of interconnection between parts. But to describe something as a part of a social or cultural system is itself a rather arbitrary affair. It is true that no social system is a 'seamless web' of institutions, beliefs, etc.; there are always areas of discontinuity between different, institutional sectors; and different 'parts' may be 'whole' sub-systems.* But the decision to label something 'a part' is already influenced by some conception of discontinuity. To talk about the power structure of a society is to make certain assumptions that one set of norms, interests or activities can be conceptually distinguished from others. If this can be done easily, then it means that a certain set of activities is carried on with a great degree of independence of many others, though it is not independent of them in all respects. Scientific activity in certain respects is one of the most autonomous sectors of modern industrial societies: the canons of scientific inquiry are not strongly influenced by extra-scientific norms and beliefs. But this does not preclude the possibility that scientific ideas are influenced by modes of thought which are not themselves considered to be part of science; and the choice of scientific problems, and the manner in which scientific activity is organized, are very strongly influenced by other social factors. Of course the results of science, as translated into technology, clearly affect the social conditions which are themselves necessary for scientific progress. In short, a definable part of the social system can have a high degree of autonomy with respect to others, but at the same time influence and be influenced by them.

There are two slightly different senses in which the parts of a social system may be said to be relatively autonomous with respect to other parts. In the first sense an institution or social sector is autonomous if it is *protected* from potential influences which would otherwise affect its operations. It is in this sense that one may refer to the autonomy of judicial, academic and artistic activities. In the second sense, a system part is autonomous insofar as it operates without much influence from other parts and needs no protection against such influence. All social institutions, organizations, systems of beliefs, etc., are, in this second sense,

* See D. G. MacRae.[20]

to some extent, and in some respects, independent of many others. For example, the internal organization of industrial firms in Britain may, to a considerable extent reflect the state of British technology, British class structure, and British attitudes to work; on the other hand, such organizations will also have characteristics which they share in common with similar organizations in other societies—and these will derive largely from the goals and functions of the organization and from the internal and external exigencies which arise in the pursuit of such goals. Similarly, the feudal institutions of different European societies and of Japan will all reflect the influence of other institutions and aspects of social structure and of ecology which are part of the local context in which feudal institutions function; but, at the same time, each society will have a core of such institutions which are common to them all and have a degree of autonomy of other items of social structure and culture.

Functional independence is one possible antinomy of functional integration or interdependence. But another possibility is functional malintegration or what Merton calls 'dysfunction'.[21] Here the parts are not independent of one another but, instead of supporting, they actually obstruct one another. To assert this is to assume one of three things: that the members of society have some ideal notion of how institutions should work and that, in terms of these, certain items are experienced as obstructive; or that an institution has been working in a certain way and ceases to do so because of the effects of some other social item; or, it can mean that the effect of some social process is to reduce the general level of predictability within a particular sector. If the term 'dysfunctional' is used in any other sense, then it clearly carries highly evaluative overtones. For example, to say that caste is dysfunctional for Indian industrialization is to imply that Indians want industrialization. For if they do not want it, and have it foisted upon them by their leaders, then caste is *functional* in preserving India from rapid industrialization. Putting it another way, one might say that the sluggish pace of industrialization in India is compatible with the preservation of some features of the caste system. This example demonstrates only too well what Merton emphasized long ago: that it is always possible to abstract some features of social and cultural life and to demonstrate that they are functionally integrated, while simultaneously showing that some or all of these same features are not functionally integrated with others. And it is as well to remember that two or more institutions or beliefs or other parts of social systems can be in some respects integrated and in other respects malintegrated; *for functional integration is an aspect of abstracted social processes, not of institutions, systems of ideas, or institutional sectors treated as real entities.*

As I showed in an earlier part of this chapter, the degree of integration varies from one type of system to another and from one part of a system to another. On the whole, simple societies are more integrated than complex ones: and if simple societies do change less rapidly than complex ones there is less chance of the emergence of characteristics which are incompatible with one another; for while incompatibility may be a cause of change it may also be a consequence of continous but uneven change.

This brings us to the final pair of opposites, persistence and change. It has already been shown that there is nothing para-doxical in asserting that social systems simultaneously persist and change. For the study of social change is concerned with changes in the structure of societies; and structure implies endurance.

The Two Models of Society: A Critique

One of the principal substantive issues in the recent literature of social theory has been the debate concerning the compatibility of two models of society: the first is called the 'consensus' or 'integration' model, while the second is called the 'coercion' or 'conflict' model. It is clear from the two alternative sets of names that the proponents of the first model are alleged to emphasize the importance of both consensus and integration in society, while the proponents of the second claim to emphasize the significance of both coercion and conflict; the assumption is that consensus and integration are either the same thing or that they are empirically correlated, and that coercion and conflict are similarly connected.

One might characterize the controversy, such as it is alleged to be, by saying that one model attributes to social systems the characteristics of commitment, cohesion, solidarity, consensus, reciprocity, cooperation, integration, stability and persistence, while the other attributes to it the characteristics of coercion, division, hostility, dissensus, conflict, malintegration and change. One could also say that the first model emphasizes the significance of norms and legitimacy, while the second emphasises those of interests and power. These two opposed models can now be set out as below.*

Model 'A'		Model 'B'	
(i)	Norms and values are the basic elements of social life.	(i)	Interests are the basic elements of social life.
(ii)	Social life involves commitments	(ii)	Social life involves inducement and coercion.
(iii)	Societies are necessarily cohesive.	(iii)	Social life is necessarily divisive.
(iv)	Social life depends on solidarity.	(iv)	Social life generates opposition, exclusion and hostility.
(v)	Social life is based on reciprocity and cooperation.	(v)	Social life generates structured conflict.
(vi)	Social systems rest on consensus.	(vi)	Social life generates sectional interests.
(vii)	Society recognizes legitimate authority.	(vii)	Social differentiation involves power.
(viii)	Social systems are integrated.	(viii)	Social systems are malintegrated and beset by 'contradictions'.
(ix)	Social systems tend to persist.	(ix)	Social systems tend to change.

* Cf. the models proposed by Dahrendorf.[22]

Reasoned arguments underlie the defence of either or both of these two models. The theoretical defence of Model A is as follows. If social life is not possible without the existence of norms, then there must be commitment to these norms and, therefore, consensus on the values which underpin them. All divisions are countered by a fundamental unity, cohesion and solidarity. All social roles, including those which involve the exercise of power must, in the long run, be governed by norms mutually acceptable to all parties; thus all power ultimately becomes legitimate authority, and it is exercised in the pursuit of those goals which are defined in terms of the fundamental values of society. The exercise of power within a legitimate system is both a reward for special qualities as well as a facility for the achievement of social goals. The underlying system of values influences the particular sets of norms which operate in any institutional sphere; therefore, all institutions tend to be integrated through their conformity to basic value orientations.

Given all these conditions, it follows that there is a widespread interest in the status quo and a relative harmony between the different parts of the social system. The social system tends, therefore, to be in a state of equilibrium: any tendencies to deviant conduct are controlled within certain limits or call forth responses which restore support for the institutional structure: the social system tends to persist. Insofar as social change occurs it is largely an adaptive process, though some forms of change can occur largely as a result of the failures of socialization to ensure adequate commitment to values.

The argument underlying Model B is very different, but succeeds equally in linking the various assumptions. Society exists because it serves men's interests. Interests are never identical for all individuals and groups and the division of society into different statuses and classes with differential access to a variety of privileges, itself generates conflicts of interest. Insofar as there is consensus, it is the gradually formed consensus of those who share certain life-chances and whose interests are structured by these. Insofar as there are believed to be common values in society this belief is part of the ideology of the powerful; the so-called basic values of society are only the values of the ruling class. Privilege in one sphere creates favourable conditions for the acquisition of privilege in other spheres; power tends to become generalized. The maintenance of power and privilege requires inducement and coercion; coercion breeds conflict, which in turn leads to further coercion. The stability of society is constantly threatened by the fundamental conflicts of interest and by opposition to coercive power. Thus the social mechanisms which are employed to inhibit change must always provoke pressure for change. There may be some degree of institutional integration which results from the pressures of the ruling class—for example, the various forms of power are brought into close relation with one another—but this can not endure; the various conflicting interests ensure that different institutional sectors will strive for autonomy and this, ultimately produces 'contradictions' between them. Societies, except, perhaps for the most primitive, are unstable systems; normally they tend to change.

Some commentators on this matter would agree that the theory behind each model is, more or less, acceptable, even if one model is preferable to the other. Dahrendorf, who has himself constructed models similar to this, recognizes that an 'integration' or 'consensus' model, is applicable to some cases, but not, on the whole to those in which he is interested.[23] Rex gives little support to model A, except to acknowledge that consensus and solidarity may be characteristic of relationships within conflicting groups or parties.[24] But neither Dahrendorf nor Rex seems to question the theory underlying each model: *in short they assume that, on the whole, if one item in a model is accepted then acceptance of all other items follows.* This view is not quite accepted by Parsons who argues that conflict, tension and normative strain are inherent in all systems, but that they must be kept within certain limits if the system is to operate as a 'going concern'.[25] Coser[26] and Gluckman,[27] following Simmel, have shown that they do not accept the theories underlying the two models: they both agree that conflict, for example, does not necessarily lead to change, and they even go so far as to recognize that it may even strengthen a system; and Gluckman argues that even conflicts of principle—normative or value inconsistency—may be contained within a system.[28]

Gouldner has also questioned the theories behind these two models. In discussing the preoccupation of Comte, Marx and

Durkheim with the problems of consensus and conflict, he recognizes that these characteristics are not mutually exclusive, but may coexist, possibly in tension, within the same system.[29]

Lockwood distinguishes two separate aspects of social systems: 'social integration' and 'system integration'.[30] The first term refers either to consensus, solidarity or cohesion; Lockwood is not quite clear on this. The second term refers to functional interdependence. Lockwood's argument is both important and correct: the existence of integration in one sense does not imply its existence in another. He argues that the 'integration model' may well be applicable to societies with structured conflict insofar as it emphasizes the functional interrelation between the material base and the different parts of the institutional structure; a system may be integrated in this sense without displaying social solidarity, consensus, etc. This view is in line with Lockwood's neo-Marxism; for Marx strongly emphasized the close connection between the infra-structure and the various levels and parts of the superstructure of the social system. Lockwood applies these ideas to the analysis of several cases of social change, showing how they result as much from the interaction between incompatible system parts as they do from social conflict. But even Lockwood seems to despair of ridding social theory of the two opposed models. He finds it comforting, but not convincing to be told that some reconciliation is possible.[31]

On all this, two points need to be made. The first is that the two models do not really need to be reconciled, for the propositions of A and B are not mutually exclusive. The two models are not genuine alternatives: to say that a room is half-full is not to deny that it is half-empty. The second point is more complicated. Assume that it is recognized that the two sets of propositions are not mutually exclusive. It may still be claimed that they argue for a difference of *emphasis*, and that it is possible to establish two models of society in which two lists of interrelated predominant characteristics are opposed to one another. The gist of the second point is that this is to assume that the existence of one *predominant* characteristic implies the existence of another. The argument against this is that it is perfectly possible to conceive of models which would contain some of the predominant characteristics of model A and some of those of model B. In short, it may be possible, and desirable, to construct several models of social systems, rather than only two; this is certainly discomforting to those who think in binary terms.

The first point—that the two sets of statements are not mutually exclusive—has really been made earlier in this chapter. But it is worth repeating for emphasis. It may be that the possession of a particular characteristic in the most extreme form would exclude the possession of its opposite. But no one could surely suggest that societies usually have only the characteristics listed under A or those listed under B. They usually possess each characteristic and its opposite in tension with one another. The difference, of course, is in the degree to which they are characterized by the emphases listed under A or those listed under B. But some of the opposed items are not even mutually exclusive when both assume an extreme form. For example, the use of coercive power may co-exist with legitimate authority; though clearly the more coercive the power becomes the less it rests on legitimacy.

The second point is not difficult to establish. Consensus does not necessarily mean persistence as opposed to change: there may be consensus on the direction and forms of change; while a lack of consensus, or a marked expression of sectional interests may produce an impasse which inhibits planned change. Similarly, a recognition of legitimate authority does not necessarily suggest a lack of change; while the use of coercive power may inhibit or slow down the process of change. Conflict may be compatible with functional integration; and solidarity may be compatible with malintegration, which may cause role conflict for the individual.

In some cases several of the predominant characteristics of model A are found together. In some simple societies there is a close connection between the high degree of integration, cohesion and solidarity and the tendency of the social system to persist. But it is doubtful whether this simple, binary conception of system models is applicable to all types of society.

The assumption that an emphasis on change is necessarily linked with the other characteristics of model B, while an emphasis on stability is necessarily linked with the other characteristics of model A, probably owes much to ideology, whether conservative or radical. This is not, in itself, a bad thing; unless wishful thinking displaces evidence. It is, of course, true that much nine-teenth century sociology did emphasize the role of conflict in explaining social change and that much recent sociology has neglected both conflict and change. But while this may signify the influence of values, it does not establish a necessary logical or empirical connection between these two things.

NOTES

1. David Lockwood, 'Social Integration and System Integration' in George K. Zollschan and Walter Hirsh (eds) *Explorations in Social Change*, Routledge, 1964, pp. 244–56.
2. See for example, Lucy Mair, *Primitive Government*, Penguin, 1962, p. 115.
3. See for example, M. Gluckman, 'Anthropological Problems Arising From the African Industrial Revolution' in Aidan Southall (ed), *Social Change in Modern Africa*, Oxford University Press, 1961, pp. 77–9.
   and also, W. Watson, *Tribal Cohesion in a Money Economy*, Manchester University Press, 1958.
4. See for example, Bryan R. Wilson, 'An Analysis of Sect Development', *American Sociological Review*, Vol. 24, February 1959, pp. 3–15.
5. See Max Gluckman (ed), *Essays on the Ritual of Social Relations*, Manchester, 1962.
6. George Simmel, *Conflict*, trans. Kurt H. Wolff, The Free Press, 1955.
7. Lewis A. Coser, *The Functions of Social Conflict*, Routledge, 1956.
8. Max Gluckman, *Custom and Conflict in Africa*, Oxford, 1959.
9. Sigmund Freud, *Group Psychology and the Analysis of the Ego* (trans. James Strachey), London, Hogarth Press, 1948.
10. Max Weber, *The Theory of Social and Economic Organization* (trans. A. R. Henderson and Talcott Parsons), William Hodge, 1947, pp. 329–34.
11. A. Etzioni, *A Comparative Analysis of Complex Organisations*, The Free Press, 1961, Intro. and Part 1.
12. Gerhart Piers and Milton B. Singer, *Shame and Guilt*, Charles C. Thomas, Illinois, 1953.
13. E. Durkheim, *The Division of Labour in Society*, pp. 200–29.
14. Claude Levi-Strauss, 'The Future of Kinship Studies', *Proceedings of the Royal Anthropological Institute of Great Britain and Northern Ireland for 1965*, p. 15.
15. S. N. Eisenstadt, 'Anthropological Studies of Complex Societies', *Current Anthropology*, June 1961.

16. Max Gluckman, *The Judicial Process Among the Barotse of Northern Rhodesia*, Manchester University Press, pp. 19–20.
17. S. J. Nadel, *The Theory of Social Structure*, London, 1957.
18. See for example, C. W. M. Hart and Arnold R. Pilling, *The Tiwi of North Australia*, New York, 1960, esp. pp. 75–6.
19. A. W. Gouldner, 'Reciprocity and Autonomy in Functional Theory' (see Chap. III, reference 31).
20. Donald G. MacRae, 'The Crisis of Sociology' (see Chap. III, reference 3).
21. R. K. Merton, 'Manifest and Latent Functions' (see Chap. III, reference 22).
22. R. Dahrendorf, *Class and Class Conflict in Industrial Society*, pp. 160–5.
23. R. Dahrendorf, loc. cit.
24. J. Rex, *Key Problems of Sociological Theory*, esp. pp. 110–14.
25. Talcott Parsons, *The Social System*, esp. pp. 490–6.
26. Lewis A. Coser, *The Functions of Social Conflict*, Routledge, 1958.
27. Max Gluckman, *Custom and Conflict in Africa*.
28. Max Gluckman, ibid.
29. Alvin W. Gouldner, 'Introduction' to Emile Durkheim, *Socialism*, Collier, New York, 1962, pp. 7–31.
30. David Lockwood, op. cit.
31. David Lockwood, op. cit.

7.

Explaining Social Change

Introduction

SOCIOLOGISTS commonly complain of a lack of a theory of social change. What they explicitly mean is that while they do have a theory of social action and of social systems, they have no corresponding theory of change. One implication is that a theory of change would somehow look rather different from a theory of systems. Another, related view, is that contemporary sociology is wedded to functional analysis which is satisfactory for the study of social phenomena within a given structural context, but does not explain change. A third version of this complaint is as follows: the study of social persistence is a special case of sociological theory; therefore, what sociology needs is a single theory which also incorporates a theory of persistence and of change. There is a fourth complaint made against sociological theory which is rather different: it is that only social change is real while social persistence is a mere illusion, largely the product of conservative thought or mistaken epistemology. On this last view what is needed then, is a return to the tradition of some of our forebears who saw the aim of sociology as the construction of a theoretical history.

The first view is partly right and partly wrong. It may be true that sociology lacks *a* theory of change. But it is doubtful whether it has *a* theory of social persistence. If it did have a *single* theory of social persistence, then it would also have *a* theory of social change. For if a theory of persistence explains why societies do not, under the stated conditions, change, then a theory of change has only to state the absence of these conditions.

The second complaint is no more reasonable than the first. If Marxism, or some other theory, can really explain social change then it should be able to explain the lack of it. In fact Marx *was* partly concerned to explain social persistence, which he did in terms of economic and ideological coercion.

The view which informs the third complaint is perfectly acceptable. The study of persistence *is* a special case of the study of change; but, equally, the study of change is a special case of the study of persistence. This point has been made in the last chapter.

The fourth complaint is rather different from the others. What it often amounts to is a rejection of anything but an historical sociology. Some powerful arguments can be brought against it, but it always remains intact: for it constitutes a decision to study society in one way only.

The Nature of Social Change: What is to be Explained

Sociologists often distinguish between changes which are a necessary part of a persisting social system and those which are genuine changes of the system itself. For obvious biological reasons every system must provide for changes in its personnel. But there are many other changes which occur which are not of this kind, but which can be treated as persistent features of social systems: for example, price fluctuations and changes in party-political support. But much depends on how the system is defined. Then again, a change which is part of an ongoing system might lead to a change *of* that system. For example, if a political system normally allows for a replacement of one party by another, then the failure of such replacement over time might be said to constitute a change of that system.

Some sociologists also try to distinguish between partial and total changes in social system. Thus social reform and the extension, or even creation, of social services might be called partial changes in a system which is based on inequality and private ownership of property. Even some degree of nationalization of key industries might be considered a partial change in the social system, because this coexists with private property ownership in other spheres, and with inequality which affects the selection of personnel to positions of power in nationalized industries. On the other hand, a change to workers' control of industry might be considered a change in the system as such.

The difficulty is to recognize a change in the 'whole' of a social system. If literally everything in a social system changes then there is no way of identifying it as the same social system; in which case, to say that it has changed is logically impossible. If we say that there is a total change in the social system of an industrial firm, we must have some means of identifying it as the same firm; clearly *something* has not changed. Similarly, if one refers to a total change in British social structure one must have some means of identifying the structure as British. In fact one does not need to go to these absurd extremes. No social system ever changes *in toto*. Even the most radical changes—revolutions —are never changes in all features of a social structure. Change is *always* uneven and partial. The notion of total change is more akin to a myth than to a scientific social theory. Men dream of total changes; they almost never experience them.

There is a reasonable and realistic sense in which one might distinguish *minor* changes from *fundamental* changes in a social system. One might do this by isolating a number of *core* or *strategic* features of a system and then defining a major change as one in which such features themselves change. But even this solution raises difficulties. First, how is one to identify these core features? Second, how is one to distinguish between a fundamental change and a superficial change in these core features? This second difficulty is, I think, simply an aspect of the first.

What is meant by the term 'the core features' or 'strategic features' of a social system? Let us say that we isolate features A, B, C, D and E of a social system: then, if we assume or know that a change in A will have a radical effect on B, C, D and E, and if we also assume or know that an initial change in any one of the items, B, C, D or E would not have the same sort of effect on the others, including A, then we can call A a core feature of the social system.

If one is observing an ongoing social system it is sometimes very difficult to isolate the core features in this manner. There *are* cases where it appears very simple: for example, it is obvious that the working of the economic and political institutions of a society have a great effect on the success or failure of writers and other artists, but that artistic success has very little effect on the working of the economic and political institutions. However, there are some cases where a synchronic study would fail to reveal which factor was a 'core' or 'strategic' one in the system. For example, is the British constitution a core feature of the political system or is the structure of party allegiances the core feature? By observing the British polity as an ongoing system it is clear that each factor constrains the operations of the other; but it is not clear which is the core factor. Of course, it might be argued that neither is a core factor in relation to the structure of property ownership which is the *real* core factor. But the truth of this is not obvious to anyone but a confirmed Marxist. The matter can only be settled by a study of social change. If changes in factors A, B or C can not occur without producing changes in E, F or G, while changes in E, F or G can occur without producing changes in A, B or C, then clearly A, B and C have the greater claim to be called the 'core' features of the social system. If election results do not change the electoral system, but changes in an electoral system have an effect on election results, then it could be said that the electoral system is a core feature of the political system.

Even if there were no problems of *identifying* core elements of a system, there would still be a problem of distinguishing basic from superficial changes. This is important for the following reason: even if one identifies factor A as strategic in relation to B, C, D and E, this does not mean that these other, non-core, features do not change at all without an initial change in A, nor does it mean that changes in them have no effects at all on changes in A. It is almost impossible for one feature of a social system to change without in *some* ways affecting the others. The crucial question is: do changes in A produce *radical* changes in B, C, D or E, while changes in B, C, D and E produce only superficial changes in A? And if the answer to this question is affirmative, does one have some measure for distinguishing radical changes from superficial ones? And, if one does have such a measure, when does one apply it? For the short-run effect of B on A might be superficial, while the long-run effect might be radical!

The gist of all this discussion is that one can only know *ex post facto* whether a particular change was or was not a change in a 'core' feature of the social structure. This does not prevent one from having theories which state that certain factors are core features and are likely to produce great changes as a result of changes in themselves. But this means that the identification of core features is part of the theory of social change, and not a preliminary step in the distinction between partial and total changes.

All social changes are important: but a small number of changes in certain sectors of the social system may have greater consequences than a great many changes in other sectors. Furthermore, all changes are partial; only some are more so than others.

Problem Areas in the Study of Social Change

There are two broad problem areas in the theoretical study of social change. The first is concerned with the factors or mechanisims which produce change. The second is concerned with general characteristics of the course of social change. The rest of this chapter is concerned with mechanisms of changes and the following chapter with the course of change.

Since the eighteenth century, social theorists who have sought the mechanisms of social change, have tried on the whole to explain all or most forms of change in terms of a single factor. Their theories can be divided into two groups: those explaining change in terms of endogenous factors or processes, and those emphasizing exogenous factors. The former have dominated most sociological thinking.

The best-known explanations of social change in terms of a single or dominant factor are the technological theory, the economic theory, the conflict theory, the malintegration theory, the adaptation theory, the ideational theory and, finally, the cultural interaction theory. I shall review all of these before returning to the question: can there be a single theory of social change?

The Technological Theory

This theory, which is sometimes mistakenly associated with Marxism, has had something of a vogue recently. In one context it is used to explain the growing similarity between socialist and non-socialist industrial societies. In another context it is used to analyse and predict the process of social change in so-called developing societies. The theory can be considered in two forms: as stating the sufficient conditions, or as stating the necessary conditions of social change.

In the first form the theory is obviously true in one respect and false in others. Any technological change *which is great enough* will produce some other social change as a consequence. For example, new techniques of manufacture are bound to affect social relations in the relevant industry; new techniques of warfare are bound to affect some aspects of military organization. It would be hard to find a technological change of any significance which did not produce *some* social change. This, however, does not mean that technological change alone can produce social changes of all types.

In fact, a widely accepted idea in sociology has been the 'culture-lag' hypothesis, which tries to explain many features of modern industrial societies—its tensions, conflicts, forms of mental illness, and what you will—in terms of the failure of social organization to keep pace with technological change. There is a good deal wrong with this hypothesis. It assumes that one knows that sort of social relations would be best suited to a particular level of technology; and it probably seeks to explain far too much. But its fundamental germ of truth can scarcely be disputed: very rapid technological changes can occur without a similar degree of change in social structure and other features of culture.

Nor is technological change always a necessary condition for other social changes. It may be that certain technological conditions are necessary before other factors can produce certain changes, but these need not precipitate social change. It would require no change in technology to bring about a totalitarian regime in Britain. This is not to deny that technological change is sometimes responsible for widespread and fundamental changes in social structure. But the nagging question that remains is: why does technological change itself occur? It cannot simply be the consequence of its own momentum; for this could not explain why it is so rare in certain societies and in certain periods of history.

The Economic Theory of Change

Owing largely to the influence of Marx and Marxism, the economic theory of change occupies a major place in the discussion of social scientists and historians. This is not because the theory, at least in its Marxian version, is so widely accepted, but rather because it invites an endless series of refutations and defences. No doubt this is due in part to the enormous significance of Marxism as an ideological weapon in the struggle within and between societies. But it is also due to the attractiveness of the doctrine; for no matter how many criticisms are marshalled against it, it still invites more; and this is because it *is* so plausible, and seems to penetrate to the depths of social reality. Of course, economic interpretations of history or social change need not be Marxist; but none of the other versions of the doctrine are quite as interesting as Marxism.

The Marxist theory rests on the fundamental assumption that changes in the economic 'infra-structure' of society are the prime movers of social change. This 'infra-structure' consists of the 'forces' and 'relations' of production; the 'super-structure' consists of those features of the social system, such as the judicial, political and religious institutions, which serve to maintain the 'infra-structure' and which are moulded by it. Marx does not assert that the 'super-structural' elements are *completely* renewed with changes in the 'infra-structure'; nor does he suggest that all societies at the same stage of economic development possess identical 'super-structural features'. His is *not* a theory of the *complete determination* of all institutions by certain common, general processes of economic change.[1] It simply asserts that economic changes are fundamental and that they bring about other changes which are in accordance with economic interests. Marx's theory is not a form of technological determinism. He himself states that any social system can contain considerable, though not unlimited, developments in the 'forces of production' without breaking down. The limit is only reached when technological developments produce or exacerbate class conflict and other 'contradictions' to such an extent that the system must give way to a new one. By a change in the system Marx means a change in the relations of production, and in those other institutions which correspond to a particular form of these relations. What generates change are the 'contradictions' of the social system which stem from the social relations of production.

Although Marx's theory is considered a general theory of the mechanisms of social change, Marx scarcely applied it in form to any other system but capitalism. I do not propose to review here the many concrete criticisms of the Marxian theory: that capitalism has not been replaced by socialism in advanced capitalist societies; that the classes in capitalist society have not become increasingly polarized; that reforms and growing wealth have made revolution less likely in advanced industrial societies; and so on. All of these criticisms have been made often enough and sometimes accepted by Marxists.

The theory has also been criticised heavily for ignoring or underestimating the causal significance of ideas and political processes as such. These criticisms also are constantly rebutted by Marxists in the following way. First, they argue, Marxism does not deny an interaction between 'infra-structural' and 'super-structural' processes: for example, it does not deny that the oppressed classes may be attracted to religious beliefs which express some protest against the social system, and that these beliefs may later lend themselves to the formation of a political ideology of revolutionary activity; and it does not deny that the oppressed classes may make certain political gains through the democratic process which will, in turn, facilitate a radical transformation of the social system. Secondly, Marxism claims mainly to explain the 'significant' changes from one type of social system to another: from slavery to feudalism, from feudalism to capitalism, and from capitalism to socialism. In doing this it may show that, at any moment in time, there is an interaction between economic and other social factors, just as there is an interaction between technological and economic factors. However, in the final instance, the economic sub-structure must change before there can be a qualitative change in the social system as such.

It is this second argument which makes it difficult to treat Marxism as a testable theory of social change. For, if one adduces evidence to show that political and ideological changes are either necessary to produce certain economic changes, or that many social changes occur which are not preceded by significant economic changes, it can always be argued that this does not refute the Marxian theory, on the grounds that these changes are not 'fundamental' changes in the social structure. For example, if it is shown that political stability and ideological commitment to modernization are necessary preconditions for economic development, it could be argued by Marxists that the 'real' changes in the social structure only occur *after* economic development. If it is argued that political rivalry between nation states is as much a factor in promoting industrialization as economic factors, the reply could be that this is a stage in the liberation movement of the colonial peoples, which is itself a stage in the development and replacement of capitalism. The main trouble with Marxist theory is that it presupposes certain true and objective criteria whereby the qualitative change from one type of social system to another can be assessed. It is always possible to show that a social system is still *fundamentally* unchanged; just as it is always possible to show that it is *fundamentally* changed. The whole debate becomes purely ideological and once Marxian theory concedes some interaction between economic and other factors, it is difficult to sustain the view that economic change is the prime mover of social change. But the main defect of the theory is that it does not really account for many types of change at all. For example, much social change in non-industrial societies is due more to political and military pressures than to economic ones. Naturally, it is important to show that these other processes would not occur in all economic circumstances. But that is hardly the same thing as explaining these changes in terms of the internal processes of the economy itself. One of the interesting things about relatively stagnant economies is that they scarcely develop endogenous processes of change without certain radical changes in the structure of social relations and in those ideas which both permit the use of technological innovations and encourage their invention.

One of the great merits of the Marxian theory of change, as opposed to the technological theory, is that it is truly sociological. It seeks to explain social change in terms of the inner processes of social systems as such. And, moreover, it does not treat these processes as reifications. It attempts to use a series of models of action and interaction at the economic level, to show a continuous logic in the development of capitalism or some other system. But the trouble is that social systems do not operate in such simple ways. Each area of social life develops some *degree* of autonomy even in the simplest societies, so that each can constitute a possible source of change. Furthermore, human creativity is such that its inventions and innovations do not simply occur in response to economic demands. They too have some autonomy of their own; though, it is true, as Marx has pointed out—and for this alone modern social theory is greatly in his debt—that inventions require a favourable social environment, and a stimulus, which may well come from the economy. And when they occur, they may have consequences which are quite unintended by their inventors or by those who apply them.

It is interesting that Marx did avoid a technological determinism; for such a theory might have seemed in keeping with a materialist philosophy of history. But his avoidance was perhaps necessary. For technological changes begin not as material substance but as *ideas in the minds of men.*

The Conflict Theory of Change

In Marx's theory, economic change only occurs and produces other change through the mechanism of intensified conflict between social groups and between different parts of the social system. Recently social theorists have suggested that conflict, in its *broadest* sense, must be the cause of social change. The reasoning behind this is that if there is consensus in society, and if the various sectors are integrated, there is little pressure for change; therefore, change must be due to conflict between groups and/or between different parts of the social and cultural system.

This theory is very plausible, but it is not necessarily true. The contention that group conflict is a sufficient condition for social change is obviously false. Of course a theory of this type refers not to the sporadic formation of groups which happen to be in conflict with one another, but to the existence of *structured* conflict between groups or social sectors which are likely to have enduring interests which are opposed to one another. But it is quite common for such interests to express themselves in particular issues which are resolved by compromise: the obvious example of this is the settlement of industrial disputes by bargaining or arbitration.

It is arguable that structured conflict, when it involves a fairly equal balance of forces, actually *obstructs* change which might otherwise occur. For example, in societies where there are deep divisions between regional, ethnic or racial groups, there may be little possibility of promoting economic development or welfare policies: such 'ameliorative' changes require some degree of concensus, or at least the emergence of divisions which cut across those which segment the society into hostile units. *The simple point is that conflict may lead to impasse not to change!*

If conflict is not sufficient is it not necessary for change? Clearly the assertion that conflict is a necessary condition for change can scarcely be refuted. There is no society, changing or unchanging, which does not have conflict of some kind or another; so obviously there is no case of social change which is not associated with conflict in some way or another. The theory should state that an *intensification* of conflict is necessary to produce social change. It seems unlikely, for example, that negroes in the United States would have secured changes in their status had there not been an intensification of conflict between negroes and whites. This example sounds superficially convincing but there are a number of flaws in the argument. To clarify it one must make a distinction between the terms 'conflict' and 'struggle'.*
Social conflict exists where the goals of one group are pursued in such a way as to ensure that the goals of another group cannot

* See Weber.[2]

be realized. Struggle occurs when action is taken to remove the source of conflict by reducing the power of another party, or by eliminating another party from the conflict situation.

The intensification of struggle between negroes and whites in the United States is due largely to the increased perception of or experience of inequality on the part of negroes, and from the increased fear of greater equality on the part of whites, which results from many changes in the situation of negroes. The conflict is translated into struggle by the negroes' perception and experience of inequality, not necessarily by a real increase in inequality, and by the whites' perception of a slow, but real increase in equality.

But even when conflict becomes translated into struggle— and even collective bargaining is an institutionalized form of struggle of a rather mild nature—it does not necessarily lead to change, nor is it the necessary condition for change. The intensification of racial conflict, as with any other form of conflict, can lead to the use of oppression to prevent change. There is no doubting that the intensification of struggle *may* contribute significantly to the nature and pace of change. But it should not be overlooked that the intensification of conflict may itself be the product of other factors which are not themselves directly connected with conflict. The intensification of negro-white hostility and struggle in the United States is itself the result of increased industrialization, the growing structural unemployment resulting from inadequate educational facilities for negroes, increased urbanization and, by no means least important, an expectation of greater equality. Just as it is naïve to expect these changes to proceed without conflict and intensified struggle, so it may be naïve to expect that the 'dialectical' process of racial struggle will create racial equality.

Conflict may not be sufficient to bring about change in many circumstances; it may not be necessary in some, though it clearly is necessary in a great many. But intensified conflict is itself one of the *products* of many types of social change. It is the empirical association of conflict with change that often persuades sociologists that conflict is the major cause of change. In a society which has set its sights on planned industrialization, conflict may well contribute to the process: competition for prestige and power between states and even between segments within a state may well stimulate change; but these same forms of conflict may also inhibit change.

Much of the attraction of the conflict theory of change is the belief (often messianic in the extreme, and as unrealistic as a good many eschatologies) that conflict, par excellence, means revolution—a radical and total change in the social structure. Revolutions actually occur less frequently than they are expected, and they frequently do not result in the changes which would have been predicted in advance by those who either support or fear these revolutions most. Plato said that all revolutions lead to reactions. He was possibly expressing a fervent wish. But there is much truth in this idea. Revolutions provoke repression and counter-revolution. And if these last are overcome, they leave an aftermath of disorder and a reduced sense of legitimacy. Post-revolutionary leaders are faced with three problems: to govern, to create order, and to discourage the enthusiasm for illegitimate opposition and even violence. This does not mean that revolutions produce no changes. They may well produce many. But it is a mistake to confuse the sound and fury of revolutionary action with the slow introduction and implementation of reforms which follow on. The most successful climate for a post-revolutionary society is one in which a strong degree of legitimacy and consensus is developed. It is for this and many other reasons that the conflict theory of change, as present formulated, often leads to muddle and simplification.

The attraction of the conflict theory is partly that it provides a simple answer to the problems of sociology; but it should be emphasized, that social conflict is often as much the product of social change as the cause. And it is commonly a great obstacle to certain types of change.

The Malintegration Theory

Closely allied to the conflict theory is one which explains change in terms of incompatibilities between different parts of social systems.

There are a number of sources of inconsistency or incompatibility within social systems. The most obvious is the possible tension between personality and the demands made upon it by social institutions. If men are perfectly socialized they are constantly motivated to act as required by the social norms. But, for at least two reasons men never are perfectly socialized. First, if socialization is too rigid, it leaves men incapable of dealing with unforseen events; but if it permits some flexibility then it also allows some personal interpretation of social roles. Second, all socialization makes conflicting demands and, therefore, produces some antagonism to socializing agents, thereby creating a possible source of motivation for social deviance.

A second source of incompatibility, closely associated with the first, is inherent in the nature of role expectations. Social roles are prescribed by *general* norms. However, the concrete situations in which these norms are expressed, vary considerably. The very fact that role expectations are general enough to be applied to a variety of situations means that they must allow some room for personal interpretation. It is here that personality and conflicting obligations may have their effect.

Social systems and parts of social systems vary in the degree of flexibility allowed to roles, and they also differ in the degree of variability which occurs in socialization. Insofar as these two factors jointly constitute a source of tension, making for social change, it is likely that the potential for change will itself vary from one system to another. One of the merits of the socialization-role-flexibility theory is that it not only indicates a source of social change but suggests reasons why some societies or social sectors are more likely to produce change than others. The weakness of the theory is that it does not really explain why change does occur, only why it *might* occur. Roles may be so flexible as to allow for a great deal of variation of conduct without leading to changes in the institutional system.

The principal version of the 'malintegration' theory explains change in terms of the conflicting pressures or demands of different sectors of a society or culture. The assumption underlying this is that if actions in one sphere inhibit those in another then, one or other must change.

In some cases the opposition between sectors corresponds to an opposition between social groups or quasi-groups of one kind or another; in other cases the system incompatibilities may cut across group division or simply remain within a particular social group or quasi-group. This second type may take the form of role conflict within the same individuals; or it may take the form of conflict between individuals within the same social group. An example of the first type is the conflict between traditional authority and bureaucracy where bureaucracy represents the urban sector and traditional authority the rural. There may, of course, be some social ties between the two sectors, particularly those of kinship; but these ties may be too few and too weak to minimise the conflict. This is not simply a case of group conflict, for each group or quasi-group represents different institutions. Out of this type of conflict there may emerge a different structure of relations between town and village, or between the centre and periphery of political life. An example at the other extreme, is the conflict between family roles and occupational roles which occur in industrial societies: such conflict may affect everyone, leading not only to change in family structure but also, possibly, to a change in the occupational system.* Intermediate examples would be the conflict between Church and State in mediaeval society, or between traditional Hindu values and those of modern industrial society in present-day India. In these last two cases the conflict may be, for some individuals an internalized one, but for others it will be between individuals who may well be connected by ties of kinship, friendship, class, status, etc.; and in some cases the conflict may be both internalized and interpersonal.

This theory is as plausible as the group conflict theory; and the two together seem to account for a good deal of social change. But there is a possible weakness in it. Let us assume that we are trying to explain change in terms of the incompatibility between two items A and B. Now if A and B were incompatible in the past then they would have brought about some change. Since they did not, they must have been compatible. But in order for them to *become* incompatible they must have changed. This suggests that the changes in A and B, which must have occurred to make them incompatible, were due to something other than their incompatibility. In other words, incompatibility is not a necessary condition for change. Of course, it might well be that

* One example of this is discussed by N. Smelser.[3]

the changes in either A or B, or in both, were due to incompatibilities between them and other items, C and D, and that these changes created further incompatibilities between A and B, which created yet more changes. This way, it could be argued that all change is due to incompatibilities, but that the locus of these incompatibilities itself changes. Alternatively, it could be argued that each item, such as A, B, C or D, is itself composed of parts, A_1, A_2, A_3, B_1, B_2, B_3, etc., whose incompatibilities bring about changes in the wholes, which then become incompatible with one another. This way it could be argued that all social change is an endless series of adjustments between incompatible parts of social systems. But the question still remains: *why should any parts ever become incompatible with one another in the first place?*

Of course the theory need not aspire to answer this last question; for it may merely state that incompatibilities are *sufficient* to bring about change. However, it is doubtful whether the theory is true even in this form. Of course, if two things are *highly* incompatible then they cannot, one presumes, coexist. And if they cannot coexist, then their ceasing to coexist in a particular state, is a change. To say this is to say that the definition of true incompatibility between items is that they must change in orders to coexist. If, however, the theory states that no incompatibilities are tolerated within a social system then it is clearly false: for the truth of the matter is that men will tolerate a good deal of inconvenience from social institutions if it is in their interests to do so, or if they have no alternatives; and they will react to some forms of inconvenience by changing their institutions because it is equally in their interests to do so. Not only can seemingly inimical institutions and values coexist; but their coexistence can also inhibit certain courses of social change. The persistence of internal caste ties and inter-caste exclusiveness in Indian society is, in some spheres, encouraged by some modern developments; but these persistences actually inhibit other modern developments.[4]

An historical instance that is often quoted of institutional conflict producing radical change is that of the Church-State conflict which helped to encourage the growth of Protestantism and of science, both of which are thought to have promoted 'liberal' economic and political developments. But the incompatibility between the Church and the State—if it can be called this—was due to a struggle for power; the Church may not have been separated from the State, as in many modern societies, but it did owe allegiance to a political power of its own. Where religion does not have its own 'political' organization, incompatibilities between religious morality and interests, and those of the state or the economy, are often kept within manageable proportions.

This is not to say that conflicts of principle, conflicts between the demands of different institutions, and conflicts between different sets of norms and values, do not provide one source of social change. But in the final instance the medium of such change is interaction between men performing a complex of social roles, pursuing manifold interests, constrained and guided by a variety of perspectives, norms and values, and enmeshed in a network of social ties based on sentiment, interest and obligation. Where there is a felt or experienced net balance of disadvantages in pursuing a given set of norms, and meeting a given set of expectations, there will be pressure to deviate from these. Such pressure will be greater where different sets of institutions make conflicting demands. Where institutions like the family are concerned, the pressures affect everyone, though not equally; where other institutional spheres are concerned—such as the effect of changing bureaucratic structure on political decision-making—the incompatibilities will be immediately experienced more in some social roles than in others, but may be transmitted further afield by interaction.

It is possible for incompatibilities to be predicted and for action to be taken to modify institutions in advance of some clash of interests. It is also possible for incongruities to be morally or aesthetically 'sensed', as Oakeshott suggests, and for this to influence the pressure for change.[5] But deliberate manipulations of this sort occur more in complex societies with elaborately specialized organizations whose task it is to modify institutions; though it may be the lack of historical evidence which leads one to think that it is not characteristic of the simpler societies. It is probable that the Zulu king Shaka deliberately fostered the development of regimental age-sets and commanded the presence of their members at or near his court, in order to combat the conflict between tribal and national allegiances. The experiment seems to have been successful—at least for a while.[6]

There is a version of this theory which explains social change in terms of the 'need' for compatibility between parts. But this is really a separate theory which attempts a functionalist account of social change. It can be called the 'adaptation' theory.

The Adaptation Theory

It is commonly stated that functionalism does not or cannot explain social change. Yet, as I have argued earlier, functionalism must be a theory of change if it is also a theory of social persistence. One form of the doctrine comes very close to using the biological analogy in explaining functional processes in terms of survival value, and proposes an explicit theory of social change in terms of adaptation. What the theory states, in effect, is that social systems, as wholes, adapt to external environments. Of course, the term 'system' is used here to refer to any interrelated set of social processes in which there is sufficient evidence of 'feedback' (or circular causation) to warrant the assumption of some degree of self-maintenance. In this sense a system could be a family or *the* family, a local community, an organization or type of organization, the economy of the Common Market, the British polity or economy, a tribal society, and so on.

One of the first difficulties to deal with is the meaning of the term 'external environment'. If by this is meant the natural environment then the ambiguities are relatively slight. For, although the natural environment of society is *not* purely natural —it is transformed both destructively and constuctively by human action—it can be treated as external to the social system. In other words, the human collectivity with its institutions, beliefs, interests and values can be treated as one complex and the external environment as another, and the interaction between the two as an 'ecological' system. The fact that part of the external environment is man-made is of little importance; for what one is explaining is a change in a society from a given state, not from its initial state in a *purely* natural environment.

However, this interpretation of the theory has relatively little value. If one is dealing with simple societies, then the assumption that the 'raw' natural environment considerably affects social structure, is to some extent, warranted. This is because the absence of a complex technology to transform the environment makes men highly dependent upon nature; and this sets limits to the variability of social structure. But this still fails to explain why societies with similar physical environments have rather different social structures. The application of this theory to complex societies is even less rewarding. This is not to say that men in complex societies do not interact with their natural environment. But what they do with it is related to the goals which they pursue; and these are more a product of social and cultural environment than of the natural one. On the whole, the study of men in relation to their physical environment probably contributes more to an understanding of why social systems do *not* change than of why they do.

In fact, what some proponents of this theory have in mind is the process of adaptation of social systems to one another. Thus, one can explain changes in the economy as adaptations to other economies or to the polity, or changes in the family structure in terms of adaptation to other institutions, and so on. One of the specific assumptions of this theory is that a particular form of change—namely, differentiation, or increased complexity—can be explained in these terms. The argument, which stems from Spencer, seems to be that differentiated structures are more likely to survive in any given environment than simple ones; therefore, the development of differentiation is due to the process of adaptation to the environment.[7]

Confirming instances immediately spring to mind. For example, one can explain the development of complex organization in industrial firms in the following way: such firms, in order to survive in a competitive world, must become increasingly efficient; and efficiency requires complex organization; hence this development is due to the adaptation of the organization to the external environment of other industrial firms. Another example would be the development of military bureaucracy: armies must be able to defend themselves in combat against other armies; effectiveness in combat is increased by organization; hence, increased military organization is adaptive. Even some instances which seem to refute the theory can be shown to support it. For example, it could be argued that although the family structure of modern industrial society is less internally differentiated than that of non-industrial societies, this is necessary because the functions of the family have become differentiated from other social functions—such as those of economic production and formal education—*thus making the whole system more complex and, therefore, more adapted to the external environment of other systems.*

This last example illustrates, better than anything else, the real weaknesses of this theory; terms like 'system', 'environment', 'differentiation' and 'adaptation' can always be defined in such a way as to demonstrate the truth of the theory. Of course, one can specify certain goals of a social system—provided these goals are recognized or can be recognized by those who participate in these systems—and show that the pursuit of these leads to changes in the system which result from the effects or anticipated effects of other systems upon them. But to do this one does not need a complicated theory of adaptation; and the assumption of differentiation should, in any case, be kept quite separate; for differentiation may, in *some* circumstances, characterize the process of adaptation and in others it may not. It would not be difficult to show that differentiation is sometimes highly maladaptive in relation to particular goals. In war it may be advantageous to integrate a whole range of decision-making processes within a single authority; but in times of peace this may be disadvantageous in terms of the goal of freedom or economic prosperity, or both.

This brings one to the next serious weakness in the theory: it assumes that the goals of a system are clear-cut. But they may not be; and one of the reasons for this may be that a system has a number of competing goals*; one of these goals may be the preservation of the system itself, as far as this is possible. It is much simpler to analyse changes in business organizations, armies and the structure of 'command' economies in terms of adaptation than it is to analyse changes in the structure of families, religious organization and non-command economies; this is because the former examples all exhibit *a relatively simple priority of goals which, on the whole, are specified by those who represent the organization and who have power to ensure that other goals do not assume more than a subsidary importance.* But even in these simpler cases it is not always clear whether changes are adaptive: they may be

---

* To say that a system has goals means only that some participants in a system *impute* certain goals to it.

adaptive in some respects and not in others; they may be adaptive in the short-run and not in the long-run.

A far more satisfactory formulation of the adaptation theory is that of Wilbert Moore, who prefers the term 'tension-management.'[8] Moore suggests that theories of social change should aim to locate the points of greatest tension in social systems and identify them as sites of social change. This view rests on the assumption that one of the necessary processes of social systems is the reduction of tension, and that such processes may occur through change. This tension-management may be called a process of adaptation of one system, or system part, to another; but Moore emphasizes the point that change is as likely to produce tension as to create it. Thus Moore's theory does not require any criteria of success in tension-management to explain change; it requires only the assumption that tension produces some process of management. Presumably, since social systems do not strictly manage anything, Moore must imply that the intended or unintended consequences of tension, as experienced through interaction, can be interpreted as forms of management. One should not assume that all system tension necessarily leads directly to a form of management which constitutes change. Social systems, like individuals, can tolerate a good deal of tension.

The Ideational Theory of Change

The ideational theory of change has periodically suffered considerable unpopularity amongst sociologists. This aversion is largely due to the influence of Marx, and partly to that of Durkheim's interpreters, particularly Radcliffe-Brown.

Marx rejected ideational theories of social change mostly because he rightly recognized that many of these theories simply reflected an ignorance of social processes and, possibly, a tendency for ideologists and theorists to overestimate the importance of their own activities. (This last failing seems to be common amongst some contemporary Marxists who appear to be obsessed with ideology.) Marx's objection was primarily to the kind of theory which explains the existence of sovereignty, democracy or parliamentary institutions as mere embodiments of doctrines, whereas *he* argued that institutions existed as a result of social interactions largely governed by 'real' forces, as opposed to 'ideal' ones.[9]

Durkheim's aims both resembled and differed from those of Marx. He too wished to establish that the only true causes of social phenomena must be social processes, not the processes of individual thought. But he did not really deny that ideas, as social phenomena, could influence the course of social change.

All social phenomena are, in an important sense, ideational. A social relationship does not exist unless men have some expectations concerning the likely conduct of others. These mutual expectations, which are a fundamental element in social relationships, are of course ideas. This does not imply that these ideas can be articulated as consistent systems by those who hold them.

In addition to those ideas which are *inherent* in social relationships, there are, in all types of society, ideas which men have *about* social institutions, structures and systems, as well as about the physical and 'supernatural' world.

These two ideational levels do not necessarily remain separate. On the one hand, ideas which are implicit in social relationships may become explicitly formulated into doctrines, which may then be exported from one society to another; when this happens then may also become causes of social change. On the other hand, explicit doctrines about society may be applied to particular social conditions and, ultimately, become ideas within the social system. In the process whereby ideas within social systems become explicit doctrines, and those about social systems become implicit expectations, considerable transformation usually occurs.

Of course, ideas within and about *society* are not the only ones which are alleged to influence and cause social change; in fact some theories attribute all important processes of social change to technological ideas.

An ideational theory of social change could take one of three forms. First, it could assert that all social change *is* ideational. Second, it could assert that ideational changes are *necessary conditions* for certain types of social change. Third, it could assert that ideational changes are *important contributory factors* to many or most types of change.

The first theory is this: if it is agreed that all social and cultural phenomena are, at least in part, ideational, then all changes in these phenomena must be, at least in part, ideational.

This kind of theory has been attacked as tautological or meaningless by the philosopher, Alisdair MacIntyre, who argues that such ideas can only be said to exist insofar as they are acted upon; the idea is inferred from the action and therefore bears only a logical relation to it, not a causal one. MacIntyre would conclude from this that the explanation of social change—insofar as it is causal—cannot be ideational.[10]

There *are* cases which are clearly subject to this criticism. Many social expectations change because conduct is no longer reciprocated in certain ways, or because the conditions of a relationship change and therefore enable one or more parties to it to command different expectations. For example, if widespread disease causes a shortage of peasant labour, and if money is available from an urban sector of an economy, then the conditions of serfdom may become commuted; or, if insufficient slaves are available through conquest, or if the price of slaves for other reasons is too high, or if the supervision of slaves becomes unmanageable, then slavery may decline in favour of other forms of dependent labour. To say that the changed expectations of master and slave are associated with the change in structure is, in fact, to say that the conditions of the relationship have changed. Of course, these conditions can only be transmitted by way of expectations; but the initial causes of the change are 'material': for example, a change in the supply of labourers. Thus, it is argued, even if social and cultural phenomena in some respects are ideational, this does not make the ideational theory of social causation acceptable.

But there are cases where an expectation may change *prior* to a change in a relationship and thereby affect it: an arms race does not occur simply because two or more parties increase the level of national armament; it occurs because such increases are *believed* to occur; the original belief may even be mistaken; but its consequences may be no different from those which follow from an actual change in the level of armaments.

Ideas are communicated by social interaction; they may or

may not be dreamed up by single prophets or seers. But once they are communicated they become public property and affect expectations. If this is not social causation it would be difficult to establish what is.

The second theory is that ideational changes are necessary but seldom sufficient conditions for social change. The gist of this is that no material or other social factors can produce change unless there is *also* a change in ideas within society and, possibly, ideas about society or nature. Here one must distinguish two different types of case. In the first changes in the 'natural' conditions of social life may have far-reaching consequences which are not themselves dependent upon ideational changes: for example, changes in demographic structure, which may be caused by changes in mortality rates, themselves due to natural causes, will, in themselves, produce changes in the ratio of bread-winners to dependants. However, such a change can itself have consequences for the structure of family, kinship, political and other institutions, *only* by influencing expectations and beliefs. It is in this second type of case that changes in ideas are necessary conditions for social change.

The counter-argument to MacIntyre is strengthened by those cases in which the consequences of ideas cannot, by any means, be said to be logically entailed by the ideas themselves. This brings us to the third type of theory.

An example of the third theory is Max Weber's hypothesis concerning the causal connection between Calvinist Protestantism and modern capitalism.[11] Briefly, Weber's argument is that Calvinist Protestantism motivated men to seek worldly success in order to prove—to themselves as well as to others—that they had achieved salvation that they were predestined to a state of grace. Weber considered that this religious development was not simply an epiphenomenal consequence of capitalism, since many of its characteristics developed, in his view, prior to the development of certain significant features of modern capitalism, such as the emphasis on rational calculation, the willingness to accumulate for long-term profit and success, and the emphasis on entrepreneurial success as a virtue. Weber considered that these attitudes and values were quite *anti-traditional* and that they had little chance of developing without the powerful impulse of a new belief which gave men religiously sanctioned goals to pursue.* Weber did not simply explain capitalist development in terms of religious belief, but argued that the religious factor combined with others, of a political, economic and social nature to produce a certain type of social change. A significant point concerning Weber's explanation is that the secular conduct of capitalism is *not* logically entailed by Calvinism—the religious doctrine does not urge men to accumulate capital and to invest it rationally—but results from a psychological change in motivation and values. It certainly cannot be argued that Weber's hypothesis is tautological, or purely logical, unless one insists that he attributed to Protestantism characteristics which are indistinguishable from those of the 'spirit of capitalism'.

Weber's hypothesis has been strongly criticized by historians of religion and of capitalist development. But whether Weber was right on the particular matter of capitalist development or not, the general view which he proposed is now widely endorsed: that changes in values and other ideas are necessary or at least contributory factors in certain types of social change. And the corollary, that the persistence of values and other ideas do inhibit certain changes is also endorsed by contemporary sociologists.

If sociology has often reacted with good sense against ideational theories of change, or even against any view of social change which gives prominence to ideas, it has also tended to develop its own vested interests in such explanatory concepts as 'structural needs' or the 'ideological requirements of the ruling class'. Social phenomena are—in varying degrees and in different ways— ideational phenomena. It is not surprising that the source of social change may sometimes be found in changed ideas concerning social reality and the natural and supernatural world.

The sociological reaction against ideational explanations of social change is understandable. It is also responsible for some of the truly important discoveries in social science; for earlier theories, which emphasized the causal significance of ideas, tended to explain social phenomena largely in terms of *intention* and, more specifically, to exaggerate the influence of elaborate reasoning as a source of social change. (It is not surprising that men who devote so much of their time and energy to the

---

* This is what Weber meant when he asserted that it was not so much ideas as ideal *interests* which affect social conduct.

examination and construction of theories should accord them so much importance.) The reaction resulted in a far greater emphasis on the importance of the *unintended* consequences of social conduct and, indeed, on the unintended consequences of attempting to put certain ideas into practice: this has become the cornerstone of almost all sociological explanation. On the other hand, the rather extreme forms of structuralism which resulted from the influence of either Marx or Durkheim, or of both of them, took as its cornerstone the doctrine that ideas—at least culturally standardized ideas, such as myths, ideologies, political and other doctrines, including those purporting to be scientific, and, possibly, even the ideas of natural science—are the product of social influences or 'determinants'.

This last doctrine, known as the sociology of knowledge, came in roughly two forms: the first, in the Marxian tradition, treats the content of ideas as reflections of social interests, especially national, ethnic, class or status interests; the second, in the Durkheiman tradition, treats the structure and form of ideas as symbolic representations of the structure and form of social life. Both treat ideas as epiphenomenal and social structure as the true underlying social reality.

These theories have been heavily criticized on the following grounds: first, it can be shown that certain ideas which are thought to reflect underlying social structures have themselves developed independently of those structures and sometimes have preceded them historically: thus, certain Christian doctrines arose prior to the establishment of the Church, and cannot, therefore, be said to exist as mere reflections of Church interests or of the form of Church organization; similarly, certain myths can be shown to have existed before the rituals with which they later become associated. Second, it can be shown that a number of different sets of ideas can co-exist with the same social structures, while a number of different social structures can co-exist with the same sets of ideas; this being the case, it must either be conceded that social structures do not govern the form and content of ideas, or it must be shown that different sets of ideas have common elements which reflect particular social structures, or that different social structures have common elements which are reflected in a particular set of ideas. It is always possible to discern common characteristics in different sets of ideas as well as in different social structures; it is equally possible to 'demonstrate' that the ideas fit the interests or forms of the 'underlying' social reality; and it is, doubtless, easy enough to 'establish' that a social determinant is the historical antecedent of a set of ideas. Since this can always be done, and since one can guarantee the success of this intellectual exercise in advance, it would be quite impossible to imagine an empirical counter-example to this theory; in view of this the theory is scientifically suspect. (It may, of course, be a valuable guide in the investigation of certain cases.)

The third objection to this doctrine is the most telling: it is that the sociology of knowledge is itself an idea which is either a social product or must be an exception to the rule. If it is a social product, then there is no reason to believe that it has any foundation in fact, but is merely an ideology expressing the interests of a political movement or of sociology itself; if, on the other hand, it is an exception to the sociological rule, then it suggests that there may be other ideas which have some autonomy with respect to the social structure and which may, therefore, act as causes of social change and not only as consequences of them.

Once it is recognized that ideas, whether they be ideologies, scientific theories, myths, etc., can develop independently of certain factors of social structure, then it must be conceded that they *may* also be causes of social change. However, it does not follow that they *must* be causes of social change; to establish this requires more argument and evidence. In other words, to refute the doctrine of the structural *determination* of ideas is necessary but not sufficient to show that ideational factors may be causes of social change. But once it is agreed that they *may* be causes of social change, ideas enjoy the same status as any other factor. Thus, although it is accepted that economic changes or changes in the structure of power, or the intensification of struggle, or the growing incompatibility between different institutional structures, may be causes of social change, it does not follow that any one of these factors *is* the cause of a particular change, or a particular type of change.

To bring ideational factors into an explanation of social change requires the use of some model or set of models such as those suggested in Chapter V. In any social system or in any social situation, there are certain factors which are, more or less, external constraints; some of these are inanimate objects or non-human objects, while others are human and social. There are also, in the same system or situation, certain internal constraints which a number of social actors may share: some of these are, more or less 'natural'; others are far more 'cultural'. External, physical constraints which limit social conduct can change in one of two ways: they may change spontaneously; or they may *be changed* by human action. If the first occurs, then the resultant changes in social life may still be partly influenced by ideas; but the initial change stems from nature itself. If the second occurs, there are still two possibilities: (a) that the effects of human action were not intended, as in a case of soil erosion resulting from over-grazing; (b) that some of the effects of human action were intended. If it is this last which occurs, then clearly ideas have played a part in bringing about any social change which results from the change in the physical environment. These may be new technological ideas, or they may be new ideas concerning the possibility of applying existing technological ideas. A new idea of this last sort may be an example of creative innovation, similar to a technological innovation, or it may occur as a result of a changed situation. Clearly, the extent to which ideas are considered as true causes of social change will depend on the degree to which they are considered the product of creativity on the part of human actors.

External *social* constraints can change in a number of ways: for example, they may be due to demographic changes, or to changes in the structure of power, to changes in interests, values, or perceptions of social reality. A change in the structure of power may itself be the direct consequence of other changes; but it may be due to the creation of a social movement whose intention is to bring about such changes, or whose action results, quite unintentionally, in an alteration of the structure of power. If this last is the case, then ideas clearly play an important part. And they may play an equally important part in changing group interests. That they may play a part in changing values and perceptions is obvious.

Internal constraints may be altered as a consequence of changes in external constraints, or they may change independently. But even if the former is the case, once they have changed they can, in turn, produce further consequences. 'Natural' constraints do not, by definition, change; all the same, social conduct is governed by a number of these whose relative power can vary considerably, depending on how they are affected by external constraints and by internal, cultural ones. Internal *cultural* constraints do vary considerably, and there is good reason for believing that they are not simply the internal counterpart of external social factors, but that they do have some sort of 'life' of their own. This being so, they may also change, possibly in response to changes in external constraints, and thereby bring about further changes in themselves and in the external constraints.

The extent to which ideas can be thought of as exerting an influence on the course of social change depends partly on the level of ideas which is being considered and also on the nature of the social system concerned. The first point has already been made above, and requires little elaboration. Clearly, if one is referring to ideas which occur *within* social relations, then they play some part in bringing about almost any social change, for all cases of social change involve changes in social expectations, or changes in the definition of social roles.

The second point requires more elaboration and is, altogether, more interesting. In a relatively closed and fairly stationary social system the various sets of ideas will be formed largely by the social system and will tend to reinforce that system: in these circumstances there is little scope for ideational innovation. But in a more open changing system actors have greater freedom for creativity; furthermore, they are subject to the kinds of variety of experience which stimulate the innovative capacity in at least a small minority of them: in these circumstances the social system generates new sets of ideas some of which may, in turn, promote changes within it. Thus complex systems can be seen as containing a genuine interaction between ideational and other factors within the system; while simpler systems can be seen as containing sets of ideas which underpin and reflect other features of social life. Of course, these two conceptions of simple and complex systems are models, not full descriptions of reality. In real social life there is always some scope for ideational creativity; but whether this can, in turn, promote social change will depend on whether certain forces can break through the over-determined 'deadweight' of interdependent elements; where this interdependence is great the 'deadweight' effect is powerful indeed. Here, the mutual reinforcement of external and internal constraints can only be loosened by some impact from outside of the social and cultural system. One such form of impact is interaction with members of other cultures.

The Cultural Interaction Theory

An ingenious theory which has been suggested to explain change in simple societies and some historical societies, is the cultural interaction theory.[12] This states simply that when the members of two cultures interact there is a tendency for cultural change to occur or for an acceleration of cultural change to occur. The reason for this is not simply that each brings new items of culture to the other, but that the increase in the number of cultural items available to each leads to the possibility of new combinations of these items.[12]

Cultural interaction might also be used to explain change in simple societies in another way. Such interaction often, though not always, results in new forms of social relationship, particularly in the form of conquest. Such processes may also expand the range of social relations which can occur, thereby stimulating the development of new institutions. Such a theory is clearly needed if the assumption is made that simple societies tend, otherwise to be stagnant systems. But, in fact, few simple societies known to us are truly isolated from outside contacts; and many have been able to maintain such contacts without undergoing radical change. It is also possible that some forms of contact encourage a resistance to change.

The cultural interaction theory also stimulates thought on the causes of change in complex societies. For it suggests that there may be endogenous processes of stimulation in complex systems which are analogous to the exogenous stimuli which affect change in simple societies. The intention of this argument is that the different parts and sections of complex societies constitute, to some extent, separate sub-cultures which, when they interact, stimulate change. The more complex a social system becomes the greater the number of such parts it creates; therefore, the more likely it is to provide sources for further change.

The Search for a Theory of Social Change

The idea that sociology can provide a single theory of social change is a myth. Social systems provide many sources of change. To attempt to reduce these to a single factor is to believe that social change is a very specific phenomenon which must have very specific causes. Most attempts to discover a single theory either seize on one factor—like technology—or else they result in rather empty, though high-sounding notions concerning 'shifts in equilibria', the effects of 'negative-feed-back', and so on.

The assertion that there is or should be a single theory of change is often linked with the false notion that there is a single theory of social persistence. If there is such a theory it has yet to be stated.

One can only say in defence of such ideas that it is possible to construct a model of interrelated processes, some of which reinforce one another in their present state, others of which disrupt one another, and yet others of which reinforce certain tendencies to change. Such a model would take account of the many pressures, counter-pressures, tensions and conflicts in social systems, in an attempt to locate the main sources of change.

This general model can serve to guide the analysis of social change by providing a format for the construction of particular models to deal with different types or cases of change.

This brings us back to the question of the functional or systemic approach to sociological explanation and its application to problems of social change. A number of arguments are marshalled against the functional approach in this connection. First, that it does not incorporate the idea of action, without which the explanation of social change is not possible. Second, that it involves some idea of equilibrium and can, in effect, and at best, only provide a model of a persisting system. Third, that it so emphasised the multicausality of social phenomena—that is, the mutual interdependence of all factors in a system—that it cannot explain the occurrence of anything without referring to everything else.

The first objection has been shown to be invalid. (See Chapters

V and VI.) To explain the phenomenon of functional interdependence and variations in the degree of this which can occur, one must proceed by way of certain assumptions concerning social action and interaction. In other words, features of social structure must be treated as standardized forms of social action and interaction; and the systemic connections between different structures can only be demonstrated by analysing the processes whereby different areas of action and interaction affect one another. On the other hand, it must also be recognized that the assumptions of social action and interaction do not enable one to deduce very much about the properties of social structures and systems; for these must be taken as given when analysing the processes of action and interaction. But this does not mean that one must treat all forms of action as simply governed by the so-called pressures or requirements of a system; there is always room for innovatory potentials in social action, at least in certain types of society and in certain sectors of social systems.

The second objection is equally invalid. First of all, the idea of social equilibrium, if it is to be of any scientific value, requires some ability to measure different social forces and to show that they balance one another; if this cannot be done, then to explain the absence of social change, ex post facto, in terms of 'equilibrium' is simply to state, in other words, that no social change has occurred. Similarly, to explain the occurrence of change, ex post facto, in terms of disequilibrium is equally jejune. Since sociologists have, as yet, no way of measuring the many forces which are part of social systems there is no point in using the idea of social equilibrium. All that one can do is to show that certain types of system are more likely to persist in a given state than others.

The third criticism is both relevant and telling. There has been a depressing tendency for social theorists to abdicate the responsability for locating the more important sources of social change by arguing that all factors are relevant; they may all be relevant, but some are more so than others. (What is highly disturbing is the tendency to advocate a multicausal approach as general policy, while in practice explaining social change almost entirely in terms of changes in one factor, such as the value system, the technology, and so on.) Clearly the relevance of social factors is governed by the type of change to be explained.

It is sometimes said that the one true cause of most forms of social change is an increase in relative deprivation: that is, a change in the expectations of what one hopes to achieve, as of right, in any social situation. It is certainly true that much social change is strongly influenced by this factor; but some forms are more influenced than others. At present times great pressures for change are coming from those who previously enjoyed fewer rights than they enjoy now because they cherish the hope that, having discarded the 'deadweight' of the past they may now enjoy even greater rights which are or have been minority privileges. But not all social changes result from this type of pressure at least quite in this form. The direction of social change is often governed by slow and almost imperceptible influences stemming from the demands or exigencies of each situation as these appeared to the actors in them without their necessarily having some expectation of improvement of their lot. The idea of improvement or progress, though it has existed in the past, is very much a product of the last few centuries.

NOTES

1. See Alfred G. Meyer, *Marxism, The Unity of Theory and Practice*, University of Michigan Press, 1963, pp. 11–46.
2. Max Weber, *Basic Concepts in Sociology* (trans. and introduced by H. P. Secker), Peter Owen, London, 1962, pp. 85–9.
3. N. Smelser, *Social Change in the Industrial Revolution*, Routledge, 1959.
4. See M. N. Srinivas, *Caste in Modern India and Other Essays*, Asia Publishing House, London, 1962.
5. Michael Oakeshott, *Rationalism in Politics and Other Essays*, London, 1962, p. 124.
6. See A. T. Bryant, *Olden Times in Zululand and Natal*, Longmans, 1938.
7. Talcott Parsons, *Societies, Evolutionary and Comparative Perspectives*, Prentice-Hall, 1966, pp. 21–9.
8. Wilbert E. Moore, *Social Change*, Prentice-Hall, 1963.
9. T. B. Bottomore & Maximilien Rubel, 'Introduction', *Karl Marx*, London, 1956, esp. pp. 14–28.
10. A. C. MacIntyre, 'A Mistake About Causality in Social Science' in P. Laslett & W. G. Runciman (eds) *Philosophy, Politics and Society: Second Series*, Oxford, 1962.

11. Max Weber, *The Protestant Ethic and the Spirit of Capitalism*, trans. Talcott Parsons, London, 1948.
12. See for example, Hornell Hart, 'Social Theory and Social Change' in Llewellyn Gross (ed) *Synosium on Sociological Theory*, Row, Peterson, 1959.

8.

Directions of Social Change

Introduction

IN the eighteenth and even more in the nineteenth century, it was commonly believed that sociology could and should aim to discover the laws governing the development or progress of societies. Later, cyclical theories were added to the stock of sociological ideas, partly as a reaction against those emphasizing progressive development. But cyclical theories share with developmental theories the common belief that societies pass through certain determinate stages, and that the process is an inevitable one. Many reasons have been suggested for this widespread belief; and, indeed the whole problem provides a fascinating subject for the sociology of ideas.

Nowadays most of these theories of inevitable social development have been discredited. Yet there is still a tendency to accept certain broad notions of the general trend of social development; and there is still a feeling that the concept of stages is useful or even indispensable.

Stages of Social Development

The sociological concept of developmental stages—and henceforth I shall use the term to refer only to *developmental* stages—has been used in a number of different ways. The first usage treats stages as necessary steps in the process of change of all societies; an assumption underlying this usage is that each society contains inner mechanisms which ensure that it must change in one way and one way only.

The second usage treats stages in terms of the total history of human society. According to this view, it is not necessary for each society to traverse the various stages, though no single society can reach a particular stage before it, or another society, has passed through a preparatory one. For example, this view would concede that societies at a low level of agricultural development could become industrialized without passing through all the stages of later agricultural and early industrial development, but it would not concede that mankind in general could have leaped from primitive agriculture to industry.

A third usage applies the concept of stages to the study of particular historical processes. In this case there may be no assumption that one stage necessarily precedes or succeeds another. The stages are simply ways of characterizing actual processes of change and classifying them in some sequence.

The first usage has been almost totally abandoned. From time to time it has been used to support a particular theory or policy; for example, Russian Marxists accused 'narodniks' and other populists of failing to recognize that peasant communalism must be undermined by individualistic, capitalistic agriculture before agrarian socialism could succeed. (Such an argument could, in fact, be defended without resorting to any idea of a law of social development.) But, on the whole, such usages have been discredited. Particular societies need not traverse the same path of development of others, especially when they may benefit from the experience of these others.

The second usage is still retained by some social scientists, but treated with caution or scepticism by others.

The third usage has been subject to some criticism, and it is sometimes suggested that particular schemes of development are highly arbitrary constructions and are no truer than a host of others.

Diffusionist Critique of Theories Asserting Stages of Development

One of the earliest critiques of the stage theory of social development came from the diffusionists. In its most reasonable form—and the diffusionist ideas were often far from reasonable—

this critique asserted that since societies often obtain cultural traits from others, they could not be said to develop them spontaneously; in these cases societies could possess characteristics which they ought not to have according to some scheme of social development.

This argument is unassailable; but it only dispenses with the first doctrine of stages, and does not affect the second and third ones. Thus, it could be argued against the diffusionists, that while some societies may possess bronze implements because they have obtained them from others, and have not themselves invented them, those who did invent them must first have used stone or iron implements, while those who invented iron implements must first have used stone ones.

Another argument which has been levelled against the diffusionists is that no society can obtain a cultural item from another unless it is ready to use it. The third, and final argument against diffusionism is that it can not explain why certain items originate in the first place except by assuming that at least one society has reached a certain stage of development.

These arguments can not be lightly dismissed and have a bearing on a number of live issues in historical interpretation. For example, Marxists and others contend that certain feudal institutions would have developed in England whatever the outcome of the Battle of Hastings. But many historians deny that the English system of political clientship was like, or would necessarily have become like, that which was imposed by the Norman conquerors. Furthermore, it is arguable that English feudal institutions after the Norman Conquest developed differently from those in Western Europe because it was a conquest state in which power had been highly centralized.

On the whole, diffusionist critiques are treated as true, but trivial. The methodological critiques usually receive more attention.

Methodological Critique of Theories of
Social Development

Functionalist anthropologists have often criticized evolutionary developmental schemes for engaging in 'conjectural history' based on little or no evidence. The burden of these criticisms has been that the evidence of existing primitive societies can not be used for establishing the characteristics of earlier stages of development, on the grounds that these contemporary societies have had long histories of their own, and may be quite unlike historically extinct simple societies.

This kind of objection is partly in order, but partly disingenuous. For example, one can hazard a reasonable guess that early hunters and gatherers lived in small bands or even in separate family units—depending on the kind of foraging and hunting that was engaged in—and one could not be far wrong in assuming that foraging and hunting represented an earlier stage of human history than agriculture. This does not mean that one can also assume that the earliest forms of religion were totemism or ancestor worship simply because such religions are found in fairly simple contemporary societies.

A far more powerful and interesting assault on the whole idea of stages of development has been launched by the logician K. R. Popper, who has attacked all such doctrines under the name of 'historicism'. Popper's arguments are directed largely against Hegel, Comte and Marx; but they are meant to apply equally to a great many other writers, such as J. S. Mill and Arnold Toynbee.

According to Popper the aim of historicism is to establish laws which state a necessary sequence of historical or developmental stages.* This doctrine rests on a number of assumptions: that social development can be studied scientifically; that it is the aim of science to establish causal connections; and that it is the aim of social science to find these causal connections in the sequence of stages of social development. Popper adds that many historicists, particularly Marx, believe that with the aid of such

* Popper, in fact, makes a distinction between two kinds of historicism: 'anti-naturalist' and 'naturalist'. Here I am concerned only with the 'naturalist' variety. (See K. R. Popper.[1])

laws social science will permit the prediction of the future stages of development. He considers the claim to predict future social stages quite consistent with the view that there is a law governing the historical process, for it is in the nature of scientific laws that they permit prediction: if one states a law-like connection between any two variables X and Y, then this means that one can use at least one as a predictor of the other.

Popper refutes the doctrine that there are laws of social development with the following arguments. First, historicism makes false claims for natural science and, therefore, for social science. Second, the analogies between social entities and physical or organic ones are misleading and are partly responsible for absurd historicist claims. Third, large-scale social changes are logically unpredictable. Fourth, the role of ideas makes social knowledge and social prediction different from physical knowledge and prediction. These arguments are connected.

The first argument amounts to this. Theoretical science, says Popper, does not assert the existence or occurrence of any particular event: it is not its intention or purpose to state that events of type X or Y do occur, but only that events of type X *can not* occur, without being followed by events of type Y, or that events of type Y *can not* have occurred without being preceded by events of type X. But the so-called laws of social development *do* state that certain sequence of stages occur according to a law. This, in Popper's view, is to confuse statements of trends, which are statements of fact, with theoretical statements, which are not. Popper does not deny that there are fields in the natural sciences in which it appears that laws can state a sequence of stages: for example, laws governing the growth of organisms, or the movements of planets, all of which refer to regular or recurrent sequences of events. His comment on this is that such systems are, or can be treated as, relatively closed, and the conditions of such changes or movements can be stated as precise, constant factors. None of this applies to societies or social institutions, which do not move like planets or grow like organisms, because the conditions of change within them also change.

The third argument, linked to the first two, is that large-scale changes in social systems are, in a sense, logically unpredictable. The gist of this is that every change in social structure is the product of intersecting causal chains which are, to some extent, independent of one another, and whose convergence is, therefore, in an important sense, partly accidental. This argument is intended as a counter to Marxist and other similar doctrines which assert that the characteristics of one type of social system simply arise out of those of a previous one—that one type of system simply 'gives birth to another'. For example, the Marxist view is that the breakdown of feudal agrarian society, resulting from its internal 'contradictions' gives rise to the beginnings of capitalism. The opposing view would be that had it not been for the development of trade and the possibilities of centralization of power, which are by no means predictable *within* a feudal system, feudal agrarian society would not have changed in the way that it did. Proponents of this view would also throw in the suggestion that such significant events as the Black Death, are also not predictable. In short, the transition from feudal decentralization and agrarian subsistence to greater centralization and increased trade was not simply an inevitable development resulting from a single chain of casual connections or from a closed system of interrelated variables. This does not mean that the development of feudal-type institutions is necessarily a unique historical process. There is an intermediate position between complete historical contingency and complete developmental determinism: feudal-type institutions have developed in a number of different societies and historical periods. But this does not mean that such institutions are a necessary stage in social development.

There is a counter-argument which asserts that every major historical development may involve the conjunction of separate causal processes, but that such conjunctions are themselves inevitable and, therefore, predictable. This is like saying that if two objects are moving towards one another, one can safely predict that they will collide. Some social changes are possibly of this kind, rather like those studied by meteorologists: here there is a probability that independent casual chains will intersect, but though there are always a number of unknowns that may alter the nature of the interaction. But few major social transformations are even as simply contingent as that; they result from so many different casual chains, that the outcome can not be said to be determined in any meaningful sense. Even the parallel with the meteorological study of changing weather conditions is of limited value; for meteorologists can assume an unchanging, mechanical regularity of the solar system, whereas in the study of social transformations, no such assumption of a closed system can be made.

Popper's ultimate argument seeks to undermine any remnant of defence of historical determinism: for, he insists, changing ideas and the growth of knowledge must, to some extent, affect social development; but future ideas and states of knowledge can not be predicted in advance—if they were predictable they would be present conditions not future ones, so that one can have no theory of how such ideas will affect social development; in which case one can not know what future stages of social development will be. And if this is so, then there is no logical defence of the doctrine that *past* stages have been part of an inevitable development; for a past stage could have been predictable from a previous one.

Popper, unlike many others who deny that there can be laws of social development, does *not* deny that there can be any kind of sociological laws. He defends the view that there can be sociological theories which simply make *conditional* statements, such as: if governmental activities increase, then bureaucratic organization will increase. These general theories do not state that one stage of social development will necessarily succeed another, or that one set of conditions will necessarily occur; they only state what will occur *if* certain conditions arise.

Evaluation of Developmental Doctrines

At least two versions of the developmental doctrine can be rejected. The first is that every society must pass through a determined series of stages. The second is that there is one and only one series of stages for human society as a whole. But there are three weaker assertions which can, I think, be defended. And these, together, can be used to reconstitute a tenable doctrine of social development.

The first assumption is that some stages of development must be achieved for human society, as a whole, before others are achieved. For example, it is scarcely disputable that agriculture must precede industrialization, and it is at least plausible to suggest that a political structure of personal attachment to a leader precedes institutionalized, hereditary chieftainship. But if one turns to other areas of culture and social structure the difficulties of establishing some order of priorities are greater: totemism or ancestral cults may precede the development of polytheism and monotheism; but whether they are necessary preconditions for them is another matter. Much that is objectionable in developmental doctrines results from the confusion of *actual* historical sequences with *theoretically* necessary sequences: it is hardly disputable that feudalism preceded the modern nation state in most of western Europe; but it is by no means clear that feudal structures are a necessary precondition for the development of the nation state.

The second assumption is that some stages are more likely to precede others because they are more easily achieved. This does not assert that one stage is a *necessary* basis for another, but simply that it is a more *likely* occurrence in particular conditions. For example, early man is more likely to adopt foraging and even hunting than some form of agriculture, since the former would require less invention on his part; this clearly does not mean that foraging and hunting are necessary conditions for the development of agriculture. Similarly, it is plausible to suggest that man requires less intellectual sophistication to attribute sacred qualities to natural objects than he requires to invent the idea of an impersonal or personal God.

The third assumption is similar to the second: it is that in any given conditions certain developments are more likely than others: for example, in a society based on hoe-culture and segmentary organization the development of hierarchical clientship is politically more likely than the development of a fully centralized state organization. This limitation of the likely form of development is bound to be greater in very simple societies: the lower the level of technology the greater the influence of physical environment on social structure; and the simpler the social structure, the narrower the range of developments which can occur within it. This does not mean that there are only small differences of social structure and culture between simpler societies, even in the same or similar physical environments; major differences are well documented by anthropologists; for, the development of culture itself interposes an influence between the forms of social life and the natural environment, so that societies with cultural differences will establish different ecological systems. But there is, for all that, a qualitative difference between simpler and more complex societies and cultures in this important respect. A complex technology can transform the physical environment in such a way that it can sustain a wide range of social structures and cultures: this means that insofar as there is *any* determinism in the stages of social development it will be more apparent at the simpler levels.

These three propositions do constitute a weaker version of the doctrine which has enabled some contemporary anthropologists, such as Steward,[2] Sahlins and Service[3] to attempt some meaningful reconstruction of social development (or social evolution, as they prefer to call it). But what is usually produced is an 'ideal series'.* This is a theoretical series of developmental stages which portrays what would have occurred if human society, as a whole, had developed as a single closed system unaffected by any elements of contingency. Some critics might argue that if one discounts the contingent factors one is left with very little. Steward and other American evolutionists try to cope with this problem by making a distinction between the evolution of human society in general, and the specific paths of evolution of particular societies or culture areas.[5] What is implied by this suggestion is that the 'ideal series' does roughly describe and explain the evolution of human society, in general, but that it can not be applied so easily to the particular developments which have occurred within each region or society. There are several reasons for this. First, it must be recognized that the kind of technology and economic organization of each society will be strongly affected by the particular characteristics of its physical environment: whether foraging is carried out by a band or by a small family unit will depend on the kind of foraging and hunting that are possible. Second, in each region, the social structure and culture will be affected by the influences of the surrounding culture: nomadic pastoralists who live within a wider civilization which uses the territory of the pastoralists for trade and communication may possess cultural items, such as money and fire-arms, which are not possessed by

* A discussion of Comte's use of an 'ideal series' and of related matters is to be found in Teggart.[4]

other pastoralists and which are highly important factors in their social life. Third, interaction between societies, particularly when this takes the form of conquest or political union or absorption, may result in some societies or cultures 'retrogressing' in certain important respects, while others 'skip' certain stages.

When all this is conceded, one must sympathize with those who argue that nothing much is left of the 'ideal series'. But this judgement might be a little too hasty. The usefulness of an evolutionary or developmental scheme depends greatly on the problem to which it is to be applied.

But even if one can construct some 'ideal series' of social evolution, should this really be called a general theory? Even in biology there is no general theory which states what the actual evolutionary process is, though there are certainly general theories which explain the *mechanisms* of biological evolution such as those of natural selection, genetic transmission and mutation. But there is no theory of the overall process as such. In fact, what biologists emphasize is the highly accidental nature of the whole process.* One can, at best, propose a general interpretation of evolution which emphasizes the process of increasing complexity of organisms, or greater adaptability of organisms, or an increasing variety of species.

But the fact that a theory of evolutionary process is not found in biology does not rule out such a possibility in sociology; it does, however, mean that sociology can not model such a theory on the example of biology, for no such example exists.

The chief fault of most earlier developmental 'theories' was that they overemphasized a 'limitation principle' in tracing the emergence of one type of social system from another: that is, they operated with a rather closed model of the social system and of the mechanisms whereby it changed its form. The nineteenth-century theorists tended to forget that the conditions of change themselves change: writers like Comte assumed a constant tendency for intellectual development, while Marx assumed that economic 'contradictions' and class conflict must be the source of change from any one stage to the next. And

---

* According to some estimates the chances of any mutation actually recurring in the same form are not much better than 1/10,000,000. Even if the odds are much better than this, it can hardly be said that the evolutionary process is itself an instance of a natural law.

while all of these writers paid lip service to the historical method, few acknowledged the complexity of history. Of course, Marx himself did concede that abstract theorizing was no subsitute for detailed history; but he did not seem to realize that abstract theorizing can not be about the *process* of history itself but only about the nature of social action, social structure and the forms or mechanisms of social change.

An exaggerated concern with stages of social development sometimes inhibits sociological insight by obscuring important similarities between societies which are not in any obvious sense at the same stage of development. For example there is a clear structural similarity between systems of political and military clientship as found in primitive African states and in European feudal societies. But in terms of criteria of agricultural and military technology, literacy and other cultural characteristics, the societies of feudal Europe are at a much 'higher' level of development. Nor can these structural similarities be explained in terms of cultural diffusion. They are due almost entirely to the same political conditions which make a form of hierarchical clientship one of the few viable modes of organizing and maintaining some degree of centralized authority in the absence of some means of raising and maintaining an army and an administration responsible only to a head of state or his representatives.

Most of these criticisms seem to leave little worth salvaging from the wreck of nineteenth-century thought. But one should at this point consider the use made by Max Weber of a development typology. For although Weber's procedure is not without defects, it suggests certain fruitful possibilities. Weber was not particularly concerned with the general question of social development and was not bent on constructing a full developmental scheme. He was, however, concerned to write sociological history. This does not mean that he tried to establish laws of social development, but that he sought to analyse the structural changes which were discernible in historical processes; he also tried to show how and why a certain trend of development was started and maintained, particularly in the history of European societies; and, finally, he aimed to explain how one set of conditions of social structure and culture could *set limits* to the possible changes which could emerge out of them. Unlike Marx, Weber

did not believe that each type of social system was simply transformed by its own inner 'dialectical' processes. For him social
and cultural structures were abstractions, not real things. In
historical reality, different currents could join together to produce
unpredictable results. But Weber recognized the possibility of
combining a genuine historical explanation with a sociological
analysis of the emergence of one type of system from another.
To do this he made use of what he called 'ideal types'. Among his
best-known ideal types of social structure are those of patrimonialism, feudalism and rational-legal bureaucracy. Weber used
these as descriptions of the forms of social reality to establish
landmarks in the historical process; by emphasizing certain
dominant characteristics of a period, he could then trace the
conditions which had led to a change in these characteristics.
In this way he hoped to trace and explain trends such as that of
increasing rationalization of administration from patrimonialism,
through patrimonial bureaucracy, to bureaucracy itself. Weber
also sought to link changes such as these with the major forms of
change in the economy, and, in particular, with the growth of
impersonal markets, the use of money and rational calculation, and
the gradual 'liberation' of economic relations from the influence
of traditional obligation.[6]

Weber's discussion of these processes is one of the most
significant contributions to modern sociology. But he was to
some extent the victim of his own method, and also of the errors
which he sought to avoid. For, while recognizing the abstract
nature of structural conceptions, he continued to assume that
one could somehow elicit from historical inquiry *the* essential
features of a period or social system. This is not to doubt that
there are some features of a social system which are, in a
certain sense, essentially characteristic of it: an example is the
difference between the personal bonds of feudal relationships and
the impersonal, almost abstract relations, of the modern market
economy. But, for all that, to choose one set of characteristics
and to attempt to interrelate them and explain the process of
their transformation, is to a large extent to exercise a degree of
arbitrariness. Weber did concede this in his methodological
writings.[7] But he denied that the ideal type was an hypothesis,
and insisted that it was simply a description of a type of social
or cultural phenomenon which exaggerated its principal character-

istics in order to contrast them more clearly with the characteristics of other such phenomena.[8] For example, he deliberately
emphasized the rational, impersonality of bureaucratic rules in
order to highlight the difference between these and the norms of
personal obligation which are characteristic of patrimonialism
and feudalism. In this way he could provide a clearer statement
of the process of development to be explained. But when Weber
turned to explanation he did, in fact, use his ideal types as explanatory models by translating structural and cultural factors
into courses of action. He showed, in effect, how the courses of
action which are characteristic of an expanding exchange economy
may become increasingly incompatible with those which are
characteristic of a patrimonial structure of authority. (Not that
he explained the political change simply in economic terms, or
the economic change simply in political terms.) But to do this
Weber had to close off a system of interrelated processes in rather
arbitrary fashion and to work out the mutual consequences of
these processes for one another through an analysis of social
action. *This meant treating ideal types as sets of hypotheses.*[9]

When this is acknowledged, some of the criticisms of Weber
take on a different light. Weber is commonly criticized for not
recognizing the importance of those informal, personal relationships in bureaucracies which are thought to be necessary for
their functioning. But while this objection may pinpoint a
defect in Weber's model of how bureaucratic organization works,
it does not weaken his explanation of a developmental process
from feudalism or patrimonialism to bureaucracy. The models
used for this explanation carefully select certain elements of
social structure and culture which are thought, by hypothesis, to
be related: the growth of impersonality, the reduction of arbitrary
decisions and the increased application of universalistic rules all
constitutes *selected aspects* of bureaucratized relationships which are
functionally interrelated with the expansion of an exchange
market.

This discussion of Weber's contribution does show that
constructs of development stages are not simply dissolved in the
process of explaining change.* But it does also show how cauti-
ous one must be in using concepts of developmental stages; these
should not be reified—they are not entities whose boundaries

* Cf. Gellner.[10]

are readily observed—but, like many other sociological concepts, should be treated as theoretical models: they are sets of interrelated assumptions which artificially simplify the structure and processes of that area of reality being dealt with, and which thereby permit some kind of explanation.

The idea of a unilinear process of development, which is now scarcely accepted by anyone, was necessarily linked to the hypothesis of monocausality and determinism. If one major factor is responsible for all social change, then developments which spring from this factor must all be in line with it. But if the source of change can be traced to a number of points in social cultural life, and if changes in one area of social life do not determine all others, then it is possible to find that societies are more 'advanced' in some respects and less 'advanced' in others.

These difficulties indicate that if there is to be any progress in analysing the course of social change in a developmental manner, this will have to be done only by constructing models using a small number of factors at a time. The assumptions linking these factors would not necessarily be applicable to all or even a great number of the developmental stages; though a scheme of this kind would certainly make use of certain very general assumptions about the nature of social interaction, the characteristics of social systems and the likely causes of social change.

Some contemporary sociologists would begin this task not by trying to rank societies in terms of rather specific characteristics of technology or other items of social structure and culture, but rather by using more abstract notions concerning levels of technological, social and cultural development. These ideas call for separate discussion.

From Simple to Complex Social Systems

One of the most influential ideas in contemporary sociology which has survived from the nineteenth century is that human society has developed from simple to more complex forms and that this development has been accompanied by certain qualitative changes in the nature of social and cultural life. This view was, in the past, closely linked with two assumptions: (i) that social evolution is a continuation of biological evolution; (ii) that the mechanisms of social evolution are the same as those of biological evolution. These assumptions have recently been revived in one form or another by a number of writers including Parsons.[11]

Assumption (i) is either meaningless or wrong. There is no law of biological evolution which describes and explains the actual process of increasing differentiation, specialization and adaptability. The fact is that most cases of biological mutation were evolutionary failures, and the 'story' of biological evolution is a 'success story' only insofar as it is a deliberate selection of the facts of increasing adaptability. In any case, the time-span involved in the analysis of social evolution is infinitesimally small compared with that of biological evolution. This does not mean that a knowledge of biological evolution is irrelevant to the under- standing of human society. The evidence of primatology, no doubt, does throw some light on the origins of human society and on those psycho-biological and even social characteristics of man which have survived 500,000 years of cultural development; but it does not follow from this that social and cultural evolution can be treated as a continuation of biological evolution, unless one assumes that there are mechanisms at work in biological evolution which have ensured that, despite the many evolutionary failures, there would be a tendency for phyla, orders, genera and species to become increasingly differentiated from one another, increas- ingly differentiated within their own structures and increasingly adapted or adaptable to their environments, and which mechan- isms are also at work in social evolution. This brings us to an assessment of proposition (ii).

Students of biological evolution do justifiably make general assumptions about such mechanisms of evolution. First, they assume that mutations may occur and that these are genetically transmissable and transmitted; though they recognize that although the processes of mutation are law-like, the actual occur- rence of any particular mutation is *very* much a matter of chance. Second, they assume the laws of genetic inheritance and trans- mission. Third, they assume the principles of natural selection, though ideas about this have changed greatly since the nineteenth century to include behavioural as well as anatomical and physiological characters. In addition to these assumptions, which are now scarcely disputed, there is one other which asserts that with every increase in adaptive efficiency and in the degree of differentiation between genera, species and so on, there is an increased likelihood that yet further processes of this kind will occur.

How applicable are these assumptions to social evolution or social development? The first, the assumption of mutation is scarcely applicable in any meaningful sense. One does not need any equivalent of the mechanism of mutation to account for social change.

The second assumption is equally unnecessary. Of course, human procreation is affected by genetic laws, but the transmission of social characteristics occurs through the process of social interaction itself. For this reason, there is a sense in which societies transmit acquired characteristics, while biologically this can not occur. Since this transmission is also very much influenced by conscious intentions and unconscious motives, there is yet another respect in which the biological analogy proves not only misleading, but totally unnecessary.

The third assumption, of 'natural selection', does appear to have greater applicability. The argument is that more complex and differentiated forms of social structure and culture have a better chance of surviving than have simpler ones because they are either better adapted or more adaptable to their environments and are therefore able to compete favourably with simpler societies.

That complex societies are better adapted to their natural and social environment than simpler ones is very doubtful. Of course, it is difficult to know what is meant by the term 'better adapted'. But if it means that there is some obvious 'fit' between the social structure and its environment then there are no ready criteria for estimating this. But, intuitively, one would think that most simpler societies were, indeed, better adapted than more complex ones. For example, there seems to be little or no tendency for population growth in simpler societies to outstrip the means of subsistence, if only because natural conditions are supplemented by cultural practices such as infanticide, to ensure a high infant mortality rate.

One can, of course, say that complex societies are more *adaptable* than simple ones in the sense that their technology enables them to survive in a greater variety of environments. It would also, perhaps, be correct to say that the different parts of complex systems are more flexibly interrelated with one another than those of simpler systems, so that complex systems can adapt more successfully to the introduction of new elements.

But to use the argument of greater adaptability to explain the greater survival value of complex social systems is clearly indefensible. For the evidence simply does not exist. For all one knows a thermonuclear conflict may destroy all societies, or at least all complex ones.

The one proposition which may well be defensible is that which states that the more complex social systems become the more likely they are to develop in the direction of greater complexity. For increasing complexity introduces increasing indeterminacy —the greater the number of processes going on within a given system, the greater the possible number of mutual influences which can occur, and hence the greater the number of outcomes. The more indeterminate social systems become, the greater the degree of autonomy achieved by their parts. This increases the possible number of sources of social change, which in turn increases the likelihood of greater complexity.

The most valuable and certainly the most intellectually distinguished contribution to the analysis and interpretation of the process of increasing social complexity has been that of Emile Durkheim in his book *The Division of Labour in Society*. Durkheim starts out with a very significant problem which arises in the work of Comte and Spencer. Comte argued that the growing division of labour would, by increasing the differentiation of interests, beliefs and values, promote increasing conflict and lead to the disintegration of society. His solution to this problem was the creation of a new religion, or pseudo-religion, based on science, which would constitute a new basis of social consensus. Spencer contradicted Comte's view by asserting that the division of labour would, in fact, foster a growing social interdependence, therefore making dissolution less likely than in simpler societies, which consist of a number of homologous units barely held together by some form of authority.

Durkheim senses that both Comte and Spencer are right, in

some important aspects, and wrong in others. His own argument is as follows. Primitive societies have little division of labour; a point agreed upon by Comte and Spencer. Such societies, according to Durkheim, consist of a number of homologous units, such as families or clans; they have a 'segmental' structure. These are bound together solely by their uniformity of practices and beliefs. This Durkheim calls 'mechanical solidarity'. The measure of this form of solidarity is a type of social control which is largely punitive: there is a great reliance on repressive law. As the division of labour progresses, a number of things occur; the 'segmentary' structure of homologous social units is replaced by an increasing differentiation of units, which are interdependent; and, in addition, the uniformity of ideas, including moral ideas, decreases. But this does not spell the end of solidarity, as Comte believed: for there is a new solidarity—an 'organic' solidarity, based not on uniformity, but on a moral foundation of *interdependence*, which involves the acceptance of difference. The measure of the development of this form of solidarity, which corresponds to the new, differentiated structure of society is the gradual replacement of repressive law by a form of social control which emphasizes restitution, and which is manifest particularly in the emergence of contractual law. Durkheim is at great pains to show that the emergence of contractual law is an *expression* of the new form of solidarity, for Spencer sought to show that contractual obligations *themselves* create a basis of social morality. Durkheim does not argue that the decline of 'mechanical solidarity' means the end of all moral consensus; rather, he insists that 'organic solidarity' is characterized by a rather vague moral consensus, which does not specify particular norms of conduct for all members of society, but merely serves to *underpin* a variety of norms, particularly the legal norms of contractual obligation.

Thus, in effect, Durkheim's argument is that the growth of the division of labour brings with it a new form of social solidarity to replace the older form which disappears with the breakdown of the segmentary structure of society: 'organic' solidarity meets certain needs (or fulfils a particular function) which were previously met by the 'mechanical' form. Durkheim recognizes that one cannot explain the emergence of the division of labour by showing that it is beneficial for the social system. (And he is insistent that the growth of the division of labour is not itself responsible for the disappearance of the segmental structure and of mechanical solidarity.) He provides an explanation for the effacement of the segmentary structure and for the decline in 'mechanical solidarity' which is as follows. At some time there occurs a population increase in 'segmental' societies. This causes an increase in 'moral density' or social interaction: this condition is threatening to the cohesion of society because it is accompanied by intensified competitiveness; thus the only lasting solution to this problem is the creation of a division of labour which reduces competition by demanding differentiation and interdependence.

The boldness and ingenuity of Durkheim's conception is unrivalled. But there are a number of defects in the argument. Since these are constantly emphasized, it might be as well to list some of the great merits of this system of ideas.

Firstly, Durkheim does not treat the classification 'segmentary-differentiated' as simply dichotomous; he recognizes that there are degrees of 'segmentariness' and he suggests that the ladder of social evolution can be constructed in terms of the *relative* decline of segmentary characteristics and the relative growth of differentiation, which is its logical opposite: thus, Durkheim recognizes that each village or town or district in a complex agrarian society is, in some aspects, a replica of each other one; and to this extent the society is still highly segmentary, though also differentiated.

Second, Durkheim also recognizes that the decline in the significance of one type of law is relative: in other words, what he is suggesting is that the ratio of repressive to restitutive laws changes in favour of the latter as society becomes more complex.

Third, Durkheim goes far beyond Comte and Spencer in that he makes a clear distinction between two different aspects of social systems: that which can be called the articulated structure of social relationships ('segmentary'/differentiated); and that which can be called the form of social consensus ('mechanical'/'organic').

Fourth, Durkheim realizes that the only viable theory or model of social evolution or development is one which disavows any attempt to force every social institution or institutional form, set of ideas or symbols into an evolutionary scale, but which attempts rather to characterize levels of social complexity in terms of abstract variables and the relationship between these: though this does not then exclude the possibility of showing how different social and cultural forms exemplify such variables.

The defects of Durkheim's theories are glaring. First, his characterization of simple societies is, in some important respects, little better than that of Comte and Spencer. What he fails to realize is that the cohesion of simple societies—that is, their capacity to survive as social units—depends not so much on the detailed consensus of ideas, particularly moral ideas, as on the actual network of ties which links the constituent individuals and groups together. In other words, simple societies do not consist of a number of distinct, homologous units, with scarcely any links between them. Even when they are divided into segments, such as lineages, the members of different segments are linked together by ties of affinity—and, therefore, of kinship, since affinial ties in one generation create kinship links in the next—of ritual participation, and by political alliances. The gist of this is that the articulated structure of intersecting ties which provides the cohesive framework of simple societies is no less real and important than the articulated structure which results from social differentiation. Thus Durkheim, in seeking to refute Comte, accepts Spencer's mistaken premise concerning the looseness of the structure of simple societies. It is at least arguable that, in *some* respects, simple societies are more cohesive than more complex ones.

Second, Durkheim over-emphasises the punitive nature of social control in simple societies and, in some ways, misinterprets it. First of all, the principle of restitution does operate in very simple societies: if an individual or group is deprived of its rights in persons or in property, then it seeks to have these restored. If this fails, then there is resort to force; that is, where the normal process of restitution does not or cannot be made to operate, then punitive measures may be taken. But Durkheim insists that such measures are a collective expression of disapproval of or horror of some moral delict. They sometimes are: but not when they are taken against some *other* group. In fact, it is arguable that at some 'stages' of social development the importance of punitive law increases and does not decrease with the growth of differentiation: thus, it is with the formation of primitive states that many actions—such as alleged witchcraft, rape, homicide, including fratricide, and even incest—which were previously not punishable, become criminal offences. One of the reasons for this is that the holders of power cannot permit others to take action on their own behalf lest this be turned against the authority of the State.

Third, Durkheim is probably also wrong in thinking that the growth of the division of labour is necessarily accompanied by a decline in the significance of punitive law even in industrial societies. It is quite possible for advanced industrialization to be accompanied by increasing centralization of power and an extension of the idea of criminality: for example, in a state-controlled economy, actions which were previously considered in breach of contract might become criminal offences. Durkheim measured the ascent of contractual law by counting the amount of legislation; but this is unacceptable: what is important is the qualitative significance of a piece of legislation.

Fourth, Durkheim assumes that the growth of contract is an expression of a new moral basis of social life. His argument is that without such a moral basis there would be no expectation of the legitimacy of contract. There is a good deal to this argument. But it is at least plausible to suggest that expanding trade makes it necessary for contracts to be made and honoured and that the growth of contractual relationships itself contributes to the formation of some morality of contractual obligation. It is very typical of Durkheim to explain the emergence of institutions by reference to the underlying values and attitudes which support them; but it is, at least, no less plausible to explain the development of attitudes and values as a consequence of the emergence of institutions. But there is no need to choose between these positions in many cases, for it is doubtless true that there is an interaction between the two sets of processes.

And this brings us to the fifth major defect in Durkheim's theory: his tendency to refer to the 'needs' of society. This is particularly obvious in his discussion of the State. For Durkheim, the State is a co-ordinating agency which is required by the growing complexity of social life. The State therefore expresses the moral basis of social life. Now one can sympathize with some aspects of Durkheim's view. Clearly he reacted against those who explained so many characteristics of social life in terms of the wishes of the powerful. He wished to show that the State was one institutional complex within a wider social system, and that its characteristics were, to a large extent, governed by the pressures of these other parts of the social system. But even if one accepts this, it does not follow that the State simply reflects the moral basis of social life. It is one thing to say that State institutions are affected by other institutions; it is quite a different thing to say that all institutions are governed by a single set of moral values. (This theory is strongly criticized in Chapter VI.) Durkheim under-estimates the significance of power; he fails to recognize that the powerful can to some extent fashion morality; and that they can also act, whether in subtle or blatant fashion, in defiance of public morality. In any case, in most societies, particularly in complex ones, there are many different moral principles and it is always possible for those who wield power to appeal to one set of principles rather than to another. Furthermore, it is not simply true to say that state institutions are no more influenced by others than these others influence them.

Of course, many of these defects are related to the sixth, which is Durkheim's unfortunate tendency to treat societies as organic entities. This clearly emerges when he states that the division of labour functions to create a new moral basis of social life, following a decline of 'mechanical' solidarity. It is as though society were an entity which, having lost one organ to perform certain functions, is fortunate to acquire another. But, in fact, the statement that the 'segmental' structure is replaced by a differentiated one is almost tautological: for to say that there is an effacement of a 'segmental' structure is to say that there is a more differentiated structure, since the one is the logical counterpart of the other. For that matter, to say that cultural uniformity is replaced by increasing diversity is a fact; but to say that the emergence of the latter performs a function for the social system is almost meaningless, for the characteristics of normative uniformity or diversity are simply *aspects* of social systems. This is not to deny that there is much value in Durkheim's assertions. But the value does not always lie where Durkheim thinks it does.

In fact, one could state a relationship between the variables used by Durkheim without accepting a major part of his argument. The theory would run as follows. The application of new techniques of production and communication and the expansion of the universe of social interaction results in increased specialization of tasks. This leads to the breakdown of kinship, vicinal and other traditional solidarities. It also leads to the creation of greater cultural diversity within society. Furthermore, the growth of trade and the increased emphasis on specific, instrumental patterns of economic relations, encourages the growth of contract, which replaces the moral obligation which inheres in diffuse social relationships. There is far less consensus on detail norms and far greater reliance on a vague moral consensus which is sustained by certain symbols of identification. Solidarity of large collectivities is hard to maintain and scarcely important: for large-scale collective action, whether for military or for other purposes can be achieved by inducement or even by coercion; though where defence of a territory is concerned solidarity may be mobilized effectively. This statement at least has the merits of not treating abstract conditions such as solidarity, consensus, etc.—which Durkheim tends to confuse—as though they were equivalent to the health of an organism. Altogether, Durkheim's biologistic conceptions do more harm than good.

But what emerges from Durkheim's discussion and from his remarkable penetration of a number of issues are some important questions: what is the connection between cohesiveness, solidarity and integration in society, and to what extent is there a decline in all of these during the process of social development from simpler to more complex structures? In Chapter VI I suggested some models which indicated that in simple societies a particular form of cohesion was associated with a high degree of cultural uniformity, a high degree of interaction between the members of society, an intense solidarity, and a high degree of institutional and cultural integration in all senses. (See pages 151–5.) But does it follow from this that the form of cohesion changes in a single direction, and that there is a corresponding decline in the degree of solidarity, consensus, integration, etc.? Durkheim would, on the whole, have assumed this, because of his tendency to view the overall development of society as a continuous progression. (A view which he changed in his later work.) But there is reason to think that the relationship between these variables is by no means as simple as this. It is probably true to say that social development has displayed a tendency towards an increase in functional autonomy, and an increased reliance on universalistic rules which can be applied to wide categories of actors with whom one has little true sense of common identity and with whom affective bonds are weak. But this process is not inevitable; much depends on the nature of a regime, on the stability of its institutions over a long period, and so on. In fact, fairly stable industrial societies, such as Britain, enjoy a greater degree of consensus, solidarity and institutional integration, to say nothing of cohesiveness, than many less complex societies which are struggling towards 'modernization'. Of course, Durkheim would have agreed to this and would have explained it by showing that 'transitional' societies have not yet found their 'organic solidarity'. In my judgement this is not a true explanation, but only a way of characterizing the situation by linking a number of its elements within one category. It would be a sounder explanation which showed that these societies lack the divisions and ties which undermine parochialism, ethnicism and regionalism, that they lack a firm, effective and co-ordinated administration which can ensure the provision of services and which can be looked upon as a symbol of a wider unity, and so on. The lack of institutional integration in these societies is due to the fact that the modern sector is, as yet, largely isolated from the traditional sector: though despite their relative isolation, the characteristics of the one sector may adversely affect the development of the other.

The process of modernization is commonly held responsible for the growth of individual isolation and of what is called 'alienation' and 'anomie'. Durkheim himself considers that the process of individualization is not necessarily a process of atomization. In other words, he agrees that social development is associated with an increasing detachment of the individual from the compulsive bonds of a circumscribed and intimate network of social relations; he also considers that this results in a greater sense of individuality, because each individual is the centre of a network of social relations which are somewhat peculiar to him, and that he is relatively free to enter into relationships which are not bound by the framework of kinship and community; finally, he considers that each individual personality is more highly differentiated from the personalities of other individuals than is the case in simpler societies. But Durkheim denies that this means atomization, for he points out that this is a type of social structure not an absence of social structure. However, Durkheim also fears that the breakdown of 'mechanical' solidarity does produce anomie—a condition in which the norms of society are unstable and malintegrated and in which the individual is prone to states of malaise. He explains this as due to an insufficiency of 'organic' solidarity: but what he seems to mean is that until, and unless, complex societies can provide some forms of social organization in which the individual feels committed to its goals, there is bound to be a condition of potential anomie.

A similar line of argument is followed by Marxists, existentialists and others, who speak of the growing 'alienation' of the individual from the product of his labours, which results from the division of labour, and also of the 'alienation' of man from man and, moreover, of man from *himself*. The plea behind this is for a socialist society in which individuals and groups are committed to collective goals, and fulfil their true selves in work, social participation and the enjoyment of civilized pursuits. This is doubtless admirable: but is there convincing evidence of increasing 'alienation'? 'Alienation' in work in modern industrial organizations is doubtless a reality: in short, much factory work is boring and unsatisfying. But is there any good reason why most men should enjoy their work, rather than their leisure activities? As for the 'alienation' of man from man, it is true that the 'organic' communities of rural society no longer exist: but does this mean that the relationships between kinsmen, friends, workers, members of voluntary associations, etc., are without meaning? It is true that multiplex relationships are less predominant, except within the family: but why are friendships and other relationships less meaningful because they are not also work relationships and kinship relationships? The myth of the 'meaningful gemeinschaft' is a powerful one.

Finally, what is one to make of the assertion that Man, in modern industrial societies, is 'alienated' from himself? Is there a 'true self' concealed behind the 'masks' which are needed for the performance of different social roles? And if there is such a self, how does one know of its existence? One may attempt an answer to these questions along the following lines. In most relatively simple societies children grow up in a community or household which contains a number of adults as well as other children, and in which the variety of adult social roles which are performed to some extent constitute a microcosm of the social world in which the adult participates. In these circumstances the early process of personality formation, in which the child first learns to identify with adults and to 'internalise' them as part of the mechanism controlling his conduct provides a fairly adequate basis for the performance of adult social roles. In more complex societies, conditions are very different. The child first identifies with a very small number of adults, particularly parents, with whom alone strong effective ties are developed: thus the first conception of 'self' is one which mirrors these highly charged relationships in which one adult cannot replace another. But at a certain point the child moves out into the wider society, particularly at school and among peer-groups, and must perform social roles for which the early years do not equip him: therefore, the child begins new processes of identification and this becomes a part of growing up; at each point in his personal and social development a new range of social roles is learned as part of the adult world, which is perceived and reacted to, as part of the world of the child. Thus, the effect is of imposing one identity upon another. This is one aspect of the matter. There is another important difference between simpler and more complex types of society. In the former the individual has neither the need nor the opportunity to choose to enter into certain types of social relationship; the range of types of relationship is highly limited, and the obligation to enter into most of them is, for practical as well as for moral reasons, binding. In more complex societies there is greater need for and a possibility of choosing between different types of relationship, and there is a wider range available. Thus, the individual comes to see himself rather than a group or segment as a separate unit of social life. For these two reasons—the greater need for individual self-consciousness, which encourages some speculation concerning the 'self'; and the greater sense of a layer of selves, one of which is felt as primal—there is a greater likelihood that the individual may, in certain circumstances, feel that he is isolated from others and 'alienated' from himself.

So much then for an attempt to identify the phenomenon of 'self-alienation' and to explain its existence. Is this theory acceptable and does it lead one to expect a growth of 'self-alienation' in modern society? I think not. In the first place, the theory tends to exaggerate or dramatize the rather tortured sense of identity which results from this type of upbringing and this form of participation in the social system: the transitions are not usually so sudden, nor do we know that the effect is really to create an experience that different persona are imposed upon one another. There is possibly some such experience, but there are good reasons for thinking that the personality is also capable of integrating these different elements. Secondly, where is the evidence that this process creates some lasting and disturbing sense of loss of anchorage in the original personality? There is no evidence that the rate of mental illness is any higher in modern industrial society than in any other type. And if it is higher, this could be due to a number of factors. Nor is there any evidence that the *kinds* of mental illness which reflect this sense of loss of identity or failure to link one's 'true' identity with one's social personae are more common now than in the past. The answer that would doubtless be given to this is that the 'alienation' is manifest in the nature of social relations themselves: thus each individual is forced to compartmentalize his 'self' in order to relate in different types of social situation. But even if this is true, why is it considered so tragic? One can only conclude that those who are so preoccupied with the problem of 'alienation' have not yet freed themselves of a belief that each man has an essential soul which can be at war with his personality. The attractiveness of this belief does itself call for explanation; but not here.

The process of development from simple to more complex forms of society has no doubt brought with it many changes in the quality of social relationships, in the structure of personality, and in the nature of the relationship between the personality as a system, and the social system. The speculations of Durkheim and others have contributed greatly to our understanding of these things. But what is called for is a readiness to treat these ideas not as received wisdom, but as theories to be tested. Durkheim was almost alone among theorists in trying to do this.

NOTES

1. K. R. Popper. *The Poverty of Historicism*, Routledge, 1957.
2. Julian H. Steward, *Theory of Culture Change*, Urbana, 1955.
3. Marshall D. Sahlins and Ellman R. Service, *Evolution and Culture*, University of Michigan Press, 1960.
4. Frederick J. Teggart, *Theory and Process of History*, University of California Press, 1941, pp. 106–9.

5. Julian H. Steward, op. cit.
6. Max Weber, *General Economic History*, Collier, 1961.
7. Max Weber, *The Methodology of the Social Sciences* (trans. and ed. Edward A. Shils and Henry A. Finch), Free Press, 1949.
8. Cf. J. W. N. Watkins, 'Ideal Types and Historical Explanation', *British Journal for Philosophy of Science*, III, 9, 1952, pp. 22–43.
9. See Percy S. Cohen, 'Models', *British Journal of Sociology*, Vol. XVII, 1, March 1966, pp. 70–8.
10. Cf. E. A. Gellner, *Thought and Change*, London, 1964, p. 15.
11. Talcott Parsons, 'Evolutionary Universals in Society', *American Sociological Review*, 29, 3, June 1964, pp. 339–57.

9.

Conclusions

SOCIOLOGICAL theory should be assessed according to three criteria: first, it should be able to explain, or suggest ways of explaining, why social phenomena have the characteristics which they do have; second, it should provide ideas for the analysis of complex social processes and events; third, it should aid in the construction of models of how social structures and systems operate. That these three criteria are interrelated, is obvious.

Most of the founders of modern sociological theory, particularly Comte, Marx, Spencer, Durkheim, Pareto, Simmel and Weber were, on the whole, committed to these three aims. But in recent years, much of what passes for theory does not contain propositions which can be evaluated in terms of their explanatory or suggestive power; it does contain a number of paradigms which are constructed with great ingenuity; but whether these can be used, or whether their usage is genuine, remains very much in doubt. There are some notable achievements, but there is still too much discussion of concepts and of diagrammatic representation, and too little discussion of truly competing ideas and models, and of the evidence in favour of them.

Most sociological theory which is of any value deals with one of two levels of social reality, though some tries to deal with both. The first level is that of social action and interaction; the second is that of social structure or system. In the history of social thought there have been few attempts to bring these together. Durkheim was concerned with the second. Simmel tried both but scarcely succeeded in bringing them into relation with one another. Pareto succeeded in bringing them together, but his synthesis was a poor one. Marx, who did not really set himself this task, actually succeeded in performing it rather well; but not well enough.

The best known attempt, in recent times, to link the two

levels of social action and social system has been that of Talcott Parsons. But his scheme has a number of weaknesses. First, like Durkheim, Parsons is prone to offer explanations which treat the shared, internalized, cultural constraints as the all important independent variable. This means that the actual process of inter-action is seldom used as an explanation of how social systems come to be what they are and of how they change.

The second weakness is that Parsons is equally prone to reify social systems, rather than explain system properties in terms of action. This is most notable in his recent discussions of social evolution in which the concepts of system adaptation, system goals, etc. play a great part.

The third main weakness, which is related to the first and the second, is that Parsons is scarcely concerned with action at all, but rather with the conditions that lead up to it.[1] For example, when he discusses power—with great insight—Parsons is really concerned with the presuppositions of the use of power and its acceptance; he is not, for example, concerned with the struggle for power or with the struggle against it. This means that he does neglect the unintended consequences which flow from the exercise of power.

The main arguments of this book have been these: that when one 'demystifies'* much of what is said about social action, inter-action, social structure and social systems, it is possible to explain, or to suggest ways of explaining, why social systems persist and change, why they vary in their characteristics; and that one can do this without taking sides in rather pointless debates concerning the limitations of the 'structural-functional' as opposed to some other models of society, or the merits of the 'integration or consensus model' (which is thought to be linked up with a structural-functional one) as opposed to the so-called 'conflict-coercion model'. The unwillingness to become a partisan in these disputes does not stem from a distaste for polemics. Radcliffe-Brown once stated that there was no room for 'schools of thought' in contemporary social theory.[2] An uncharitable inter-pretation of this view would be that he found no room for any set of ideas other than those which he himself endorsed. But a more generous reading of this would be that he recognized that

---

* This now fashionable word is used by the opponents of 'bourgeois' sociology who are not averse to some remarkable mystification of their own.

many so-called debates between theories of different persuasions were really non-starters: the two sides were dealing with different problems. What sounds like a distasteful 'pronunciamento' could be a telling criticism of the condition of theoretical debate in some of the social sciences, where there is an unfortunate tendency to present theories and models which do not necessarily compete with one another as though they were genuine alternatives.

A classic case of this is the opposition between the 'atomistic' theory of society, which explains social phenomena in terms of individual actions and interactions, and the 'holistic' theory, which explains them in terms of the emergent properties of social systems. The first can be made irreconcilable with the second when it proposes to create a 'billiard-ball' sociology which would seek to build up models of social structure by starting from the irreducible properties of social action and interaction. The second can be made irreconcilable with the first when it treats individual actors as though they had no characteristics other than those ascribed to them by the social system in which they participate, and when it leads to the reification or even personi-fication of social wholes by attributing to them characteristics, such as goals or aims, which are possessed only by individuals or groups of individuals.

The second debate which I think saps the energy of some sociological thinkers is that between the proponents of the two models of society, the 'soft' model, which emphasizes commitment, solidarity, value-consensus, integration, stability and adaptive change, and the 'hard' model which emphasizes conflict, coercion, malintegration and disruptive change. This debate did serve a useful purpose at one time in correcting an excessive enthusiasm for one particular view of social systems which derived from a Parsonian interpretation of Durkheim.

The third debate is the largely methodological one concerning the validity of offering explanations in terms of social structure without hopelessly distorting or idealizing the chaotic reality of social events. This dispute is resolved by recognizing that sociological analysis necessarily makes use of models which isolate certain aspects of reality and interrelate them. In any case it is also a fundamental error to believe that any reporter of human actions, be he an historian or a journalist, can describe 'pure' events, in all their real complexity 'just as they occurred'. For there are no such events; these are always, and must be, to some extent, presented as abstractions from reality. The difference between the historiographical description of 'events', and the sociological examination of structures or systems, is a matter of emphasis and degree. To refer to capitalism, clientship or patrilateral parallel cousin marriage is, inevitably, to present a model. The systematic sociologist recognizes this, and attempts to be even more abstract and refined in his construction of models, so that they have general application of one sort or another: at best they apply to a number of different societies; at their most modest they apply to only one society but refer to some enduring features of it.

To say that none of these debates is worth pursuing further is a plea neither for orthodoxy nor for complacency; it is a recommendation that the problems which arouse theoretical speculation be redefined, or at least specified in more precise terms. The groundwork has been laid by the classical authors. It is time to become more daring and hence, in a new way, more polemical.

The Uses of Social Theory

The author of a work in philosophy—say the theory of ethics, or epistemology or aesthetics—does not necessarily recognize an obligation to justify his activity, which is thought of as an end in itself.* For quite different reasons, the author of a work in theoretical physics or genetic theory does not feel called upon to justify his exposition: he assumes, and his readers assume, that theory serves a number of functions indispensable to any natural science: it explains what is observed; it directs attention to what is to be observed; and it permits the making of predictions concerning what will be observed.

In the past, writers on social theory felt no need to explain or justify their activities: they thought of themselves as philosophers.

* Nowadays, for good reasons, some philosophers do feel called upon to explain and justify what they are doing. Some say that they are serving the interests of science, but most still assert that philosophical thinking is an end in itself.

It was when they began to think of themselves as scientists—and to have doubts about this no sooner than they had had the thoughts—that social theorists felt the need to explain and justify themselves.

There are several main views on the role of social theory. One, which has had much influence and is expounded by Parsons, is that general theory can, and indeed should, be formulated in advance of testing particular, empirical hypotheses, since these last can only be 'derived from theory'. Behind this view lies the belief that empirical observation, if it is to be meaningful and scientifically relevant, must be guided by some theory. The underlying belief is undoubtedly correct—as Comte pointed out, no scientific observation can proceed without a theory to direct it—but the view which is associated with it is, in some important respects, misleading. It is certainly not the case in the natural sciences that a theory is first formulated so that testable hypotheses can be derived from it. In any natural sciences it is usually the case that a general theory, which is simply the highest level of theory accepted at any particular time, emerges from the need to explain certain lower-level theories. There are some exceptions to this in the natural sciences: thus, the higher-level theories of physics did not come into being in order to explain the lower-level theories of physical chemistry; rather it was the existence of physical theories which led some chemists to attempt to explain certain chemical properties in physical terms. But this case also does not support the view that a general theory of physical chemistry had to exist prior to the development of chemistry.

Of course, one might argue that this particular view of the role of general theory applies only to sociology or the social sciences, and that the reason for this, which is not given by Parsons or any other proponent of this view, is that the general properties of social phenomena are more familiar to us than the less general ones, so that statements on the higher or highest levels of generality can be discovered prior to those on a lower level of generality. Sometimes allied with this argument is the assumption that the highest levels of social theory are statements about the properties of the mind, and that these can be known by introspection: this implies that all statements about social phenomena are reducible to statements of psychology, an assumption which has proved untenable. But this argument can also be allied with the view that the highest level of sociological theory concerns the general properties of social situations, and that these can be understood intuitively by anyone who takes the trouble to do so. There is some justification for this viewpoint. But it should be interpreted with some caution. It may, indeed, be possible to formulate certain very general statements about the nature of social action prior to stating anything very definite about the properties of social systems within which such actions occur. For example, a sociologist may assert that alliances tend to break when the interests and moral obligations which bind them are insufficiently strong to withstand the enmities which have developed within them; and he will tend to accept such a statement without necessarily knowing how actual types of alliance work in segmentary societies or in international relations. But this does not mean that he can derive statements of a lower level of generality from statements of a higher level; for the more general statements are usually too vague or imprecise, or they may not be true universal statements, or they may be near-tautologies, so that little can be strictly derived from them concerning the nature of social systems.

The second view of the role of social theory is that it should progress, like natural science theories, from the lower to the higher. This is, in most respects, more acceptable than the first view, since it is quite clear that general sociological theories do not, at present, permit strict logical derivation of lower-level hypotheses; if they are to do this they must be formulated, as are the theories of the natural sciences, with the intention of explaining other particular theories or sets of theories. But the defect in this view is that, unlike the first one, it underestimates the value of the rather vague, but suggestive, meta-sociological theories.

The third view is that sociologists should bother less about imitating the natural scientists or about obtaining theories which permit them to derive others from them, and should attend more to the task of making statements which enable them to investigate the nature of social reality as adequately as possible. This certainly involves taking any general statements and seeking to give them a more rigorous form; and if this is done, the rest may follow. I have tried to show that in seeking to explain why certain general properties of social structure are subject to systematic variance one loses nothing and may gain a good deal. Insofar as such substantive goals are furthered by methodological and philosophical discussion, then these last are in order; but there is a depressing tendency for social theorists to discuss the nature of social theory and not the nature of social reality.

There is, of course, a fourth viewpoint. It is that all science should progress by collecting facts which provide generalizations which, in turn, can be taken together to provide higher generalizations. I do not know of any social scientist who now subscribes to this view. But there are many who come close to it. Their view is that social theory is simply an array of concepts which are used for the description of social facts which, when brought together in certain ways, provide causal explanations, or better still, meaningful correlations.

I do not propose to criticize this last position, since I hope that the reader will treat the whole of this book as an argument against it. However, I would like to say one or two mischievous things in its favour. This conception of methodology does not, at least, assume that science is logically neat; nor does it perpetrate the fallacy that there is something called scientific method which enables one to engage in 'theory construction' and which prescribes the techniques whereby these constructions are tested. Most science proceeds in a logically untidy sort of way, and there are no prescriptions for the construction of theories; and the making of causal discoveries, or the establishment of meaningful correlations, is usually a hit-and-miss affair. The rigorous examination of theories is part of the scientific process. But whether anything fruitful comes of this activity depends on chance, ingenuity, and the state of the science to which one tries to contribute. This last condition is determined not only by theoretical speculation, but also by empirical enquiry.

The relationship between theory and research in sociology is far from satisfactory. This does not mean simply that particular enquiries do not constitute rigorous tests of high-level theories: this is, perhaps, too much to hope for, at least at present. The complaint has a different intention. It is that not enough empirical enquiry is used to decide between the rival claims of different theories, at least to establish whether these claims are or are not incompatible with one another. The community of empirical sociologists should establish itself far more as something like a court of law in which judgements are made on the presentation of rival arguments. This may not commend itself as methodological perfection. But, in the present state of sociology, that *should* bother no one.

Concluding Remarks

In this book I have attempted a sustained argument concerning the nature of social action, social systems and social change, and of the relationship between these. I have tried to show that certain ideas, which derive from a number of different authors, some living and some dead, can play their part in refining certain problems and in showing how they may be solved. If and when such solutions are found it will be time to examine *their* weaknesses.

NOTES

1. Cf. Max Black, 'Some Questions About Parsons' Theories' in Max Black (ed) *The Social Theories of Talcott Parsons*, Prentice-Hall, 1961, pp. 274–5.
   and G. E. Swanson, 'The Approach to a General Theory of Action by Parsons and Shils', *American Sociological Review*, Vol. 18, 1953, pp. 125–34.
2. A. R. Radcliffe-Brown, 'On Social Structure', in *Structure and Function in Primitive Society*, p. 188.

Index